*American Diplomacy
and the Israeli War
of Independence*

ALSO BY FRANK W. BRECHER
Negotiating the Louisiana Purchase: Robert Livingston's Mission to France, 1801–1804 (McFarland, 2006)

American Diplomacy and the Israeli War of Independence

Frank W. Brecher

McFarland & Company, Inc., Publishers
Jefferson, North Carolina, and London

The author gratefully acknowledges permission to use the following:
Frank W. Brecher, "America's First Ambassador to Israel: James G. McDonald," *Foreign Service Journal* 87, no. 9 (2010).

Frank W. Brecher, "Secretary of State George C. Marshall's Losing Battles Against President Harry S Truman's Palestine Policy, January–June 1948," *Middle Eastern Studies* 48, no. 2 (2012).

The Library of the New York Historical Society for permission to quote from the Robert Lovett Diary in its Brown Brothers Harriman Collection.

LIBRARY OF CONGRESS CATALOGUING-IN-PUBLICATION DATA

Brecher, Frank W.
    American diplomacy and the Israeli war of independence / Frank W. Brecher.
    p.   cm.
    Includes bibliographical references and index.

    ISBN 978-0-7864-7426-4
    softcover : acid free paper ∞

    1. United States—Foreign relations—Israel. 2. Israel—Foreign relations—United States. 3. United States—Foreign realations—1945–1953. 4. Israel-Arab War, 1948–1949—Diplomatic history. I. Title.
E183.8.I7B74 2013
327.7305694—dc23   2013005137

BRITISH LIBRARY CATALOGUING DATA ARE AVAILABLE

© 2013 Frank W. Brecher. All rights reserved

No part of this book may be reproduced or transmitted in any form or by any means, electronic or mechanical, including photocopying or recording, or by any information storage and retrieval system, without permission in writing from the publisher.

On the cover: President Harry S Truman (Library of Congress)

Manufactured in the United States of America

McFarland & Company, Inc., Publishers
   Box 611, Jefferson, North Carolina 28640
     www.mcfarlandpub.com

Table of Contents

Preface	1
One. Secretary of State George C. Marshall's Losing Battles Against President Harry S Truman's Palestine Policy, January–June 1948	5
Two. James G. McDonald's Unusual Path to Appointment as America's First Representative in Israel	33
Three. Truman Speaks Off-the-Record on Palestine to the State Department, July 1947–June 1948	41
Four. U.S. Policy Toward Israel and the Arab States, June–August 1948	57
Five. American Diplomacy at the United Nations, Mid–1948	77
Six. The Bernadotte Plan of June 1948	84
Seven. U.S. Policy During the Final Rounds of Fighting, Fall and Winter 1948	128
Eight. The Diplomatic Consequences of Israel's Military Victories of 1948–1949, and Final Observations	149
Chapter Notes	171
Bibliography	199
Index	203

"It is widely accepted in the Western world to speak of the decades after 1914 and especially after 1933 as an age of apocalyptic anxiety and of exceptional tensions. Such periods have been known throughout history. The present period is distinguished from preceding ones not by intensity of uncertainty or fear, but by its global character. All preceding history has been parochial history. In the middle of the twentieth century mankind has entered the first stage of global history." — Hans Kohn, *The Age of Nationalism* (New York: Harper & Row, 1962), p. xv

"The recent Past contains the key to the present time. All forms of thought that influence it come before us in their turn." — Lord Acton, *The Age of Nationalism* (New York, Harper & Row, 1898), unnumbered page

Preface

Events since the end of the Cold War have dashed hopes that the demise of the Soviet Union would ease the Arab-Israeli conflict and usher in a more stable Middle East — the basic goal of American foreign policy regarding that region. Far from that result, the past two decades have seen an intensification of regional instability and have added further religious fuel to the conflict. Moreover, we have witnessed major interventions by such non–Arab states in the region as Iran and Turkey.

The consequence of all this for the United States is that its long-term policy of seeking a credible balance in its relations with the contesting states is being strained more than ever. At the center of the problem is the need to find a peaceful solution to the imbroglio involving Israel and its Palestinian neighbors — this is an essential, if not sufficient, ingredient in any overall attainment of America's regional aspirations.

Accordingly, there is now a renewed focus on historically familiar categories of intra–Palestinian issues, just as they were experienced in 1948 at the inception of the State of Israel. These issues include borders, return of refugees, status of Jerusalem, the distinct role and status of the Gaza Strip, and policy at the United Nations. It is the purpose of this book to give fresh consideration of these root issues in the Arab-Israeli conflict, doing so mainly in light of the most recently available material, especially primary sources from the United States, the United Kingdom, Israel and the United Nations.

From Washington's point of view, this situation remains as I described it twenty years earlier, in the introduction to my *Reluctant Ally: United States Foreign Policy Toward the Jews from Wilson to Roosevelt*: "At the beginning of the twentieth century, Jewish-related foreign policy issues were at the fringes of American diplomatic concerns; by its midpoint, they were near their very center." In fact, one might well say that they are, indeed, at that very center when one considers the expansion of the geographical dimensions affected by those issues, their greater volatility both ideologically and militarily, and the unprecedented direct role being played by the United States in the region itself. If one recalls the determinedly hands-off approach the United States was able to maintain throughout the Cold War in protecting its interests in the Middle East, carefully avoiding investing its military might directly in regional wars, it is clear that the stakes have now been raised considerably, especially regarding "homeland security."

The kinds of problems of worldwide concern that arose during the period of 1947–1948 have been so intractable that, sixty years later, not only the language describing those problems but also their substance are still featured in today's headlines. For example, the Palestinians openly demand, in effect, implementation of the "two-state solution" that was embodied in the basic UN resolutions starting in November 1947; Israel is still resisting any large-scale "right of return" by Arab refugees; and the United States, along with the bulk of the UN membership, remains adamant, pending a final peace settlement, in its non-recognition of Israel's claims of sovereignty over West Jerusalem, let alone the entire city. Furthermore, as in that earlier period, there are strenuous, ongoing diplomatic debates as to (a) whether Israel is trying to have it "both ways" by insisting not only on its right to the full extent of territory allotted to it by the United Nations in 1947, but also, as its leaders have maintained, on its "right of conquest" since that date as a consequence of its "defensive" wars against the Arab states; (b) whether negotiations between Israel and its Palestinian neighbors must necessarily be conducted only with the help of third-party intermediaries, as the Arabs demand, or, as Israel urges, more directly and bilaterally; and (c) the role of the international community in enforcing arms controls within the region.

The leaders of all the nations actively involved in the events leading up to, and including, the first Arab-Israeli conflict had to struggle not only with a matter of great import diplomatically, strategically and religiously, but also with one that engaged, in a more emotional way than usual, their domestic constituencies — not surprisingly, given the place of the Holy Land in human history. This profound interrelationship between foreign and domestic challenges had its inevitable effect on interactions at the personal level within governments, none more so than in the case of the U.S. government. The tensions and open displays of disagreement and inconsistencies in policy during the late 1940s regarding the Palestine question were the subject of great controversy and even public ridicule, to the acute embarrassment of many of the individuals concerned. Not least of those affected individuals was President Truman, whose revealing, off-the-record telephone comments to Under-Secretary of State Robert Lovett, the point man on Palestine, are uniquely presented and analyzed in this volume. The widely observed conflict of interest between

White House staff and the top leadership at the State Department, with Eleanor Roosevelt and her Democratic Party colleagues also playing a partisan role, is the stuff of which high political drama is made. That this is so is made clear by the fact that *Time* magazine in March 1948 put portraits of two of the drama's top public protagonists on its front covers: Clark Clifford of the White House staff on the 15th, and Lovett on the 29th.

It is the goal of this volume to bring to life these diplomatic issues, and these personal and institutional conflicts, so that readers will have an enhanced appreciation for, and deeper factual understanding of, the still-relevant origins of what remains a nettlesome, persistent, clear and present danger to world peace. Remarkably, the first important signs of this danger came into full view for the world community within one compact period of time—1948—and it is on that basis that the present study, more than others dealing with American foreign policy, concentrates its full attention. In sum, the stakes may have been enlarged for the United States since 1948, but the issues attached to them remain basically unchanged, at least regarding the core problem: the conflict between Israel and its Arab neighbors.

One

Secretary of State George C. Marshall's Losing Battles Against President Harry S Truman's Palestine Policy, January–June 1948

"The press this morning announced a complete change in the UN of the policy of the US in regard to the partition of Palestine. The President told me that this change was made without his permission and without his knowledge."—Admiral Leahy's diary, March 20, 1948[1]

Marshall-Truman Break, March 1948

With one exception, the top two men at the State Department in 1948 were never absent from their posts at the same time. The one exception occurred in the days surrounding 19 March, when Ambassador Warren Austin of the U.S. delegation proposed to the United Nations Security Council the suspension of efforts to implement the General Assembly's Palestine partition decision of November 29, 1947.[2] The U.S. government, at Truman's specific direction, had voted in favor of that decision and, in the last but key days, had successfully urged other delegations also to do so in a budding close contest. It would take extreme credulity to believe that the absence from Washington just before, during and after that crucial day by Marshall and his deputy, Robert Lovett, was purely a coincidence. Rather, it was clearly designed by Marshall to avoid any possibility of a presidential cancellation of his 16 March telegram, not specifically cleared with Truman, instructing Austin to make that proposal.[3] Their absence, the secretary visiting university campuses in California and the deputy on vacation in Florida, helped ensure that Truman would not be made aware of the impending move, which the department had good reason to fear would be prevented were he given the opportunity.[4]

While details in support of this analysis will be provided when the issue is treated in its proper chronological context, suffice it to say here that the heart of the matter was as follows: Truman's standing orders during February and March were that nothing should be said at the United Nations that "could be interpreted as a recision" of support for the November resolution, and that the U.S. delegation should "attempt to get approval of implementing" that resolution by the Security Council; however, "if we did not get it we could take the alternative step" of seeking to replace the partition plan with a UN trusteeship over all of Palestine as a successor to the expiring British mandate under the League of Nations.[5] Truman well recognized that the State Department during this period was already determined to convince the United Nations to suspend implementation of the partition resolution, which from the start it believed to be contrary to the national interest. The closest step the department had taken to meet the president's expectation of a straightforward up-or-down vote prior to any such drastic action as that embodied in the 19 March Austin statement was a 5 March procedural vote it pressed the Security Council to take without delay on its own draft resolution proposing that the Council accept the enforcement responsibility requested of it in the General Assembly resolution. The State Department knew in advance that that vote would go against it in favor of the logical alternative being offered by Belgium of delaying such acceptance pending the outcome of a ten-day consultation simultaneously being requested of the permanent Council members — the "Permanent Five" (P-5) holding veto power.

It was this procedural vote that the State Department would use in its subsequent efforts to convince the president that the United Nations no longer supported partition. That this was a shaky argument, and known to be so well before 19 March, is quite evident in the 16 March telegram's reference to the 5 March vote as only having "tacitly" rejected the Assembly's resolution, and also in the fact that Austin, upon receipt of his 16 March instruction, was at first intent on personally clearing the statement with the president (Austin had to be persuaded by his colleagues not to do so).[6] The upshot of all this maneuvering was that Truman, once he "read in the papers" on Saturday, 20 March, of the U.S. statement at the Security Council, was outraged and had his counselor, Clark Clifford, conduct an investigation as to how his Palestine policy had been reversed without his express approval. Only on Monday would he have the opportunity to meet with his secretary of state in person.

Of course, nothing but the most profound conviction that the president's Palestine policy was undermining important national security interests, and was instead being driven by irrelevant domestic political interests, could have led the secretary and perhaps his deputy, two of the most trusted and admired leaders in the government, to have indulged in such skullduggery and disloyalty.[7] And, indeed, they were acting not only on their own personal judgment but also on the basis of a multi-agency, in-depth, top-secret review that had taken place in October–November 1947 with a similarly high-level British delegation from London.[8] That review focused on strategies to counter the perceived Soviet threat to Western interests in the eastern Mediterranean and Middle East. The conclusions the Americans drew from that review, as certified by the newly created National Security Council mechanism, would serve as a guide to the secretaries of state and defense — Marshall and James Forrestal — during the next momentous year in Cold War history. Moreover, the president himself had signed off on those conclusions, which will be summarized below.

In addition to the strategic concerns identified in the bilateral review of the autumn of 1947, there was a great sense of urgency in the State Department as it moved to block the partition of Palestine. The British were scheduled to end their mandatory role on May 15, 1948, and the neighboring Arab states were openly determined, once that date passed, to enter Palestine in force and

President Harry S Truman seeing off Secretary of State George C. Marshall for the London Conference of Foreign Ministers, November 20, 1947 (courtesy Truman Library).

block the establishment there of a Jewish state of whatever size. The Jews, for their part, while full of trepidation about their military prospects, were nevertheless undeterred in their intent to proclaim a state on that very same date. Thus, the stage was being set, in January–May 1948, for a violent international conflagration that the entire Truman administration believed had to be avoided at all costs if the Soviets were not to reap the harvest of the havoc at Western expense, and if, according to a survey of U.S. ambassadors in the Arab world, Western influence and interests in the Arab world were not to disappear overnight given the close American association in Arab eyes with the Zionist cause.[9]

U.S.-British Secret Talks, Fall 1947

The U.S.–British strategy session of 1947, known as the Pentagon Talks, focused specifically on the "Middle East and Eastern Mediterranean"— that is, the Arab world and also Greece, Turkey and Iran.[10] However, the Palestine issue was seen as a "thing apart" and hence "not debated."[11] Of course, this was a recognition that Truman, since 1945, had taken a personal interest in Palestine policy, including having countermanded a 1946 agreement seen by the Zionists as unfavorable to their cause that had been negotiated in London by the Department of State and its British counterpart.[12]

The more salient results that came out of the talks, from the American perspective and for the purposes of the present study, may be summarized as follows[13]:

a. For the first time, the U.S. government developed a coherent, comprehensive policy and strategy for the area, having recognized the justice of Foreign Minister Ernest Bevin's complaint, which led to the talks, "that the policy of the American Government was unknowing" to the British government.[14]

b. The main U.S. goal in the Arab world was to curb the growth of nationalism and consequent intra–Arab conflicts with attendant competition between the West and the Soviets and the possibility of "World War Three."

c. Another major goal was the retention of the British as the power most responsible for Western military security in that area, where the stakes were so high. As shown by the recently concluded conflict, "in a world war, the Middle East must at all costs be held." Toward that end, Italy, Greece, Turkey and Iran must be kept out of Soviet hands and the British must "follow parallel policies" of those of the United States in the eastern Mediterranean and Middle East. Were the Soviets to control that area, the United States would be pushed back to the Atlantic and, therefore, into a western hemisphere defense in a "war of attrition which would spell the end of the American way of life."[15] (As for the British, they perceived that area as "a strategic whole," the loss of which would be a "mortal danger" to their empire.[16])

d. It was "essential that Kuwaiti and Saudi oil be brought to the Mediterranean as cheaply and easily as possible."[17] In this regard, the short supply of "steel pipe" must be corrected so that planned construction of pipelines could go forward.[18]

e. The United States should not get ahead of the United Kingdom regarding recognition of Transjordan. Palestine was the "main" issue connected to this matter, and premature recognition would provoke the Zionists, whose "aspirations in Transjordan" must be shown to them as impossible.[19] Therefore, recognition must await the solution of the Palestine problem. The Holocaust had led to a situation that had "distorted beyond all recognition" the intent of the Balfour Declaration.[20]

f. Aside from oil, the United States had no "particularly outstanding" economic interests in the Middle East, although its oil supply to Europe was essential to the success of the European Recovery Plan (Marshall Plan). The United Kingdom did have oil and "many other economic interests" there.[21]

g. The United Kingdom should leave the Suez Canal but with a right to return, if necessary. Relatedly, the boundary lines between Arabs and Jews in a partitioned Palestine should meet Transjordan's need to have access to the Mediterranean. This would also enable the British to extract maximum value from their military bases in Transjordan and Iraq. If the British proved unable to retain bases on the Mediterranean shore at Egypt or Palestine, they should be able to retain Cyrenaica bases along that sea.[22]

h. The British reported that they did not initiate the Arab League in 1945 but were "not averse to it," although lately it had shown "anti-foreign tendencies." Were it to break up, there would be two camps and an opening for the Soviets. The United States concurred in this assessment and wanted to see the League focus on socio-economic development rather than political and military activities. "Communism was not widespread in the Middle East and the Moslem religion was not favorable to it."[23]

Change in American Policy, March 1948

While it is beyond the purview of this study to touch in detail on each of the above results for the United States, the germane point is that the stage was now set for a clash over Middle East policy between Truman and his subordinates.[24] Those at the State and Defense Departments were deeply wedded to the validity of the stark, even apocalyptic, conclusions reached at the Pentagon Talks. Notwithstanding that Truman signed off on the course of action based on those conclusions a few days prior to the fateful UN vote of 29 November, those officials remained fearful that the president would not abide by it once pressured by domestic political or personal humanitarian concerns.[25] Their fears were fulfilled by the very next presidential move, endorsing partition and closely associating the United States with the partition plan and the prospective establishment of a Jewish state. (Even prior to that event, Truman had instructed Marshall to drop his efforts at the General Assembly to make a basic change in the territory being proposed for the Jewish state in the majority report of the UN Special Committee on Palestine [UNSCOP]: Marshall was urging the Assembly to give the southern part of Palestine — the Negev, with its access to both the Mediterranean Sea and the Gulf of Aqaba — not to the Jewish state, as the committee envisaged, but to the Arabs.[26])

It would not take long for the State and Defense Departments to begin a campaign to reverse the favorable U.S. and UN vote for the partition resolution, or at least to delay its actual implementation. For example, a State

United Nations Secretary-General Trygve Lie, January 1, 1952 (UN photograph).

telegram of 3 December to London endorsed the British rejection of the plan by the UN secretary-general, Trygve Lie, to field in Palestine early in 1948 the UN Palestine Committee (UNPC), whose assignment under the Assembly resolution included helping the Jews and Arabs to organize their respective states.[27] The British position was that the Arab opposition to the partition resolution was so strong as to pose an unacceptable security risk for the UNPC's members were they to circulate in Palestine — the British stated that they would only allow them in two weeks before the 15 May expiration of the mandate.[28] A few days later, the department publicly announced an arms embargo over the Middle East — it was not expressly imposed by the United Nations and had been tentatively decided upon within the government a few days before the 29 November vote.[29] The embargo's stated rationale was to help curb the violence surrounding the Palestine issue, but it was generally recognized as designed specifically to press the Jewish authorities, who were the most handicapped by it, to seek an accommodation with the Arabs by accepting something short of a sovereign state.[30] The Jewish Agency response was, on the one hand, to deny that an international force was "essential" for Jewish defense, but also, on the other, to insist that the Jews must be allowed to obtain arms and that any embargo should not be against both sides but only against the Arab aggressors seeking to upset the UN partition plan.[31] (As late as 2 and 19 May, the British Foreign Office was privately pointing out to the State Department that the United Nations still had not "proclaimed" an arms embargo. A Security Council resolution of 29 May was finally generally accepted by the member states as, in effect, calling for an arms embargo in the area.[32])

Other early U.S. steps to discourage implementation of the resolution included a firmly stated policy that it would not send military troops to Palestine in the face of opposition to the partition resolution by either party — even if those troops were to be part of a UN–sponsored international force to enforce the resolution[33] — and its opposition in December to Lie's proposal to the Security Council that it accept the resolution and remain seized of the matter pending developments in Palestine.[34] It is not surprising, therefore, that as early as 19 January, the Jewish Agency's representative in Washington, Eliahu Epstein, was accurately reporting that the State Department was planning to revise the November resolution, including the calling of a "special session of the UN General Assembly."[35]

On that same date, the State Department circulated a memorandum prepared under the direction of two Soviet specialists — George Kennan, head of the policy planning staff, and Loy Henderson, head of Near East affairs — which gave sundry reasons for reversing U.S. policy on partition, including the following: a possible Saudi "break with the U.S."; a likely closure of the

American University at Beirut; widespread attacks on Americans throughout the Arab world; endangerment of the Marshall Plan due to an Arab oil embargo; and an opportunity for the Soviets to "outflank" the West in Greece, Turkey and Iran by penetrating of an Arab world in turmoil. That document also ascribed to the Zionists inordinate territorial ambitions, terrorist behavior, and the use of unauthorized U.S. citizens, organizations, and members of Congress to lobby foreign powers, notably in favor of the 29 November vote.[36]

In the context specifically of UN affairs, the memorandum questioned the legality of the Assembly's November resolution, which it described as at best a recommendation that went beyond the Assembly's charter role and certainly one not binding on member states or the Security Council; in sum, the resolution could not be imposed on dissenting parties in Palestine.[37] While not rejecting the main arguments of this January memorandum, ex-colonel Dean Rusk, the head of UN Affairs in the State Department and a protégé of Marshall, in keeping with his particular responsibilities, presented some counter-arguments that he felt had to be answered before the department could seek full U.S. government authorization for it actively to try to revise the partition resolution.[38] Rusk pointed out that (a) the memorandum failed to show that a new situation had already arisen since 29 November warranting revision by the Assembly of its resolution; (b) nothing could be done in the direction of revision without the prior approval of the president and "leading members of Congress"; and (c) the State Department needed clearly to demonstrate that, as Rusk himself suspected was the case, there was not a majority in the 11-member Security Council to accept the enforcement responsibilities requested of it in the Assembly's resolution. Rusk also believed the Security Council would never declare the Arab states as aggressors were they to enter Palestine to oppose the partition plan, as they were openly declaring was their intention — to Lie's open chagrin — once the mandate expired. The only circumstance Rusk foresaw under which the Council *would* send in an

Chief Loy Henderson, Near East Office, State Department, 1946 (courtesy Truman Library).

international force would be to save the Jews from a "slaughter" by invading Arab forces, but never for the purpose of enforcing partition.[39]

The end result of these internal exchanges was a consensus favoring the initiation within the department itself of a course of action in February with the agreed-upon goal of revising the partition resolution while somehow remaining within the confines of the president's strictures regarding a change of policy at the United Nations. That "somehow" would lead it into some slippery maneuvers at Truman's expense, but it also would provoke some rather direct presidential moves at variance with known departmental positions at the United Nations. One important consequence of these conflicting moves would be the exposure of the administration to public criticism and, at times, ridicule, as to be discussed further in the present chapter.

Dean Rusk, Secretary of State, ca. 1965 (courtesy Truman Library).

Return of the Palestine Question to the UN General Assembly

February brought the first explicit, public intimation at the United Nations that the United States was receptive to a change in its pro-partition position. Based on long-distance written communications with the president, who was vacationing in the Caribbean, Marshall informed Austin on February 23 that he had obtained Truman's approval for the delegation to state its view to the Security Council that the UN Charter did not authorize the Council to impose a political settlement on any people—it could only act with force against a threat to, or breach of, international peace and security.[40] Austin duly made that debatable statement on the following day, 24 February, and it was quickly denounced as inaccurate by Lie, who laid particular emphasis on the legitimacy of the United Nations enforcing this particular settlement in Palestine given the special responsibility unavoidably thrust upon it by the withdrawal of the British mandatory power.[41] The key departmental documents preparing the way for Austin's statement were Rusk's 3 and 11 February memoranda to Lovett outlining "the logic by which this Government or other Governments might contrive a 'new look'" to the Palestine question.[42] The essence of Rusk's contrivance was the establishment at a special General Assembly session of a UN governing authority in Palestine under the direction of the Trusteeship Council and accompanied by a truce over all of that land. Rusk's suggestion for accomplishing this while barring the Soviet Union from Palestine was to convince the United Nations that the appropriate member states to administer the governing authority in the field were the British, French and Americans, who were the "remaining three of the Allied and Associated Powers of World War One" and thus the most logical successors to that mandated territory. (Philip Jessup, a prestigious jurist and member of the U.S. delegation, gave credence to this desperate idea in his 5 May memorandum to Austin, who wisely did not push it given its historical and diplomatic

From left to right: Folke Bernadotte, UN mediator, with Ralph Bunche, personal representative of the secretary-general (and Bernadotte's successor following the mediator's assassination in Jerusalem on September 17, 1948), and Ambassador Philip Jessup, deputy to Ambassador Warren R. Austin, U.S. permanent representative to the United Nations, July 14, 1948 (UN photograph).

flaws — for example, the United States was neutral and not a belligerent against the Ottoman Empire, and the French were too controversial in the Levant to be an acceptable power there once again.⁴³)

Even with the Austin statement of 24 February, the State Department recognized that it was not yet in a position to call outright for a suspension of the implementation of the partition resolution. After all, Truman had added to his approval of that statement the admonition that nothing should be said that "could be interpreted as a recision" of the partition policy.⁴⁴ The department also recognized that Truman expected a clear, high-profile, up-or-down vote on the November resolution before any such "recision." (The president would, as late as 8 March, explicitly restate this requirement in an instruction to Lovett.⁴⁵) Therefore, some further preliminary steps were deemed necessary if the department was not blatantly to disobey Truman's policy.

The first such step followed on the heels of the 24 February statement. The very next day, the United States submitted a draft resolution to the Security Council that gave lip service to the goal of "the implementation of the General Assembly resolution of 29 November" even as it proposed a procedure that intrinsically could well lead, as in fact it would the next month, to a halt in that implementation. As finally approved on 5 March, the resolution had

Truman with Robert A. Lovett, Secretary of Defense, ca. 1952 (courtesy Truman Library).

the Security Council call upon its five permanent powers "to consult and to inform it" within ten days "regarding the situation with respect to Palestine" and to make recommendations to it that it might then offer to the UNPC "with a view to implementing the resolution of the General Assembly."

That this entire exercise was a farce from beginning to end, given the State Department's determination never to allow the implementation of partition, is made crystal clear by its post–5 March private assurance to Arab leaders that they "should not be unduly concerned" by the language in the resolution calling for that implementation.[46] The most important change made in the text of the U.S. resolution when it was still in draft form between 25 February and its final adoption on 5 March was a key one initiated by a proposed Belgian amendment to drop the provision that would give immediate Security Council approval to the three-part request made to it in the Assembly's resolution that it effectively accept responsibility for enforcement of partition. The Belgians had argued — quite logically, if at the cost of diluting the positive impact on the partition plan of the prospective resolution — that such acceptance should properly await the report being requested of the "P-5." However, the United States, in keeping with its ultimate goal of demonstrating that there was a lack of majority Council support for partition, chose to escalate the substantive importance of this clearly procedural issue by demanding a vote it knew it would likely lose on the acceptance provision as contained in the original American draft. Even more significant and eyebrow-raising was the delegation's assertion, in advance of that vote, that if immediate acceptance of the Assembly's request were rejected, this would be taken by the United States as meaning the Council was against "support for the implementation of the partition plan."[47] In seeking to justify that assertion, Austin resorted to a classic example of circular reasoning: He could not accept the Belgian amendment because its stated purpose was to block the Council's approval of immediate acceptance of the Assembly's request "until after" the Big Five "had made its report" in ten days.

It was on those strained grounds that the United States on 5 March successfully insisted on a vote rather than an adjournment for a week, as others were suggesting, with the result that the Council indeed rejected that portion of the draft resolution regarding immediate acceptance of the Assembly's request.[48] The stated American interpretation of the significance of that rejection, as just described, was surely incorrect, as is evident, for example, in the statements made to the Council by several delegations (notably France and Canada) that their opposition to immediate acceptance was not to be seen as a rejection of partition itself but rather was based on the hope that the P-5 might come up with a peaceful solution to the problem, and that the ten-day period might reveal further avenues for conciliation between Jews and Arabs.[49] (As throughout this period, procrastination and resorting to procedural devices represented the prevailing attitude at the United Nations.[50])

Notwithstanding its doubtful validity, the State Department would stress its interpretation of the 5 March vote in its consultations with the president, who did not yet fully appreciate what the department planned to do on the basis of that interpretation.[51] The department now believed it had a plausible basis henceforth to maintain that the United Nations had indeed voted against partition. The patent falsity — one might even say absurdity — of this position is vividly demonstrated by the fact that the Jewish Agency (along with its most reliable supporter at this time at the United Nations, the Soviet Union) saw as "satisfactory, under the circumstances," the 5 March resolution and its stated goal of having the P-5 recommend ways for "implementing the resolution of the General Assembly."[52] The resolution had passed by 8 in favor and 3 abstentions (Argentina, Syria and the United Kingdom).

A Distraught President Truman

The State Department, having created a sufficiently plausible paper trail with which to bamboozle the president, now felt itself in a position to embark upon the final phase of its campaign to stop the partition plan. Its delegation took the lead in conducting the P-5 consultations with the acquiescence of China, the helpfully cooperative president of the Security Council for March. Secretary-General Lie, perhaps because he saw through the machinations of the United States, studiously absented himself from much of these and later consultations, leaving that duty to his Soviet deputy. The British retained their neutral posture, in keeping with their abstaining vote of 5 March, when they reaffirmed their determination to end their governmental and security responsibilities in Palestine on 15 May and to have all their military forces out of the country no later than 1 August (in reality, this withdrawal was completed by the end of June).[53] They also recalled to the Council their previous warning to the General Assembly, which "ignored" it, that the United Nations would need to have "means of implementation" if its partition plan was to be successful. Finally, and despite the failure of the United States to obtain Council approval on 5 March of its original provision that would have authorized the P-5 also to "consult with the [UN] Palestine Committee, the Mandatory Power, and representatives of the principal communities of Palestine," it did so, in the face of Soviet objection, describing those consultations merely as "informal communications."

At the expiration of the consultations, Austin on 19 March made his report to the Council, acknowledging that it only "had the agreement" of three of the P-5: the United States, China and France.[54] He said that the report's conclusions were based on "facts" that were in part obtained during the "informal consultations" with the Jewish Agency and the Arab Higher Committee representing the Palestinian Arabs. The key "fact," of course, was that "if the mandate is terminated prior to a peaceful solution of the problem, large-scale fighting between the two communities can be expected." He added that "the UN cannot permit such a result." The Soviet representative rebutted that the prospect of war was known well before 5 March, and the Council's duty, therefore, was not to investigate whether the partition plan should be implemented, but rather to agree on measures to implement it. He also charged that the United States was unfairly using the Jewish Agency's ready acknowledgment that violence was probable in order to bolster its own campaign to block further implementation of partition. This, he said, was a distortion of the position of that agency. The latter's representative at the debate then emphasized to the Council that the charge in the U.S. report that both sides were using violence to undermine a peaceful approach to the problem was not borne out by the facts as reported by the mandatory power — that violence was "due solely to the attempt by the Arab States to frustrate" the decision of the United Nations, he said.

Austin then proceeded to unleash his headline-making announcement: a call to suspend all efforts to implement partition, specifically that of the UNPC, in favor of an "immediate" special session of the UNGA, whose purpose would be to consider establishing a "temporary trusteeship."[55] The reaction at the United Nations and throughout the world was stupendous. Delegations were stunned (one even threatened to quit the organization itself), and the secretary-general the next day privately suggested to Austin that the two resign in protest at this sudden turnaround (Austin laughed the suggestion off).[56] As described at the beginning of the present chapter, none of this reaction was unexpected at the State Department. Even the "third and fourth levels" there, against whom Truman would rail in his diary in keeping with his public line that he, Marshall and Lovett all saw things "eye-to-eye," knew it was coming and made themselves scarce that afternoon lest they be called on the carpet by the White House in the absence of their top two bosses.

That middle-level group of staffers committed an even more important breach of discipline when they manipulated the system to avoid alerting the president on 18 March as to the planned Austin statement. The problem was that the department knew it should seek Truman's approval of the major new policy initiative it was about to authorize Austin to make. That initiative would potentially commit the United States to sending troops to Palestine as part of a UN international military force that might be required to enforce the prospective trusteeship the United States was about to propose for that land in place of partition. Austin had at nearly the last minute asked the State Department for authority to make that new commitment in the likely event that other delegations inquired as to what the United States was prepared to contribute to such an international force. The department agreed with him on the need for that authority and quickly obtained the concurrence of Defense Secretary Forrestal. As this proposed new policy would go beyond Truman's frequently stated position that he would not commit American military (as distinct from "police") forces to Palestine under any circumstances, it was generally understood that he should be consulted on it.[57] In fact, Lovett — in an act adding credibility to his reported comment (see above) that, had he been in Washington, Austin's 19 March statement would not have been made — gave a specific order to that effect to Rusk's aide, Robert McClintock, by phone from Florida on 18 March.[58] But, in the absence of Marshall and Lovett, the staff members allegedly failed to locate in time the next most appropriate senior official to go to the White House — the department's counselor, Soviet expert Charles Bohlen. (The nominal acting secretary of state was the uninvolved assistant secretary of state for economic affairs, Willard Thorp.[59]) When Clifford on 22 March inquired in the State Department as to why the White House hadn't been consulted on this change in military policy, among other actions related to the events of 19 March, he was wrongly told by McClintock that the exercise had taken place on that same day, the 19th, and that time had run out before Austin was to make his démarche. (Bohlen's rather unusual formal memorandum to McClintock of 22 March gives cover to the staff officer's story to Clifford.[60]) When Truman on 25 March offered to the press his personal position on the events of 19 March, he would only vaguely refer to a possible undefined American role in "enforcement measures" if they were required to quell local opposition to a UN trusteeship.[61]

At the United Nations itself, there was no question among the member states that the only practical response to the new American policy was to go along with it. There was always the hope that Washington had something in mind that would prevent the impending catastrophe in the Middle East and simultaneously save the United Nations from ruin as a mere debating society lacking the political will to implement its own decisions. Overridden in this consensus were the minority views of the Soviet Union in support of the Jewish Agency's contention that the task was not to capitulate to open and unprecedented threats by the Arab states to resort to a war of aggression to block partition, but rather to take firm measures condemning those threats to the peace and to be ready, if it came to that, to confront with force any

Andrei A. Gromyko (left), Soviet representative to the United Nations, and Ambassador Austin, February 4, 1947 (UN photograph).

actual aggression. The minority view further maintained that (a) it was precisely a posture of strength and conviction by the international community that would be the surest way to discourage any aggression, and (b) even if a trusteeship was established, there would still be a need for an international force to implement it in view of the stated opposition by both sides to such a UN governing authority in Palestine. Secretary-General Lie fully backed these minority recommendations.[62]

President Truman would have been the first to acknowledge that he had no panacea for the Palestine problem. From the time of his earliest months at the White House, he would underline that point, not cynically but as though in recognition of a political truth binding not just on the United States but on all the parties involved. His consequent uncertain, even erratic, leadership on this issue was characterized in 1947 and 1948 by a pattern of ad hoc decisions designed to allow time for his subordinates to explore avenues that might help him meet his twin goals of avoiding direct American military and diplomatic involvement in Palestine even while satisfying his humanitarian and, yes, largely domestic political needs. One of those needs, not so incidentally, was to avoid the resignation of Marshall as his secretary of state prior to the election that fall — he felt that politically he "couldn't afford to lose" Marshall.[63] In this sense, there is no doubt that Truman was complicit to a degree in the turnaround events of 19 March. It would be naïve to suppose that merely by tacking on vague qualifying conditions to his substantive approvals of the subtle steps the State Department was systematically proposing to him, which he knew were designed to water down his own previous moves on Palestine, he was under the illusion that he was adequately protecting his administration from fiascos such as that of 19 March.

Still, there is no reason to doubt his sincerity when he complained to Marshall on 22 March that, had he been alerted to the Austin speech in advance, he would have been better able to prepare the public and press for the change in direction.[64] Notice that he was not complaining that the Austin statement itself was in violation of the policies he had previously approved — only the timing upset him at first. But this is not to say that Truman deserved the treatment he received from the State Department or that, had he been more directly and freely consulted before 19 March, he would not in fact have vetoed it on the grounds that a more specific and universally understood vote on the General Assembly resolution by the Security Council would first have to be conducted. In sum, the evidence is clear that Truman was honestly taken by surprise by the timing of the move and by the enormity of the negative reaction to it. This is evident from the events at the White House once he learned from "the papers" of the Austin statement and the broad astonishment and condemnation of it worldwide. In keeping with this assessment, note that Truman, perhaps too secretively for his own good, met with Chaim Weizmann on 18 March and renewed that Jewish leader's confidence that the United States was still supporting partition.[65]

Truman's published memoir records the date of the above reference to "the papers" as 19 March. Margaret Truman's subsequent biography of her father also gives that date, as does the historical literature universally, despite its unlikely accuracy, given the time factors involved.[66] While the original so-called diary entries on which this date is based have not physically survived, according to the archivists at the Truman Library, the typewritten version prepared from the handwritten version by Truman's staff after he left the White House shows the following[67]:

> "Friday, March 19, 1948: The State Department 'pulled the rug from under me' today. I didn't expect that would happen.
> "In Key West en route there from St. Croix, I approved a speech and statement of policy by Sen. Austin to UN meeting."

"Saturday, March 20, 1948: This morning I find that the State Department has reversed my Palestine policy. The first I know about it is what I see in the papers! Isn't that hell? I'm now in the position of a liar and a double crosser. I've never felt so in my life.

"There are people on the 3rd and 4th levels of the State Department who have always wanted to cut my throat. They've succeeded in doing it. Marshall's in California and Lovett's in Florida."

"Sunday, March 21, 1948: I spend the day trying to right what has happened. No luck. Marshall makes a statement [in California, at Truman's request by phone, on 20 March to the press, where he asserted that 'he recommended the course to the President']. Doesn't help me a mite."[68]

Dr. Chaim Weizmann (left), president of Israel, with Eddie Jacobson (right), friend of Truman, and unidentified man in the middle, ca. 1949 (courtesy Truman Library).

Any fair reading of the record, and not just of the above lines, must admit that Truman was indeed taken by surprise and was upset by the Austin speech.[69] Nevertheless, once placed into this position, Truman apparently felt it best to swallow the *fait accompli* by issuing the 25 March release to the press accepting that partition could not be implemented at the present time peacefully, necessitating the U.S. proposals of 19 March; he insisted, however, that partition was still a possibility once the "temporary" trusteeship was no longer required.[70]

Marshall's 20 March statement to the press made two other points relevant to our subject: (a) the president's crisis speech of 17 March to a joint session of Congress (which he made as a result of the February communist coup in Czechoslovakia amid other signs of a heightened threat from the Soviet Union requiring new military mobilization measures) further emphasized the "importance of preventing the outbreak of open warfare in Palestine"; and (b) while the 19 March Austin statement did not foreclose any future peaceful solution there, including that of partition, the Security Council on 5 March did "refuse" to "accept" at this time the General Assembly's 29 November resolution favoring partition.[71] It is no wonder that Truman saw this statement as not helping him a "mite."

Even prior to the California statement by Marshall, Truman was on the phone early that Saturday morning asking Clifford to come quickly to the White House in light of the Austin statement. This call was in keeping with Truman's having assigned Clifford the task of keeping an eye on the State Department's Palestine moves. Prior to March, the president basically was "winging it" in his consultations with State and Defense over that subject. Therefore, bringing in Clifford following the controversial statement by Austin of 23 February, as discussed above, marked an important phase in how the White House handled the problem. Recall that the National Security Council was barely getting started and would lack a national security advisor and substantive staff for years to come. Moreover, Truman did not initiate that office, which he saw as largely a congressional attempt to limit his presidential authority. He tended in this early period to ignore the mechanism; accordingly, Clifford may be said, at least for the moment, to have picked up the national security advisor role by default, accounting for the great personal animosity that arose between him and Marshall, who seems never to have gotten beyond his image of Clifford as merely Truman's domestic political advisor.[72] This tension would come most memorably to the fore at the White House strategy meeting of 12 May regarding whether and when the United States should recognize the soon-to-be proclaimed new Jewish state. At that meeting, Marshall told the president that Clifford had no business being there, while Truman's response was that he was there at his (Truman's) request and would be presenting the case for immediate recognition, in opposition to Marshall's position.

But before we pick up the next calamitous development — the sudden U.S. recognition of Israel minutes after its proclamation and while its UN delegation was still pressing for a trusteeship and truce over Palestine — a brief final observation would be in order regarding the historical record surrounding the events of 19 March. That record includes frequent quotations from the president's diary, but they should not be taken at face value. As described to the author of this book in communications from a Truman Library archivist:

> Truman kept a sporadic diary during his Presidency. He sometimes used a conventional, bound "diary book," but more often wrote on loose pieces of White House stationery or scratch paper. Occasionally, he jotted notes on his daily appointments calendar. I found Truman diary entries for March 19–20, but none for March 18 or May 12–14.
>
> Many of Truman's original, handwritten entries as President have survived, either in annual bound diaries for the years 1947, 1949, and 1951–53, or in dated longhand notes spanning the period from 1949 to 1953.... I was unable to find a handwritten Truman diary entry from March or April 1948.
>
> We believe that there was once a bound diary for the year 1948, which had not survived.

Given this situation, including the earlier noted discrepancy between what Truman may or may not have written on 19–21 March and the sequence of actual events, it would be reasonable to conclude that some manipulation of the presidential record for 1948 occurred in an effort to make the following case: (a) Truman was not prepared to drop partition on 19 March; and (b) that action was not carried out at Marshall's and Lovett's direction but was due to the decisions of their underlings. Note, for example, that the unpublished 21 March entry (above) clearly showed irritation at Marshall, and that Truman and Margaret seem unduly to harp on the role of the "third and fourth levels," as though staff members could have wrought the policy-level damage on their own.[73] In sum, we are left with the more direct evidence, which in itself is sufficient to give us confidence that, as some observers put it at the time, there was a kind of mutiny by the State Department that hurt both the White House and the reputation of U.S. diplomacy generally.[74]

General Assembly, Partition Resolution; Truman, Marshall, May 1948

The balance of the story of the struggle between Truman and Secretary of State Marshall over Palestine policy is less burdened by a murky historical record and consequently will take up less space here. But there are two specific questions that deserve further factual examination at this time: Was the U.S. delegation at the United Nations truly unavoidably caught short on the General Assembly floor on the late afternoon of 14 May by the news report that the president had just announced the recognition of the new State of Israel? Was the State Department truthful when it denied that it tried to use the bait in late May of offering Israel a higher level of recognition (*de jure* versus *de facto*) and exchange of diplomatic representation (minister versus special representative) if it would agree to give up to the Arabs part of the territory — notably the southern, "Negev" part — allotted to it by the Assembly's 29 November resolution?

Even as the General Assembly duly began its special session on 16 April pursuant to a request by the Security Council in its resolution of 1 April, pessimism already reigned as to whether the United States indeed had a workable plan for preventing the outbreak of international violence in the Middle East after 15 May. The British had begun their gradual withdrawal of soldiers from Palestine, increasing the scope for Jewish-Arab conflict as the two communities jockeyed for optimum strategic positions in anticipation of the larger scale of warfare ahead. Moreover, thousands of armed men were slipping into the country from the Arab states and participating as an Arab Liberation Army in the still ostensibly domestic battles conventionally labeled the "civil war" phase of the Arab-Israeli conflict in 1948.[75] The Jews, too, were building up their military strength, whether through their establishment militia, the Haganah, or through the more radical and terrorist underground forces, Irgun and Stern Gang. On top of that, thanks largely to successful, legal fund-raising in the United States (the Jewish Agency's Golda Meir was able to collect some $100 million largely from American Jews during the period covered by the present chapter),[76] they were able to purchase, principally from the supplier of both sides, Czechoslovakia, the heavy arms that they lacked and that began to arrive only in early April, once the Jewish Agency was able to organize a safe delivery port on the Mediterranean as well as secure airports.

At the United Nations itself, the American initiative was soon stalemated by a number of problems. The British, much to the inadvertent advantage of the Zionists, remained adamant that they would not extend their stay in Palestine under any circumstances (barring a Jewish-Arab agreement) or for any period of time, short or long.[77] The truce called for by the Security Council on 1 April failed to materialize. The very rationale serving as the basis of the U.S. plan — a UN governing authority under the policy control of the Trusteeship Council and acting with the help of a modest international police force in a calm atmosphere — was seen as faulty and a pie-in-the-sky fantasy.[78] Despite this negative atmosphere, the American delegation soldiered on into mid-May at the General Assembly and in the Trusteeship Council, where it labored over the draft of a municipal charter for the planned internationalization of the Jerusalem area. The delegation also went so far as to circulate a lengthy text of the prospective trusteeship agreement for the UN governing authority in Palestine, and to obtain the appointment of a Philadelphia lawyer, Harold Evans, as the head initially of the United Nations' Jerusalem apparatus but hopefully also eventually over the Palestine-wide UN governing authority — he barely got to his post in late May when he realized the futility of his role and promptly returned to the United States. In early May, the State Department even obtained Truman's approval for the use of his personal plane for a last-minute, Rusk-inspired contrivance to fly what he considered the key New York–based Jewish, Arab and other negotiators to Palestine to work out on the spot a ten-day truce or cease-fire so that the General Assembly would have more time to agree on the "temporary trusteeship" replacing the British mandatory power. The effort was aborted amid open skepticism.

With that failure, and time having run out to block the proclamation of a Jewish state, the State Department, at the last minute in the General Assembly, ended its campaign for a trusteeship and settled instead for a resolution, adopted late in the evening of 14 May, that established a mediator position and a demand for an immediate truce.

In these circumstances, one didn't have to be a State Department insider to know that the United Nations was merely spinning its wheels while Palestine was heading toward its own destiny. Nor would one have been surprised at Lovett's reported guidance to the delegation not to do any "unusual" lobbying or at Rusk's privately expressed comment that the United States, having called for the special session, must now at least be seen as having a plan for the Assembly to wrestle over lest the Americans be perceived as having acted merely to help the Arab cause.[79] Certainly, the Truman White House did not need to be told by others of this dead-end situation. Time and again, after 19 March, the State Department had wrongly assured it that a truce agreed upon by both Jews and Arabs was in immediate view, first by 7 April and then by the end of that month, and finally well into May. Whether for its own domestic political reasons or out of recognition of the realities in Palestine, the White House was set on making the most of the situation for the U.S. national interest and, presumably only incidentally, for the political benefit of the Truman administration in the November election.[80] The reasoning seemed unassailable: the Soviets clearly were going to recognize the Jewish state, and it behooved the United States not to leave the field to that adversary;

the Jews by mid–May were seen as better able to defend themselves and to establish their state than at first thought (even Forrestal revised his previously pessimistic estimate of Jewish military prospects, at least for the immediate future); recognition would be consistent with the historical trend of American policy and, especially after the Holocaust, with majority public opinion, which was in favor of a Jewish state; and the State Department's own general counsel, Ernest Gross, wrote a memorandum that was made available to the White House which assured that the United States would be perfectly within its legal rights under existing circumstances were it to choose, once the present special session of the General Assembly ended without revising its 29 November resolution, to recognize either or both independent states in Palestine, but not a unitary Palestinian state, as that would be contrary to the provisions of that resolution.[81]

The dramatic 12 May White House meeting on Palestine referred to earlier in this chapter left the impression with the State Department participants that

On October 26, 1949, Israeli ambassador to the United States Eliahu Elath (formerly Epstein) gave Truman a silver ark to hold the Scrolls of Law, which Weizmann had presented to Truman on May 25, 1948 (courtesy Truman Library).

Truman was still with them. But, as was typical of past such policy debates on this subject, Truman hesitated to come down firmly one way or the other, and it could not have been that much of a surprise to the department when Clifford informed Lovett at lunch on 14 May that the president would announce recognition of the Jewish state minutes after it came into existence at 6:00 P.M. Washington, D.C., time. The official record and later reminiscences as to what happened on that day, once again, fail to add up. They raise questions in the reader's mind. A brief chronology, based largely on Lovett's Diary, follows:

10:00: The beginning of a White House–Jewish Agency (Eliahu Epstein) drafting collaboration on a letter requesting U.S. recognition; by noon, the draft is completed and a copy sent to the secretary of state.

11:35: Lovett has McClintock double-check regarding any British "recognition" plan; the answer is that, on 8 May, they informed Ambassador Lewis Douglas that they will "wait a while."

11:45: Former department legal advisor Charles Fahy, who, like Lovett, was a naval aviator during the First World War, phones him to request that the United States pressure the British to get the Arab Legion out of Palestine now, as promised, and stop attacking Jewish villages.

Noon: Clifford informs Lovett of the recognition decision and agrees that the department should take every precaution to alert the field in advance so that protective measures might be taken. The two also agree that, as regards the UN situation, the department should try to ensure that there be no delegation leaks prior to the president's announcement.

12:05: Lovett assures Marshall that he has "nothing else" this morning and then lunches with Clifford.

2:40: Rusk phones to say he has "just arrived" from New York. Lovett: "come up."

3:50: Legal advisor Gross phones to report a "misunderstanding as to exactly what kind of recognition we are giving to the provisional government in Palestine"—followed immediately by a meeting of the two plus Rusk, Henderson, "et al."

4:00: Lovett informs Clifford that Marshall does not approve of the recognition but will not oppose it.[82]

4:35: Clifford phones to say that he will get to Lovett by 5:30 the "formal request" for recognition being prepared with Epstein and Ben Cohen, the former counselor in the department. Lovett: "If you approve, we'll send out to Chiefs of Mission in the Middle East" a telegram giving advance notice at around 5:00.[83]

5:40: After turning down Lovett's 5:30 appeal to delay the announcement at least until the end of the General Assembly session around 10:00 pm that evening, the White House confirms that Austin should be informed.

5:45: Clifford agrees to be the one, rather than Lovett, to call Rusk and have him inform Austin. Rusk, according to Clifford's memoirs, gave him the impression that the recognition decision was news to him. Rusk then protested it on the grounds that the United States already had a majority for obtaining Assembly approval of its proposals. However, Rusk does telephone Austin, who famously leaves the floor of the Assembly to receive it and then goes home without having informed his colleagues. The delegation (specifically, Jessup) then continues to speak from the podium in favor of a truce and the creation of a mediator post, even as news reports begin to circulate of the recognition, at first denied by the Americans but soon acknowledged as accurate.[84]

6:10: Lovett tells Clifford that, contrary to what he'd told Clifford earlier in the day — that Austin's likely response to the recognition would be to "get mad and resign"— Austin actually informed Rusk that "he is supporting the President's position."

The incongruities in this chronology are striking. It is inconceivable that the State Department, hours before informing Austin, could have sent out a circular telegram without Rusk (who had just been summoned to the department from New York and had just met Lovett) knowing of it before Clifford's call. Moreover, once that telegram went out, it was extremely unlikely that no one in the department would at least informally have told its delegation in New York of the situation. If, indeed, Austin had been informed hours prior to Rusk's call, as could well have been the case given the history of the gamesmanship between the State Department and the White House, then it would be entirely natural in this scenario for Rusk, in another of his contrivances, to have feigned ignorance of the president's recognition decision until Clifford called him minutes before 6:00 P.M. This would make credible the official State Department version that the fiasco that followed at the United Nations could not have been avoided and was entirely spontaneous rather than staged. Creating such an impression was important to the department, which surely wanted to make it clear to the world that it had no advance knowledge of, nor approved (as Marshall informed Truman), the president's recognition, and that it had been negotiating a different course of action in good faith up to the last hour. Finally, Clifford and not Lovett making the call to Rusk is unusual and invites the suspicion that the department, while badly wanting to separate itself visibly from Truman's action, also wanted to avoid giving the White House the impression that the UN events were designed to embarrass the president personally. Therefore, giving Rusk the opportunity to tell Clifford of his ignorance of the decision until that last minute adds to the impression the department surely hoped to make on the White House that those events in New York were unplanned. That Lovett was bitter enough about the timing of the recognition to help carry out such a scenario is clear from his 17 May memorandum summarizing the events of 14 May, which ends with these words: "the President's political advisers, having failed last Wednesday afternoon [12 May] to make the President a father of the new state [by having him recognize the Jewish state even before it officially came into existence and while the General Assembly was still in session], have determined at least to make him the midwife."[85] (It would seem that each of the two sides in this political struggle was more prepared to blame the lower levels than the responsible principals themselves.)

The second murky point remaining to be analyzed here concerns Clifford's charge that the State Department tried on 29 May to pressure Israel to agree to territorial adjustments in exchange for a higher level of diplomatic recognition and representation than would otherwise be the case.[86] The department's Loy Henderson is the official in the middle of this controversy, whose very nature reflects the new, post-recognition phase of U.S. relations with the Jews of Palestine. Whether the Clifford charge is valid or not, there is no question that the department after 15 May necessarily dropped its effort to nullify Truman's pro-partition policy and was now focusing on what might best be called "damage control" to limit the negative effects of the president's action on American interests in the Middle East. One way to achieve this goal, which included finding a formula to win Arab acceptance of the Jewish state, would be to accord Israel less than full diplomatic recognition and a low-key level of representation unless it agreed to a rollback of its claim to all the territory allotted to it under the 29 November resolution. Henderson's biographer writes that "Clifford's tale is hard to credit," as there was no evidence to contradict that official's denial that he offered Epstein, now the Provisional Government of Israel's Washington representative, the above-described deal.[87] In fact, as will be shown shortly, there is contemporary evidence that the offer was indeed made. But first, some context will be provided.

The Soviets by then had given the higher level of recognition and representation that Henderson now was allegedly dangling before Epstein. Nevertheless, after the Henderson-Epstein meeting, the United States decided to accord Israel representation only at the *de facto* and special representative levels (making the Soviet minister the senior foreign diplomat in Israel).[88] The State Department at the time justified its decision on the legal grounds that it had no other choice given that the American act of recognition was only of the "provisional government as the *de facto* authority of the new State of Israel."[89]

It also accompanied that final decision with the nomination to the White House of a career mid-level Foreign Service officer to be the "temporary Acting U.S. Special Representative" to Israel.

While the White House went along with the department's decision regarding the initial level of diplomatic relations with Israel, it most definitely bucked at the effort to send only a Foreign Service officer to Tel Aviv, strongly preferring a high-profile, political appointment.[90] Therefore, and to Marshall's great disgruntlement, it on its own, on 22 June, as described below, plucked a well-known, active Zionist, James G. McDonald, from the private sector to help demonstrate and protect the president's more forthcoming policy toward Israel.[91]

To return to the Clifford-generated controversy, which publicly flowered years later, a reporting telegram by Epstein (who was the source of Clifford's information), sent on the day that the alleged Henderson offer was made, informed his government that Henderson had proposed the above-described deal — specifically, *de jure* recognition and representation at the ministerial level in exchange for "frontier adjustments."[92] In that telegram, Henderson was quoted as saying that U.S. recognition had not been based on the 29 November resolution but on the need to avoid a vacuum[93]; that there was no consultation with the British over the arrangement being proposed to Epstein; and that, since the economic union with the Arab state envisaged in the resolution was not in the cards, Israel could well gain viability from frontier changes (but he then declined to offer details on this suggestion and dropped the point).[94]

Epstein went from that meeting to one with Lovett, who had been briefed beforehand by Henderson. Lovett, in what he acknowledged to be only a "delaying tactic," made clear that the United States would only proceed at the *de facto* and special representative levels.[95] (McDonald arrived in Tel Aviv on 12 August as the only member of his mission holding diplomatic status in Israel.[96] His second in command, political counselor Charles Knox, proved to be a strong supporter of the president's policy and fully shared McDonald's aspirations for the Jewish state. Incidentally, Knox was the very Foreign Service officer the State Department had originally nominated to act as the special representative before the White House turned to McDonald.[97])

Perhaps a fitting note on which to end this aspect of the study would be to quote a point of view that Rusk on 2 May offered to a visiting Saudi Arabian prince and that still resonates today: "the President considers partition a fair and equitable solution for Palestine, subject to the conditions for UN action contained in the Charter and subject to our determination not to take unilateral action.... If it were clear that such a [Jewish] state would be at war permanently with the Arab world or would serve as a base for hostile elements

James G. McDonald (left), the U.S. special representative to Israel, meeting with Prime Minister David Ben-Gurion on August 20, 1948, a week after his arrival in Tel Aviv. McDonald would be elevated to the rank of ambassador in March 1949 (United States Holocaust Memorial Museum, courtesy James McDonald. The views or opinions expressed in this book, and the context in which the image is used, do not necessarily reflect the views or policy of, nor imply approval or endorsement by, the United States Holocaust Memorial Museum).

[read: Soviet Union], the U.S. obviously would not consider it to her own interests to see such a state established."⁹⁸

Just prior to the Suez War of October 1956, Richard Rovere, in writing about the Palestine issue in the *New Yorker* issue of 21 April, concluded, "It is one of the neater ironies of modern history that the view of the informed and disinterested men turned out to be almost completely wrong, while the relatively uninformed and by no means disinterested politicians were vindicated on all counts."⁹⁹

Would Rovere have continued in his assessment had he the perspective of our present-day observers? Perhaps a point of view such as Rusk's would have received a second hearing from him in light of the events since that spring of 1956.

Two

James G. McDonald's Unusual Path to Appointment as America's First Representative in Israel

"I should like to say, in complete honesty, that you have made a valuable contribution to history.... There is a satisfaction in having been the first diplomatic representative to a country. You and I have shared this unique experience — you in Israel and I, years ago, in Canada."[1] — Former undersecretary of state William Phillips to McDonald, September 24, 1951

Unique, indeed! How many newly appointed ambassadors confront their president at a pre-departure meeting with a memorandum citing the names of mid-level State Department officials working against White House policy and in need of more senior supervision? How many had spent the immediately preceding years in the United States and abroad actively and publicly denouncing the uneven record of the American government regarding the very matters that they would now be concerned with as ambassadors? Finally, how many could justifiably claim that their very appointment was an important act of policy given their outspoken public advocacy for one side in a diplomatic dispute within the administration?

McDonald's is a most unusual story of how a 61-year-old, to his own surprise and gratification, was offered his first full-time, salaried position in the government. As the shape and fate of his ambassadorship were heavily determined by the background and circumstances of his appointment, their details are of more than normal interest. Typically, an ambassador either comes from career diplomatic service or has been an influential supporter of the political party in power. McDonald (1886–1964) was neither of these. His apolitical career was almost entirely in the private sector, and he was not an independently wealthy man. Rather, earning a decent living was a constant concern, requiring him to seek out and accept sundry positions in the New York area, which was his base starting in 1919. That year was a seminal one, because he became chairman of the Foreign Policy Association (FPA), a position that was a perfect match with his talents, interests, and personality.

FPA would be his vehicle for the next fifteen years, as he built up a reputation for independent, informed judgments on international and public affairs. Though he had been an instructor of history at Harvard and then at Indiana University, his alma mater, he never achieved an earned doctorate, and his only book, *My Mission In Israel*,[2] was published in 1951, the year he left government. As FPA chairman up to 1933, McDonald proved himself a tireless correspondent, a smooth organizer of conferences, a successful nationwide radio commentator, and a determined fund-raiser. His public speaking was often described as inspirational, complementing a sincerely warm and sociable personality and a creative mind. No wonder, then, that by the early 1930s he was personally known to essentially all leading Americans in public life and in the financial world. For example, in 1929, he escorted John D. Rockefeller III, a fresh college graduate, on a four-month, round-the-world tour, during which the two predictably had little trouble meeting world figures.

Until 1933, the main Jewish-specific question of the day, Zionism, was but one of many topics on his agenda. Starting with that year, when that question took the form of how to respond to the ever-increasing number of Jewish refugees fleeing Germany, it would dominate his work and thinking — at least until the World War II period, when winning the war was the foremost issue. Even in the year before Hitler's advent to power, McDonald would tell of having by chance stayed at a Berlin hotel where Hitler and his entourage also were staying and of how he quickly recognized the nature of that group's dangerous goals both for the Jews and for world peace. That impression from a distance was cemented by his private interview in 1933 with now–Chancellor Hitler. There, using the fluent German he had learned from his family since childhood, he directly confronted him with a warning against continuing his present course of action. The German's blunt response that the world would end up thanking him for his actions against the Jews was enough to convince McDonald that, unless Hitler were stopped, the Jews of Germany would very soon be in mortal danger.

McDonald felt that this Nazi program was a challenge to the Christian world as well. He began publicly to appeal throughout that world for firm policies to curb Hitler. Certainly, no non–Jew was as prominent as he during the 1930s in promoting awareness of the need for preventive action, not only by private organizations but, even more necessarily, by governments as well. This prominence led to his nomination and acceptance, despite justified doubts as to the extent of practical support it would get, of the office of League of Nations High Commissioner for Refugees (Jews and others) from Germany. Now, for the first time, McDonald's focus was entirely on the problem of how, literally, to save the Jews of Germany. The obstacles were quite obvious, beginning with his own sponsoring organization: the League of Nations. While granting its imprimatur to his office, that body still harbored hopes of luring Germany back into the fold. For that principal reason, the League denied McDonald office and secretarial support, let alone sustained funding. Consequently, McDonald felt it best to establish his headquarters at Lausanne, where he would periodically regroup and meet with his board members and staff after traveling the world seeking places of refuge, financial support and international cooperation at the private as well as governmental levels. His main active and financial backers, of course, came from the appreciative Jewish communities, among whom he became a very familiar face, especially in Western Europe, Latin America and his own country.

The following two years, however, were predictably frustrating and led to his long letter of resignation to the League in December 1935. It quickly became a rather famous document in which McDonald candidly laid out his detailed analysis of the problem and those responsible for it. While it didn't really change things, that letter further cemented his image among Jews as their most admirable public advocate.

During the next few years, he took on a variety of positions: first, for two years he served as a member of the *New York Times* editorial board (an irony, given the harsh criticism that would later be leveled at that paper for having "buried" the story of the genocide against the Jews); then, up to 1942, as president of the Brooklyn Institute of Arts and Sciences (although, as the editors of his published papers have noted, administration was not his strong suit); and finally, during World War II, as a regular radio commentator on a national network along with ad hoc public assignments as a member of various local and federal boards. Clearly, he had to work for a living. (The $20,000 annual salary he would receive as ambassador to Israel was about the same level of income he averaged throughout this earlier period.)

McDonald kept up his useful ties to FPA as "honorary chairman." He also retained an important public role, and access to the highest levels of the U.S. government throughout the Second World War, as chairman of President Roosevelt's Advisory Committee on Political Refugees. For example, he attended the 1938 Evian Conference on the refugee problem, but to his apparent regret only as a "technical advisor" to the president's head of delegation, Myron Taylor. This latter role seemed to especially rankle him, perhaps because his favorite title for mid-level officials who were opposing his policies, whether in the U.S., the British, or the Israeli government, was "technicians." (A good interpretation of this tendency can be gleaned from a commentary of 1976 that Secretary of State Kissinger and Egypt's President Sadat treated their "subordinates ... as mere technicians, entrusted only with details."[3])

At the war's end, McDonald intensified his job-hunting campaigns, focusing on now–President Truman's reorganization of the government's top staff. But he was in for a series of disappointments, especially regarding his expressed hopes either for an ambassadorship to a European country or for an assistant secretaryship in the State Department. He particularly urged his friends in the nationwide Jewish community to use what influence they could bring to bear on the White House and on James Byrnes, the secretary of state, and he drew on his long-time, if distant, relationship with Clark Clifford's mother, apparently in part with the same goal in mind. Despite all this, he failed even to be selected by Truman for the fateful 1945 survey of Jewish displaced persons in Europe that was performed instead by Earl Harrison, the American representative to the Inter-Governmental Committee on Refugees.[4] Nevertheless, McDonald did end up with a role even more in the public and international eye regarding the refugee problem and its nettlesome element, the Palestine question: he was selected as one of six U.S. members of the Anglo-American Committee of Inquiry on Palestine that carried out its work from December 1945 through April 1946. It was established at British initiative in response to Truman's endorsement of Harrison's call for the immediate entrance into Palestine of 100,000 Jews languishing in camps in the British and American zones of Germany.

While that committee's unanimously approved ten recommendations failed of subsequent governmental adoption, the fact that the first of them endorsed Truman's 1945 call for unconditional entrance into Palestine of the 100,000 was greatly appreciated by Jews worldwide, including those heading the Jewish Agency in Palestine. McDonald naturally reaped much of the reward for that recommendation. At a meeting with Truman in July 1946, he took the lead for New York senators Wagner and Mead, who also were present, in bluntly criticizing the president for allowing the special State Department–led Cabinet Committee on this issue to dilute his own policies in its follow-up consultations with the British. The latter were adamantly opposed to such an unconditional immigration of Jews into Palestine and instead refreshed an entirely different plan for Palestine's future that the Anglo-American Commission had already rejected back in January, but which the Cabinet Committee's three-man technical team that had gone to London for further consultations — the so-called "Grady Group"— was now endorsing. McDonald told the president in no uncertain terms that implementation of this British plan would result in an unacceptable "cantonization" of the Jewish communities in Palestine and allow the British to remain there indefinitely.

Following that meeting, McDonald sent a personal telegram to Truman expressing the hope that he hadn't come across as more concerned with the political fate of the Jews in Palestine than with the issue of most concern to the president — the fate of the 100,000 displaced persons. That telegram also informed Truman, who at their meeting had berated New Yorkers, that he, too, was a Midwesterner by background, that he had never been an employee of a Jewish organization,[5] and that he would gladly be at the president's disposal for any further assignment Truman might wish to give him. McDonald took satisfaction from Truman's subsequent forestalling of any further U.S. consideration of the British–Grady Group plan and then renewing his call for the transfer of the 100,000 to Palestine (doing so in what was widely perceived as a clear political move on the eve of the 1946 congressional elections — the famous "Yom Kippur" statement).[6]

Still, by mid–1946, McDonald found himself without the kind of position he had hoped to obtain in the postwar period. He began to travel the world as a compensated speaker, urging primarily Jewish communities to purchase bonds for the development of Palestine. In 1947, he also visited Palestine itself for the private purpose of researching a book he was writing that would analyze the thirty-year history of the British Mandate there. Although the extensive manuscript for the book was soon almost entirely completed, he proved unable to publish it for lack of the 3,500 assured advance purchasers the prospective publisher was demanding.

A measure of how pessimistic he was regarding prospects for a position in the Truman administration is that, when the White House in the person of Clark Clifford made the offer in a phone call on June 22, 1948, the McDonalds had only a few weeks earlier returned home from a long trip to South Africa and England in connection with his fund-raising role.[7] While in England, he had made several widely reported speeches berating efforts by the United States and Great Britain to gut the UN General Assembly resolution of the past November 29 (incidentally, his birthday) recommending partition of Palestine into Jewish and Arab states along with international status for the Jerusalem area. The White House, anxious to appoint its own man ahead of any public debate with the State Department over its candidates for the Israel post, insisted on an immediate response from McDonald to the offer of being made special representative in Israel. Overruling any practical issues of family or financial needs, and recognizing that the assignment was a fulfillment of his decades-long work in favor of the Jews, McDonald within the hour agreed to the position. He also was convinced that his prestige with the

Jews worldwide and with Israelis of all stripes was a unique asset for his own country, whose official policies he was determined to carry out faithfully and well.

McDonald obviously felt strongly that those policies, as enunciated by the president, were still being undermined at the State Department even at this late stage in the creation of the Jewish state. Accordingly, at his pre-departure meeting with Truman in late July, he once again, as in 1946, had occasion to press him on the need to exercise stronger control over that department. Coming armed with the memorandum described at the start of this chapter, he agreed not to submit it for the official record, obtaining in return then and there from Truman a letter that he could and would use within and outside government to show that he indeed was acting with the full and express authority of the president. That letter specifically cited as illustrative matters within McDonald's areas of responsibility, "in addition to your regular reports to the Department of State," the following: "matters as relate to the arms embargo, the appropriate time for full recognition, and the types of assistance as may be required by and can properly be granted to the new state." Truman added that he expected to be "personally informed" on those matters. McDonald would during his tenure make full use of this explicit request of the president.

Just as there was — and remains — controversy as to Truman's reasons for so quickly giving Israel (or perhaps only its provisional government, as the State Department maintained, leaving ambiguity as to whether the United States had actually established diplomatic relations with the State of Israel itself) *de facto* recognition in May, there also was — and remains as an integral element in that controversy — debate as to the appropriateness of selecting McDonald as America's representative there. Of course, the principal charge against the president regarding the McDonald appointment is that he was pandering for the Jewish vote and for their financial support in the upcoming presidential election.[8] Another is that it was not in the national interest to have chosen a man so explicitly associated with the Zionist cause. Counter-arguments, as would be vehemently articulated in later years by, for example, Clark Clifford, were that Truman correctly understood public opinion in the United States as being in favor of his decisions regarding Palestine; that those actions were in line with U.S. government policy in favor of the Balfour Declaration, the Palestine Mandate that incorporated that declaration, and most recently the UN vote of 29 November; and that McDonald's selection was in keeping with the president's recognition of Israel and his need to demonstrate an ongoing commitment to that policy of support for the Jewish state. The White House also clearly perceived the utility of having in its administration another voice to temper the unenthusiastic support it was receiving from the State Department, the consequences of which were creating a public image of uncertain and ineffective leadership on this issue. There is also evidence that Truman and his staff honestly admired McDonald's talents and intellect.

But the debate over who should represent the United States in Israel was not finished with McDonald's June 1948 selection as special representative to a provisional government. When Israel in January 1949 elected a constituent assembly and established a permanent government, it finally received *de jure* recognition from the United States, among others. This naturally elevated their respective missions to embassy status, and their representatives to ambassadorial level. The election of Truman to a new term notwithstanding, it was far from certain that McDonald would remain at his post as ambassador. The president was under pressure once again from within his administration to choose a career diplomat, or at least a person less completely devoted to the Israeli cause. Some in the private sector were also pushing their own candidates on the grounds that the ambassador would best be Jewish; to McDonald's personal disappointment, there was a reportedly self-declared candidate, Bartley Crum, who had been his most like-minded colleague on the Anglo-American Committee of 1946 and who was now publisher of *The Star*, the only New York newspaper (or so he claimed to the president) that had endorsed Truman's candidacy. In the end, to the delight of most American Jewry and probably the entire Jewish population of Israel, McDonald in late January 1949 was offered and gratefully accepted the promotion to ambassador, which the Senate confirmed in March, and he would remain in that post until his departure from the country on December 13, 1950. McDonald was thereby not only the first U.S. ambassador to Israel but also the world's first such ambassador. This leap-frogged him over the incumbent Soviet minister as the new dean of the seven-man Diplomatic Corps.

It might be well to close this chapter with a suitable matching bookend to the opening epigraph that is illustrative of the very personal heat generated by McDonald's diplomatic role in the Palestine issue. But first, it would be relevant to note that on June 21, 1948, just one day before Clifford's surprise call to him, McDonald authorized, along with two other former members of the Anglo-American Committee, a press release "deploring" Ambassador William Phillips' acceptance of the vice-chairmanship of the "Committee for Justice and Peace in the Holy Land." The three expressed "sorrow and bewilderment" at Phillips' action, and they charged that that committee backed and encouraged Arab aggression in Palestine. They also noted with disapproval the language in one of its planks opposing "extreme Zionist pressure" in the United States, including "insistence on separate Jewish nationalism." (A note to McDonald after the issuance of the press release came from an official of a Zionist organization expressing "thanks for cooperating on this.") Phillips, who was himself a member of the Anglo-American Committee, was perhaps unaware of that 1948 criticism when he penned his complimentary letter to McDonald of 1951 quoted at the beginning of this chapter. However, by 1953, he felt unfriendly enough toward him to include the following sarcasms in his *Ventures in Diplomacy*[9]:

> "[McDonald, after the completion of the Anglo-American Committee's work in 1946,] was to come out strongly for a Zionist state and was to be naturally acclaimed by the Jewish communities wherever he went. Very naturally also he became the first American Minister to Israel."

Three

Truman Speaks Off-the-Record on Palestine to the State Department, July 1947–June 1948

"Israel wasn't a problem yet but became a stinker in a short time."— Lovett, speaking in July 1971 about his early months after taking office in July 1947[1]

Lovett Diary and Conversations with Truman, July–September 1947

There has been little, if any, prior use made of Lovett's diary in the historiography of the Palestine question, although surely there is valuable insight to be obtained there regarding the concerns and motivations of the principal policymakers in the government as they made their moves to ease the diplomatic and military crisis in the Near East stemming from the coming to a head of communal and international conflict in the Holy Land.[2] Accordingly, this chapter, as will be the case in two subsequent ones dealing with the remaining phases of the present study, will offer a set of the more significant, relevant quotations from the log regarding one vital topic in the hope that it will help summarize the key issues of the period covered by the preceding chapters and that it will stimulate use of that valuable document by future historians. The material should be considered as falling under the category labeled by Court Historian Voltaire as "anecdotes," because it goes beyond the official documentation while still representing authentic contemporary evidence explaining the concerned events. To clothe this point in more contemporary, concrete terms, a modern American historian has recently written:

> Unfortunately, the [official] record itself may be harder and harder to reconstruct when it comes to the past couple of decades. On the one hand, we have access to vast amounts of information and endless, often pointless, commentary by talking heads and so-called experts. But we also know that bureaucrats

and decision-makers are increasingly reluctant to put everything on paper (or in electronic files); sensitive emails can be deleted; presidents since Nixon have stopped taping their conversations in the Oval Office; secret presidential findings may remain secret for a long time or even be destroyed; telephone diplomacy often leaves little trace of what leaders actually said.[3]

A limitation of Lovett's "diary" is that its substantive content consists only of brief, very sketchy summaries made (presumably by Lovett's secretarial staff) of his telephone conversations; the document, however, does helpfully list who visited Lovett's office and where he went at any given time of the day. In sum, it is a record in "real time" of how the two principal policymakers on the Palestine question experienced its evolution.

The selections made in this (and in a later, similar chapter) out of the large number of log entries for the nineteen-month period of Lovett's tenure are designed to demonstrate the document's value in shedding additional, focused light on one of the more important — and still controversial — aspects of the issues with which the Truman administration had to contend in formulating its Palestine policy — the extent to which Truman, either speaking "off-the-record" himself or through his personal staff at the White House, was actually and directly involved in, and generally supportive of, State Department maneuvers in responding to rapidly changing circumstances in the field; the selections will also help clarify the role Truman's personal political ambitions played in his Palestine decisions. The approach will be to provide brief but essential context to the selected entries, which will be grouped chronologically, period by period, after a general description of the dominant issues of concern to the administration, and to Truman personally, during that particular time. Where supplementary material is not drawn directly from the log's entries, it is placed within brackets and labeled as a "comment." All citations within quotation marks are exactly as they appear in the log.

However, before getting to these individual entries, a summary would be in order of the main Palestine-related conversations between the White House and Lovett, the State Department's "point man" on Palestine, in his first few months in office before the matter became a "stinker":

July–September 1947

There were few references during this period to White House activities related to the Palestine question. One concerned the unsuccessful effort of the United States to convince the British not to send the *Exodus* passengers (Jewish displaced persons seeking illegally to enter Palestine) back to Germany, even obtaining assurances from the Jewish Agency and American Jewish

Arthur Vandenberg, Republican Majority Leader of the Senate, with Mrs. Eleanor Roosevelt, member of the U.S. Delegation to the United Nations, and Austin, April 24, 1949 (UN photograph).

groups that they would provide the funds that the British were initially claiming they lacked in order to sustain the passengers in Palestine. As Lovett finally concluded, "funds had nothing to do with the matter." A second issue concerned the recruitment of suitable members for the U.S. delegation to the upcoming UN General Assembly session in New York: the White House pushed for assigning General John Hilldring, the departing assistant secretary of state for occupied areas — and a warm supporter of helping Jewish survivors living in refugee camps in Germany to find new permanent homes outside of Europe. For reasons of health and the prospect of a position as "executive secretary" of the newly established National Security Council, Hilldring hesitated until the last moment, when he finally agreed in early September to go to New York, much to the special satisfaction of Eleanor Roosevelt and others concerned with the Jewish refugee problem and the Palestine question. In a related matter, Lovett helped his chief of the Near East Bureau, Loy Henderson, to bring in from the field Ambassador George Wadsworth to serve the delegation as an advisor regarding relations with the Arab states; Lovett had to overcome White House qualms over this appointment given Wadsworth's known anti–Zionist views.

September–December 1947

Context

The president's main concern regarding the Palestine question, as the General Assembly session opened in New York in September, was to avoid having the United States bear the brunt of achieving his administration's joint policy goal with the British — which was to maintain peace and stability there while also assuring continuing Western control of, or at least dominant influence in, that country. He also had a vested, personal interest, since the end of the Second World War, in seeing a large number of Jews immediately and unconditionally enter Palestine from U.S.-administered refugee camps in Germany, a goal opposed by the Arab states and, on this point, by the British as well. The General Assembly's vehicle for considering the overall question centered on a debate over the report of its Special Committee on Palestine (UNSCOP), whose majority recommended partition and an internationalized Jerusalem. The United States supported partition, but with the important condition (one that the British held in special regard) that UNSCOP's territorial proposals be modified to give most of the Negev (which, minus the Gaza Strip, borders Egypt down to the port and Gulf of Aqaba) to the proposed Arab state versus the Jewish one. Truman ordered the delegation, headed during the initial weeks of the session by Secretary of State George C. Marshall personally, to avoid lobbying for its position, except regarding the Negev issue, although this would change in the days leading up to the Assembly vote of 29 November, a vote that gave the necessary two-thirds support for partition. In a compromise with the Jewish Agency, the Assembly resolution left to the Jewish state the UNSCOP-proposed Negev borders except for a few miles along the frontier with Egypt just eastward of the Gaza Strip, which was now assigned to the Arab state.

Following are relevant excerpts from the log. As will be true for the balance of this chapter, the reader will find paraphrased, for purposes of brevity and clarity, only the nonessential elements in the entries, leaving the rest unchanged and in quotation marks.

9 October

Hilldring calls from New York to report that the president had just told him that he "wanted make certain we are not going pick up hot bricks that British drop and put in position where they can say 'carry on'; also, we do not want any undertaking involving use of U.S. troops except as part of UN group."

19 November

President calls: (a) "would not want us to be in the minority in voting No [on partition] against the majority in the Committee" [Comment: This was an Assembly sub-group comprised of all member states — an "*Ad Hoc Committee of the Whole*," or COW — and put in charge of preparing recommendations for the plenary concerning the Palestine question]; and (b) had talked with [Chaim] Weizmann and "wanted us to be on the square with both sides.... Mr. Lovett said we proposed to vote No on the first round but to make it plain that we would accept the majority view [of the COW], which would maintain our position, but would follow the majority decision."

22 November

President phones: (a) "has had advice from certain sources in New York that it would be impossible to get our program through UN; that UN would not get support from the other countries. Under circumstances, he would not wish us to be in position of carrying the torch alone and getting blamed for failure of compromise"; and (b) orders that we "release Hilldring, Rusk and Johnson from previous instructions and take whatever steps are necessary so that we will not be left holding the bag." [Comment: Dean Rusk, head of the State Department's UN office, was with the delegation in New York; Ambassador Herschel Johnson, a career diplomat, was the deputy to Warren Austin, the permanent representative to the United Nations.]

24 November

(a) Lovett calls Rusk in New York: "president anxious that we uphold our commitment to Arabs. President thought we may have gone a little far on assurances we gave ... wants to be sure we don't step into British shoes in accepting leadership." (b) Lovett tells White House staffer David Niles that the Jewish Agency was "finagling with Commies. Has never seen a group ruin its cause so quickly; thinks best thing they could do would be leave New York."

25 November

(a) Lovett tells Secretary of Defense James Forrestal that he had "asked President not to see any more of these Jews; also, we should do nothing which would prejudice the other countries." (b) Lovett asks White House staffer Matthew Connelly to urge the president "not discuss matter with anyone."

28 November

Clark Clifford, White House staffer, agrees with Lovett that the president should not "personally inject himself" on the Palestine vote.

16–22 December

(a) Lovett on the 16th tells others he is planning to get away "for a little rest in February." (b) Truman on the 22nd urges him "to take week off to rest up." [Comment: On that latter day, Lovett declined Forrestal's suggestion that the two go together to their respective vacation homes at Hobe Sound in Florida: "no way" with Marshall also away. Lovett would finally get away to Florida only in mid–March, when Marshall, too, was away for part of that period. As described in Chapter One, it was during their common absence, apparently designed to help ensure that Truman would not intervene at the last minute, that Austin made his headline-making statement on 19 March to the Security Council that the United States now favored a "temporary" UN trusteeship versus partition in Palestine.]

January–June 1948

Context

With Palestine now in the throes of what was generally known as a "civil war," the Truman administration became convinced that partition could not be implemented without unacceptable military and political involvement directly by the United States. Therefore, beginning in February, it progressively backed off from its previous support for that approach and obtained UN agreement to hold a special General Assembly session, April–May, to consider a new U.S.-led plan for a trusteeship and truce. Realities on the ground, however, precluded adoption of this plan. Then, as shown in Chapter One, came the sudden Truman announcement on 14 May — just a few minutes after the proclamation in Tel Aviv of the new State of Israel at 6:00 P.M., New York time — that the United States recognized it on a *de facto* basis; this apparently caught the American delegation at the United Nations unawares, and it continued from the Assembly podium to urge its now-outdated plan before it finally understood that press reports of the recognition were accurate. With this development, an entirely new set of considerations entered into the making of America's Palestine policy, especially in the face of the war there, now a fully international one, with the invasion of that land by neighboring Arab states for the purpose of blocking the establishment of the Jewish state. Also to be recalled are the two notable personnel developments toward the end of this period: the White House's appointment, imposed over State Department protests, of a prominent Zionist, James G. McDonald, to serve as the U.S. special representative in Israel; and the decision to transfer to an overseas post away from the region the most prominent and controversial department official responsible for Near Eastern affairs, Loy Henderson.

30 January

Forrestal calls and asks Lovett's opinion that "it was a correct statement that the affirmations on which U.S. voted approval of partition plan were based on justice and workable features, that there was a caveat that if it did not prove workable it would be subject to review. Mr. Lovett said those were words of art ... that it was unquestionably the consideration in our mind. The implication is that if this were tried and did not work we would have to find another plan."

19–20 February

(a) On the 19th, Clifford tells Lovett the president is leaving for Florida on the 20th, to which Lovett says that he "need take position" by the 24th and therefore he would need to be in touch on the evening of the 22nd by "safe commercial facilities." Clifford: "no problem." Regarding president's planned speech in New York City on 17 March, Lovett says, "If things do not go right in Security Council, he might not want to discuss Palestine." [Comment: The point being that, if the Council failed to agree to accept the responsibility for the implementation of the partition resolution of 29 November, as Lovett fully expected and clearly hoped would be the case, then the U.S. delegation would propose effectively to cancel that resolution — as in fact it would end up doing on 19 March.] (b) On 20 February, Clifford tells Lovett that the president wants to make a press statement "after Austin presents our position at UN" to show he "had something to do with it"—that, Clifford continues, the American "course of action was reached, as a matter of policy, to sustain the UN and that Senator Austin had stated position correctly." (c) Later on the 20th, legal advisor Ernest Gross visits to express his concern over a report that Lovett wants to "bring in some other attorney on Palestine." Lovett reassures him that all he has in mind is to keep "Rusk, [Jack] Tate and Meeker [department lawyers] here ... and borrow others who had sat in on preparation of Charter and are versed in constitutional law." [Comment: The point of Lovett's concern was to recruit a lawyer who was more sympathetic than Gross and his staff to his planned argument in the Security Council that it was not empowered to impose political solutions on competing parties. One might also mention here that the State Department was unhappy with Austin's ability to reflect U.S. policies at the Security Council and more broadly with the American public, but it was unable to overcome the president's loyalty to the senator to have him replaced. For example, on 6 April, Lovett and Forrestal would share their unhappiness over Austin and agree on the need to "get two good deputies, one a ['young'] trial lawyer who will carry the burden, the other on public relations who will write stuff for the public and not just for the Security Council."]

24 February

Tells Forrestal president approved "basic paper" and Austin's speech; "Austin may have to get into constitutionality, but believe it will make perfectly clear implication in Palestine case if it's applied to other parts of world." [Comment: The issue is whether the UN Charter authorizes the Security Council to enforce a political solution on a country; Lovett's reference to other parts of the world relates to concurrent problems at the United Nations regarding Kashmir, Indonesia, and Korea.] Later that day, Lovett tells a concerned Forrestal that the State Department is to give a "background press conference" at the Statler Hotel, and other limited interviews, not to "sell our position," but to show that all "we are trying to do is interpret a document [i.e., the UN Charter]."

29 March

Tells Forrestal he has his "own great idea: we ought to make permanent base of Haifa." [See Chapter One for balance of this conversation.]

30 March

Lunches with Clifford to discuss "what authority the president has for ordering troops out for the maintenance of order outside" the United States.

14 April

(a) At president's request, Lovett calls Joseph Proskauer in New York [head of the American Jewish Committee] to have him come to Washington to have it clarified that the president, "even at considerable political risk, is determined to exhaust every reasonable possibility in UN at least of trying to stop bloodshed," and to request him to recruit "leading" American Jews to "help in efforts to stop this appalling affair." (b) Clifford calls: the president "still wants" Hilldring as "Special Assistant to Secretary of State"; Lovett: "The Secretary had promised Hilldring he would not call on him again," and, therefore, it would be a problem now. [Comment: Marshall at this time was in Bogota for a conference of the Organization of American States; while there, he was caught in a revolution that was not forecast by the CIA, forcing him to remain isolated in his hotel for a few days. Lovett's conclusion to all this was that the CIA, whose director was Admiral Roscoe Hillenkoeter, should henceforth be headed by a civilian, not a military man.]

19 April

Lovett tells Clifford about the "Department's suggestion" to get Judah Magnes [long-time pacifist and president of Hebrew University in Jerusalem] to come (ostensibly on his own) to the United States; he is a "moderate" and "leader of substantial portion of Jewish opinion," and one who does not "particularly relish idea of being slaughtered"; the State Department is also trying to get "an Arab leader" to come [Comment: It would not succeed]; both would be "off-the-record," but have now heard that Niles told some group that the "Department had invited" Magnes—"this pretty well louses up usefulness of something that was most promising." [Comment: In fact, Magnes did come to the United States, with discreet department financing, and did in early May separately see Marshall and the president, who, the department was hoping, would be unaware of how little political influence this dying old man actually had in Palestine as a supporter of a binational state. The main purpose of this Henderson-orchestrated scheme (or, rather, in the present writer's opinion, scam) was to keep the president supportive of the increasingly futile U.S. effort at the United Nations to establish a truce-cum-trusteeship in Palestine.]

28 April

At Niles' request, Lovett sees Nahum Goldmann [a leading American Zionist official] and then informs Rusk in New York that "Goldmann is completely at odds with Silver [i.e., Rabbi Abba Hillel Silver, the Republican-oriented head of the "American Section" of the Jewish Agency delegation at the United Nations] and said [he] thought Rusk's truce plan would do the job if can extend it to six months, which would bring into period of U.N.G.A." Lovett also tells Rusk he wants the Assembly resolution to provide "some basis" for a UN police force to help implement the planned UN-led regime in Palestine.

29 April

Lovett informs Clifford that "Rusk is upset because of Hilldring appointment and effect on the Arabs. Rusk is coming down tonight."

30 April

(a) Forrestal asks: "Does Hilldring's coming in mean he is going run our Palestine policy? No; Hilldring purely façade — brought in on insistence of Niles and Clifford to try to win Jewish vote back. Looks very well as though it may cost us our best man in New York — Jessup." [Comment: On March 27, Lovett had learned that Ambassador Johnson "doesn't wish to remain as number 2 man in New York." Lovett, a registered Republican who strongly believed in a bipartisan foreign policy, proposed to recruit the former chairman of the Republican National Committee, Herbert Brownell, Jr., but, at Austin's insistence, Philip Jessup, a professor of law and political appointee to the delegation, would on 1 April become Austin's deputy and item officer for the Palestine question; by the end of April, Lovett had clearly come to understand Jessup's enthusiasm for the change in American policy.] (b) Later, Clifford informs Lovett of plans for "issuance of formal directive by President regarding the truce ... wants to fix it up so that, if the truce goes over, the President will get the credit for it."

3 May

(a) Lovett informs the president that Rusk in New York will seek to arrange an "immediate ten-day, unconditional cease-fire," and then "move by air ... to Middle East ... representatives of Arabs ... Jewish Agency, representatives of three countries in Truce Commission [United States, France and Belgium] ... wants to say an airplane will be provided by the President. President agreed." (b) Later, Clifford asks, "How many are going? We'll use the 'Cow' [Truman's personal plane], which will be ready by tomorrow night."

4 May

(a) Rusk calls: "[Moshe] Shertok turned down ten-day offer"; said trip idea was bad, "too spectacular," and would have "thrown on them moral responsibility they are not prepared to accept"; Rusk also said "decision was made in New York without reference to Palestine." Lovett: "We should let them stew in their juice for a while." [Comment: Shertok was the head of the Jewish Agency delegation and, as Moshe Sharett, would become Israel's foreign minister.] (b) Later, Proskauer tells Lovett, who tells Clifford, that Silver was the block and head of the "war party," while Shertok and Goldmann favored Rusk's plan. (c) President calls to suggest possibility of Marshall inviting Shertok, Goldmann and Silver to Washington "and lay it on the line with them." [Comment: The Arab representatives in New York never gave an official response to this proposal; Shertok, on 7 May, seeks and obtains from Lovett an appointment for the next day, just prior to his departure for Tel Aviv — Clifford declines to sit in with Lovett at that meeting, which was chaired by Marshall.]

11 May

Clifford calls: need "some way of retrieving the President prior to 15 May"; Lovett: sending Rusk to see you — "we have to be utterly realistic — it would be fatal for the President to give this impression of faltering."

12 May

(a) Rusk's assistant, Robert McClintock, consults Lovett regarding Count Folke Bernadotte, of Sweden, for "UN Commissioner for Palestine." Lovett: he would "probably be ok, though hardly knows about him; UN should appoint, not us." (b) Lovett asks Clifford what the 4:00 meeting is about. Answer: "Palestine." [The meeting was then held by Marshall and Lovett with Truman and Clifford] "off-the-record," and with "McClintock and [Fraser] Wilkins" also attending [the latter on Henderson's staff. Marshall and Lovett had lunched together prior to it. They decided that, in order to help keep the meeting calm, Henderson should not attend.] (c) At 6:10, Lovett assures journalist John Hightower that the 4:00 meeting was "purely routine," and that it is not "contemplated going outside UN to deal with the matter."

13 May

Clifford agrees with Lovett "that we should do nothing which would look as if we were backtracking on partition."

14 May

(a) 11:35: Has McClintock double-check regarding any British "recognition" plan; answer: on 8 May, they informed Ambassador Lewis Douglas that they will "wait a while." (b) 12:05: Assures Marshall that he has "nothing else" this morning, and then lunches with Clifford. (c) 2:40: Rusk calls to say he "just arrived" from New York; Lovett: "come up." (d) 3:25: Clifford calls regarding Palestine. (e) 3:50: Legal advisor Gross calls about a "misunderstanding as to exactly what kind of recognition we are giving to the provisional government in Palestine"—followed immediately by a meeting of the two plus Rusk, Henderson, "et al." (f) 4:35: Clifford calls to say he'll get to Lovett by 5:30 the "formal request" for recognition being prepared with [Eliahu] Epstein [later Elath, at this time Jewish Agency representative in Washington] and Ben Cohen [former counselor to the State Department]. Lovett: "If you approve, we'll send out to Chiefs of Mission in the Middle East" at around 5:00. [Comment: Given that the department was convinced that news of the recognition would spark violence in the Arab world against its personnel and property, it is hard to accept that Lovett and Rusk sat on their knowledge for hours without sending out the alert merely in deference to Clifford's request for delay until the last minute; rather, there is evidence that the alert was sent out right after the Rusk-Lovett meeting, at around 3:00—for example, the circular telegram to Arab posts stated that recognition would be given "within the next few hours"]. (g) 5:50: Austin is called to the phone by Rusk and told of the recognition. [Comment: Contrary to Lovett's fears, as expressed earlier to Clifford, that Austin would "get mad and resign," the ambassador told Rusk, according to Lovett's call to Clifford of 6:10, that "he is supporting the President's position"—but he then famously left the United Nations without informing his delegation, which continued for a while longer to speak in favor of a truce and trusteeship.]

15 May

(a) Lovett tells Counselor Charles Bohlen "he had a definite agreement from Clifford last night not to mention the arms embargo"; Bohlen: but the White House has announced that it "will raise" that subject. (b) Later, Clifford assures Lovett that he had told press secretary Charles Ross that he should make "no comment" if questioned on this; then Lovett calls Press Secretary Charlie Ross and learns that he did comment, saying it's "under study"—Lovett got him to agree to "clear it up and say it's been under study continuously."

Three. Truman Off-the-Record on Palestine

From left to right: General Frank Stoner (Bernadotte staff member), Bernadotte, Colonel Nils Brunssen (UN chief military observer, Jerusalem), and Bunche, late May or June 1948, prior to deployment to the Holy Land (UN photograph).

20 May

Lovett tells Clifford that, according to Austin, "nobody trusts us" in the Security Council.

22 May

Lovett tells Clifford "White House has gotten us into trouble with invitation to Dr. Chaim Weizmann. Who invited him?" Clifford: only knew what was in the newspaper this morning. Lovett: Connelly got Marshall's executive secretary "to set up Blair House. If President receives him as a personal friend, that is one thing; but if receives him as head of state then he has recognized state and we have made asses of ourselves." [Comment: Lovett's point was that the United States had only given *de facto* recognition of the "provisional government" and not of the State of Israel — even to the present day, the State Department's website shows U.S. "diplomatic relations with Israel" as only having been "established" in March 1949, when *de jure* recognition was given to it.] (b) Later, Connelly calls: Truman had Niles ask Weizmann if "he would like to come down [from New York] before he leaves. Weizmann said would feel it a great honor"; Lovett: "need President to put it on a personal basis." [Weizmann on 24 May stayed one night at Blair House as a "distinguished guest" of the president and not as head of state, which he would only become in early 1949.]

21 June

Tells Clifford, regarding "Acting Representative to Israel [Charles F.] Knox," that, "at time of selection, uncertainty whether truce would stick. Therefore, had to get man who could be ordered in and ordered out quickly." (b) Later, asks Forrestal to "try and think of anyone can get for Special Representative to Israel."

22 June

(a) Forrestal calls to suggest "O'Connor of Red Cross"; Lovett says he needs someone with "background of intelligence" or senior reserve naval officer; Forrestal: "[Admiral Lewis L.] Strauss"; Lovett: "out as a Jew." (b) Later, Clifford calls: "President wants to appoint James Grover McDonald as Special Representative in Palestine" [*sic*] and wants to make the announcement today; Lovett: has the president "considered the fact that Mr. McDonald is a confirmed Zionist (he thinks), and the repercussions this would have on the [UN] Truce Commission's work"; Clifford: "sure the President had considered it." (c) Lovett, after consulting with Henderson and McClintock, calls Clifford back and asks: Does the president "realize that McDonald is a known 'fellow traveler'?" Clifford: "imagined the President knew it." [Comment: The appointment was announced that night.]

24 June

(a) Tells Clifford that the Republican plank calls for "prompt, full recognition," and he adds that this "has, of course, already been done." Clifford authorizes Lovett to say publicly that "this country takes pride in the fact that it was the first to give the State of Israel full recognition and to recognize the Provisional Government as the *de facto* authority." [Comment: Legal advisor Gross's above-cited uncertainty on the meaning of the recognition obviously continued to permeate this aspect of American policy toward Israel, giving the State Department and the White House a certain degree of useful flexibility — depending on which audience they were addressing — until the truly full, *de jure* recognition of March 1949, and the raising of McDonald and Epstein to ambassadorial level, ended all ambiguity.][4] (b) In a later conversation, Lovett informs Clifford that the previous day Marshall, who is in hospital, had written out a protest "letter" to Truman regarding the manner of appointment of McDonald, including that he "had no data on McDonald, but strongly objects to the principle of not having an opportunity to investigate the fellow or at least talk to the President about it." Lovett, however, convinced Marshall, who is still "pretty hot" about this, to agree not to send the letter but to "talk to President instead on Monday." [Marshall or Lovett regularly met privately with Truman each Monday at 12:30.]

25 June

Initial meeting with McDonald, with relevant staff members also attending.

26 June

[Comment: The following regards the State Department's nomination of Henderson to Truman as ambassador to Turkey with Joseph Satterthwaite, his deputy, replacing him.] Clifford agrees to check on the status of this proposal and that, at Lovett's request, it will not be announced until after the 9 July expiration of the Palestine truce to avoid, in Lovett's words, "injecting another problem in the Mediator's cap." [Comment: Bernadotte was the mediator, a position created by the General Assembly at the conclusion on 14 May of its special session on Palestine. He arranged a four-week truce ending 9 July — see Chapter Four.]

29 June

Tells McClintock, regarding an unacceptable provision in Bernadotte's just-released peace plan, that "there was not intention to set up Haifa on same basis as Jerusalem; thinks we should wire Bernadotte." [Comment: This is the first step toward the remarkable three-day secret mission of McClintock and a British diplomat to Rhodes, starting on 13 September, to help the mediator and his deputy, Ralph Bunche, prepare a totally revised plan to replace the failure of this first one. That mission, which will be further discussed in Chapter Six, did not remain "secret" for very long, much to the discomfort of the State Department and Bunche, who would stick to their apparently mutually agreed cover story that the mission's goal was merely to discuss how the United States and United Kingdom could assist in plans to aid the Arab refugees. At one point in late September Lovett actually dissembled to Truman, who naturally did not wish to see the United States publicly cast as dictating peace terms to the mediator, about the real mission of McClintock.]

Bunche, UN Under-Secretary-General for Special Political Affairs, February 1, 1960 (UN photograph).

Four

U.S. Policy Toward Israel and the Arab States, June–August 1948

The period between McDonald's June appointment and his arrival at his post on 12 August was an eventful one in Palestine — militarily even more than diplomatically. The long-feared and predictable expansion of the conflict from a "civil war" within Palestine to an international one occurred on schedule with the formal end of the British Mandate on 15 May and the immediately following open invasion by armies from all the bordering Arab states plus Iraq. The Arabs were intent on eliminating once and for all the Jewish state, or, if that proved impossible to achieve, at least reducing its size substantially pending further attempts. However, the results of that initial invasion did not match expectations, neither of the Arabs themselves nor of policy officials in the American and British governments. To the surprise (and often open disappointment) of many, though not to the senior-most British military and civilian leadership in the Palestine of 1946–1948, Israel's Defense Force ("IDF") proved capable, at a minimum, of defending the country's existence, and also of taking the offensive at selective fronts and times against each of its surrounding enemies — north, east and south. Recall, for example, the testimony of General D'Arcy before the Anglo-American Committee of 1946 that "the Haganah would be able without difficulty to hold any area allotted to the Jews under partition, whereas larger British contingents would be required to police any solution which involved the suppression of the Haganah."[1] On that same occasion, General Alan Cunningham, the British high commissioner for Palestine, assured the committee that no American troops would be needed were the 100,000 Jewish refugees allowed to enter Palestine, although "I should not mind having a token squad" to show U.S. support "in such a solution."[2]

Though far from having achieved definitive "victory," by the end of July Israel controlled territory extending beyond some of its original borders, as defined in the UN resolution of 29 November; however, Arab armies remained in control not only of large swatches of territory that were within those borders but also of nearly all the territory originally slated for the independent Arab state pursuant to that same Palestine resolution. In fact, the Israeli Defense Force had won victories only against Arab Palestinians and the Iraqi-led Arab Liberation Army, which, luckily for Israel, only joined the conflict after 15 May, "when the Jewish Palestinian war was already over."[3] With the exception of a partial success against Egyptian forces in southern Palestine, the IDF had suffered defeats in most cases when it fought against the regular armies of the Arab states.

This situation had developed in two distinct fighting phases: the first, from 15 May to 11 June, and the second, from 9 July to 18 July. The lull between the two phases was in deference to Security Council resolutions, especially that of 29 May, which demanded a four-week "cease-fire." That demand matched the wishes of the two parties themselves for a respite, during which each felt it could improve its military situation in preparation for a new round. As the end of the cease-fire approached on 9 July, the Israelis stated a willingness to extend it an additional ten days,[4] but the Arabs felt confident enough to reject any extension, and so the fighting was resumed in what would be termed by historians as a "Ten-Day War."[5] This time the IDF demonstrated an even greater capacity to protect and extend Israeli territory, forcing Arab acquiescence to a new Security Council resolution, that of 15 July, which demanded a much more complex set of truce conditions and contained a determination that the situation constituted a threat to the peace, warranting the application of Chapter VII against either of the two parties violating the anticipated new truce. (While the United States had been willing to cite the Arabs by name in this resolution as the aggressors, the British discouraged such a move, although, on 9 July, London had issued an instruction to its embassies in the Arab states to make it clear to them that, were they to reject a truce extension even as Israel accepted it, the United Kingdom would support a resolution citing them by name as being subject to sanctions — of course, as we have seen, in actuality, the British backed off from doing so.)[6] This was the first use the Security Council made during the Palestine crisis of the most powerful of the enforcement powers authorized it under the UN Charter — the threat of sanctions, including possibly the use of military force.

A fateful additional feature of the 15 July resolution was that it was open-ended, meaning that the resultant truce would have no time limit. The strategy underlying that feature, and strongly put forward by the United States at the Council, was that the economic, military and diplomatic pressure that would inevitably be generated on the parties by continuation of a truce that had left the armies in the field would, presumably, in relatively short order force them to reach, if not a final peace settlement, at least a more stable *modus vivendi* that, in turn, would surely lead to a peace agreement. This strategy was spelled out by a CIA-issued, inter-agency analysis of 21 July: "The current continuation of the truce is nominal ... sporadic fighting.... A continuation of the truce ... would be to Israel's advantage, and the Arabs probably would not long respect it." But, the analysis continued, if Bernadotte could be helped in an "effective means of enforcement," a prolonged truce would be possible and could lead to a settlement.

As shall be discussed below, this strategy did not succeed, with Israel in particular feeling the pinch of a stalemate seeming to have no end. On the eve of its final major offensive of this first Israel-Arab War, following that of 14 October, which drove the Egyptians from the northern Negev, the PGI, on 21 December, justified its impending move by telling McDonald that the Arab unwillingness to enter armistice talks was creating a situation where "a further indefinite and difficult truce may drag the victor into what might be tantamount to a partial defeat owing to economic and financial strain."[7] The offensives of 14 October and 22 December, unlike the first two rounds of fighting in May and July, were initiated by Israel, and these two helped bring the total of "officially legalized warfare" to 237 days for all of 1948.[8]

It was this volatile military situation that determined the diplomatic focus of the United States as it sought to curtail the scope and duration of the fighting for fear that it would otherwise spread beyond Palestine into the Middle East and even beyond, to the benefit of the Soviet Union. It follows that McDonald's task upon arrival in Tel Aviv — the *de facto* capital of Israel so long as it continued to accept the United Nations' policy of internationalizing Jerusalem — would necessarily concentrate on contributing to international efforts to keep the regional powers at the negotiating table versus the battlefield.

(To recapitulate and project briefly the rest of McDonald's personal story, it is no accident that only when the further fighting of late 1948 did in fact create the circumstances for agreements that went beyond mere truces — as well as for the election in Israel of a constituent assembly and permanent structure of government — that the United States would give *de jure* recognition to Israel and elevate McDonald in late March 1949 to the rank of ambassador presiding over a full-fledged embassy. After that landmark development and through the end of his tour in December 1950, McDonald's activities were conducted in a much calmer, less internationally eventful atmosphere — to the point that, in both 1949 and 1950, he would manage to spend months in the United States on official consultations and personal leaves. Obviously, with the armistice agreements of early 1949 and his elevation to ambassadorship, McDonald felt he had little more to accomplish in Israel and hinted as much in his unsuccessful efforts to be allowed to resign well before he finally did. Moreover, he was frequently upset during this latter period with the pressure tactics of the State Department, and President Truman personally, to coerce Israel into making concessions to the Arab states that Israel, with his support, saw as unreasonable and as jeopardizing that nation's security with no realistic likelihood of winning peace and recognition from the Arab side. As prophesied by a member of the Israeli Mission in Washington back in July 1948, any truce in the fighting would inevitably lead to a decrease in "pressure" on the American government "to be a friend of Israel."[9])

But, returning now to the period when McDonald was serving as special representative, he would directly experience periods of danger and difficult living conditions. These were fully shared by his mission staff, not least by those who had arrived on 8 July as a small advance party under the leadership of the aforementioned Charles Knox. As can be gleaned from the dates provided above, Knox and company came on to the scene just as full-scale warfare had resumed with the end of the first truce period (9 July). Tel Aviv was close to the front lines and subject to bombardment by air and sea from Egyptian forces. Both official and personal life under these conditions, including such matters as food and housing availability, is vividly on display in a reading of Under-Secretary Lovett's own diary, departmental correspondence, and Knox's personal letters home. A selection from these sources is as follows:

3 July: Lovett informs Clifford that the State Department cannot respond favorably to Epstein's urgent request to the president for transportation assistance to ship Israeli-financed "powdered milk and egg powder" from Europe in anticipation of renewed fighting on 9 July due to Arab unwillingness to extend the truce; such assistance would require the president to obtain the prior approval of Bernadotte lest it be seen by the Arabs as a violation by the United States of the terms of the present truce.

7 July: Navy Secretary Sullivan tells Lovett that not more than 7,000 U.S. citizens in Palestine need to be readied for evacuation, but more will be if the war spreads. Lovett: keep the fleet nearby, because "we have given the UN observers until 4:00 P.M. on Friday [9 July—the date the cease-fire expires]," and therefore "we cannot give the impression we are throwing in the sponge on a possible extension of the truce." [Note: As of 11 June, the United States had fielded 31 military officers, plus planes and destroyers, to help Bernadotte, the UN mediator, to staff and equip his Truce Observation Team; Belgium and France, the two other members of the Jerusalem-based UN Truce Commission (UNTC), supplied the same number of truce observers as did the United States.]

8 July: Lovett tells Clifford that "we are going ahead with plans for evacuation of ... American personnel." [Comment: This date, as the cease-fire was expiring, was the peak period of concern over the safety of American staff and families. In reality, only the observer team was evacuated, by order of Bernadotte as early as 7 July, to the great annoyance of the State Department and the U.S. delegation to the United Nations in New York; they complained that they now lacked the ability to discern key events in Palestine.]

21 July: Lovett tells McDonald in Washington that "we were unable to obtain Marine guards for Tel Aviv," but "guards from other departments of government" will be provided. [Comment: The real reason for not sending Marine guards to Tel Aviv was the State Department's and the president's firm intention to avoid having casualties of uniformed American citizens in Palestine. It was only with the greatest reluctance that they shortly would agree to the transfer of some twelve Marine guards from the Cairo embassy to protect the American consulate general in Jerusalem, where there were no international forces sent by the United Nations to back up its resolution internationalizing that city and its environs.]

Most of July and August: The only way the U.S. Mission at Tel Aviv could maintain official contact with the State Department was through the previously established consulate at Haifa or through the use of a land courier to the consulate general at Jerusalem, the courier having to travel through a dangerous, makeshift "corridor," a so-called Burma Road carved by the IDF through territory assigned by the UN resolution to the Arab state and now under the guns of Arab forces stationed on the surrounding hills. Even from Jerusalem, aside from shaky radio connections, correspondence had to be sent by way of the "Amman-Cairo route."

13 July–August: Selections from Knox's letters home written during and soon after the "Ten-Day War" of mid-July are as follows[10]: The Arabs were only 10 or so miles from Tel Aviv when "two brilliant victories ... by the Jewish Army" had "driven them back"; if the Arabs ever break through, U.S. diplomats "would have a rough time of it, but we'd make out all right"; "The night bombing is the worse," interfering with sleep; yesterday, "a 250 pounder hit a house ... 5 blocks away.... They are trying to get the corpses out from under the masonry"; "Apparently, the government can't spare any arms or planes to fight off the bombing attacks"; "2 or 3 raids a day ... a bomb hits in the center of town" [Comment: Israeli planes managed in this period to retaliate with essentially symbolic raids on Cairo and Damascus]; "What a pity it all is."

[Knox's letters continue in these early days:] "I am disturbed because I can't get on with the business of setting up the Mission"; we need an accountant; today [17 July] we are opening the consulate in a hotel room; "No meat whatsoever ... I've eaten so much chicken ... that my beard is coming out pinfeathers"; *per diem* is $10 a day, while the hotel's American Plan is $12 — "that is not too bad," although room rent exceeds our allowance [Comment: After the military attachés arrived in succeeding months, Knox later that year would write that, unlike the State Department employees, they had no "rent restrictions" and could sign a "government lease" with little limits on cost]; "This is a country where the little children are gods. The composition of the population here is, as you know owing to the Nazis, composed of new babies (from 1 to 5), a relatively small number of men below 25 who are now all fighting at the front, and many old people ... the children are the only sure future seed of Israel."

[Knox's letters written on various dates after the implementation of the second truce on 18 July:] "This blessed truce is almost too good to be true"; "The tension of this truce, such as it is, is getting on everyone's nerves"[11]; "I've received nothing in the way of letters from the States at all. Everything is sort of snarled up, but at least we have a cessation of bombing and fighting"; "Two very welcome letters from you"; "Yesterday [31 July] went for a trip to a Communal (*not Communist*, there are no Communist settlements here) settlement [emphasis in the original].... Started 20 years ago by 30 men and women in an area of desert land, it is now a beautiful place supporting 1,500 people.... The beautiful workers' rest house gardens were criss-crossed with trenches — that darn Egyptian army was only 10 miles away.... There are 40 or 50 such settlements in Palestine, of one type or another — or there were. The frontier ones have been wiped out, many with all their inhabitants, by the Arab armies. I could tell you some tragic and horrifying stories that rival any Indian massacres I ever heard of.... If the war starts again and things get tough, we have 150 cases of rations."

Notwithstanding its immensely important gains militarily since 15 May, the open-ended truce of July 18 was intolerable to Israel. Arab armies remained on lands assigned to it by the UN resolution of 29 November and were close to its major urban centers, notably Tel Aviv and the so-called New City, or West Jerusalem, where 100,000 Jews, nearly a fifth of 1947 Palestine's Jewish population, resided. (The Jewish Quarter in the Old City had by then been captured by the Arabs, and the New City's normal water source at the theoretically UN-protected pumping station at Latrun, which overlooked Israel's "corridor" to Jerusalem at a point near the coastal plain, had been destroyed by Arab forces on the very day, 12 August, of McDonald's arrival in nearby Tel Aviv.)

On 24 August, Ben-Gurion told McDonald that "the truce deprives us of sovereignty."[12] The Israelis saw the situation as no longer a mere truce, but a governmental regime with Bernadotte as the supreme authority and indefinitely curtailing sovereignty regarding issues of Jewish immigration, arms imports, and so forth. Moreover, the governments of the Arab states, despite the second truce, and to the dismay of Secretary-General Lie, were openly vowing a renewal of the war at some not-too-distant point. Illustrating this continuing danger, Lovett on 1 September advised Truman's running mate, Senator Albin Barkley, "Don't go to Tel Aviv, since it is a very tumultuous country. The Senator said he didn't think he'd go."[13] (He didn't.) Furthermore, as reported in a State Department telegram of 25 June addressed to UN Mediator Bernadotte, who was then in Jerusalem, the United States had, for some time now, been carefully screening applicants seeking passports for travel to Palestine and Arab countries.

Despite its trepidations, the Provisional Government of Israel (PGI), based in Tel Aviv, recognized that there *were* significant improvements in the country's national security, both diplomatically and militarily. For example, by mid-summer, the American government, in the view of the Israelis, had revised its estimate of Israel's military strength.[14] Their UN representative, Abba Eban, wrote Goldmann in late July that "Forrestal is no longer mobilizing the Defense Department against us," and one consequence, he wrote, was that the United States was no longer agitating against Israel at the United Nations. Eban went on to claim that Israel had rendered the world a "service" by showing it that the Arab League was "not the vast factor in strategic calculations which it was portrayed to be." Going even beyond Eban's claim, the Indian ambassador to the United States informed Israeli Special Representative Epstein (soon changed to "Elath") that Israel was considered a hero to the colonial peoples for having beaten the imperial British. This was a theme Israeli diplomats would frequently hear from their counterparts in the Third World during this early period; for example, the Turkish ambassador to the United Nations expressed pleasure to Eban that the IDF had been successful against the Egyptians in southern Palestine.

In a similar vein, the U.S. Mission to the United Nations (USUN) was advising the State Department around this time that the IDF was capable of defeating "most of the Arab States put together." A CIA analysis at the end of July chimed in that the IDF was capable of driving all the "Arab forces out of Palestine," and went on to opine that the U.S. idea in April of a trusteeship had been "the one possibility which might have prevented an Arab-Jewish war after 15 May." That agency then accurately listed the formidable new weapons purchased (mostly with funds contributed by the Jewish community in the United States) and surreptitiously delivered to Israel from abroad, mainly from Czechoslovakia but also from France and other European countries, during the period since April. The implication of this turnaround in attitude by the United States regarding the Israel-Arab military balance was that henceforth, and despite Eban's optimistic assessment of the American attitude toward his nation, the pressure would now be on *Israel* to restrain it from using its newfound power in order to capture additional Arab territory — and, more particularly, to give up in the interest of peace territory allotted to it by the November UN resolution (read: parts of the Negev) if it wished to retain captured territory beyond that original territory (read: Jaffa and part or all of the Western Galilee).[15]

Indeed, the prospect for renewed fighting at *Israel's* initiative was a clear one, and this was the great American concern toward the end of summer. The Tel Aviv government was not bashful in informing Washington that the status quo was intolerable to it, given the lack of diplomatic progress toward initiating negotiations with the Arabs for a peace settlement. Within two weeks of his arrival, McDonald stressed to a resistant Washington that the open-ended truce under the weak management of Bernadotte, who spent most of August back at home in Sweden, had to be urgently revised by a more focused UN and bilateral effort to pressure the Arab governments to begin direct or mediated negotiations with Israel. The latter, he wrote, would soon find it irresistible, even if at the expense of its relations with the rest of the world, to use its military power to end unilaterally the presence of Arab armies on what it considered its internationally recognized territory. McDonald and others also noted that Israel went further and intended to retain, by right of conquest, strategically important territory it now controlled as a result of a defensive war against enemies who remained as such, and that it would be unwilling to give up any part of the Negev in order to retain that additional territory. This point also extended to the situation in Jerusalem, where the Israelis would soon (on 3 August) declare a military government over those parts of the city it controlled, feeding the concern regularly being expressed by the new U.S. consul in Jerusalem, John MacDonald, that the Israelis were using their alleged need to control the Irgun and Stern Gang forces located there as an excuse to claim Jerusalem as an integral part of Israel. MacDonald, in this context, also faulted Bernadotte for not acting with enough urgency in establishing a creditable UN-administered demilitarization program for the city (a charge hard for an observer to fathom given the unwillingness of the UN to organize and field a sizable military force to give credence to its call for demilitarization).

The Israeli case, including its resort to offensive war in October and then again in December (and, finally, down to the port of Elath on the Gulf of

Aqaba, with minimal Arab resistance, in March 1949), rested on both military and economic justifications, along with an appeal to elementary justice for its beleaguered population. The PGI would tell McDonald and others that the Arab unwillingness to enter into armistices as a step toward permanent peace was threatening to drag Israel into a situation tantamount to partial defeat owing to the resultant economic and financial strain on its society. For example, as early as 24 August, McDonald transmitted official and personal messages to the State Department and the White House warning of a "crisis in the making," including the possibility of "armed conflict" between the United States and Israel, unless present policies were changed. The thrust of those messages was as follows:

> The truce is a "thinly-disguised continuation of the war" and does not permit Israel to demobilize in favor of essential economic development; demilitarization of Jerusalem is unacceptable in light of the military advantage it would give to the surrounding Arab armies if the 20,000 defending IDF troops were withdrawn from West Jerusalem, most of whose neighborhoods were populated by Jews;[16] the Arab refugee problem was "created by war and can be finally solved only at a peace conference conducted directly by the two parties" or "under UN or other auspices"; truce-imposed policy restraints on Jewish immigration are an intolerable infringement on Israel's sovereign rights and its *raison d'être*.
>
> [McDonald continued:] Israel is under the "illusion" that "the U.S. would under no circumstances be a party to UN sanctions" against it, and it is determined, even if "suicidal," to adhere to its position that "what we have won on the battlefield we will not sacrifice at the [Security] Council table"; Israel sees the policy of the United States and United Nations as "tantamount to taking sides with the Arabs against the Jews," and this "may finally force" it to "resume the war"; economically, a prolonged truce is "unbearable for Israel," if it must keep "70 or 80 thousand men and women under arms"; therefore, war could be seen as "a lesser burden" than "the armed truce."
>
> [McDonald's analysis further continued:] Not pressuring the Arabs to negotiate a peace would be "to confess" that they can "indefinitely call the tune"; Bernadotte in both Jewish and Arab eyes lacks "moral authority" or "dignity"; the British authorities in London continue "their record" of being "completely unrealistic" regarding the military prospects, and are not "impartial" as between Jews and Arabs — the United States must not be wed to their policies, if "unnecessary misunderstanding about the elements in the problem here" is to be avoided.

Here, in a nutshell, we see the issues drawn between Washington and its special representative in Israel. These messages were not well received by the U.S. government, which was indeed "wed" now to (a) its renewed *entente cordiale* with the British; (b) its support of Bernadotte not only as truce supervisor but also as a "mediator" whose peace proposals were to be given the fullest backing, including threat of sanctions against a recalcitrant Israel; and (c) its determination to win concessions from Israel, concessions that the United States remained convinced could bring the Arab states to acquiesce, even if only tacitly, to the existence of the Jewish state — the two principal concessions being acceptance of the return of hundreds of thousands of Arab refugees and an exchange of territory in the event that Israel wished to keep permanently any lands it occupied as a result of the war.

Another important result of these messages was that it constituted early confirmation in the Department of State that its worst fears of how close McDonald would adhere to Israeli policies at the expense of the American national interest were justified. Just how far apart McDonald and the State Department were in these summer weeks following the 18 July truce can be gleaned from illustrative memoranda it circulated to the White House and other government agencies, which argued that (a) the United States should reject Israel's 22 June demand for a $100 million loan from the Export-Import Banks, because it would be seen by the Arabs "as a unilateral action by the U.S. in violation of the present truce [and] might prejudice" Bernadotte's "mediation efforts"[17]; (b) Israel was risking the truce by its warlike behavior and, therefore, any approval of its loan request should be first endorsed by Bernadotte; (c) the department formally certified that Israel lacked the "political stability" requisite for it to receive any loan — or *de jure* recognition[18]; (c) the U.S. military government in Germany should not allow Jewish "fighting personnel" to leave its DP camps for Palestine (i.e., no "man of military age" should go without Bernadotte's prior approval — a dead-letter, because Bernadotte never would field the "observers" in the American occupation zone, as the U.S. had requested)[19]; and (d) Israel was absorbing "large numbers of European DPs" and therefore was giving the impression, due to its refusal to allow "Arab repatriation," that it was doing so "at [the] expense [of] former Arab inhabitants [of] Israel" — the solution to the Arab refugee problem, it was argued, was "intrinsic to final settlement [of the] Palestine problem.... The PGI failure to cooperate ... might create difficulties for 265,000 Jews permanently residing [in] Arab States."

Relevant to these policy issues was their clear and direct nexus with the domestic political climate, clearly illustrated by the fate of U.S. legislation regarding immigration policy. The State Department had to contend throughout the postwar years with the obvious charge by Arab states and others that the United States was being hypocritical in its support of Jewish DP and refugee immigration into Palestine while it was unwilling to open its own doors to them. The issue became exacerbated with the passage in June 1948 of the Displaced Persons Act, which Truman signed even as he castigated the law for containing "discriminating features" that explicitly banned use of its 200,000 quota for Jews who had entered the U.S.-run camps after December 22, 1945.[20] The State Department had lobbied Congress not to so discriminate against those Jews but to no avail and now, in summer 1948, was forced to weakly reassure the Arabs that the administration had not given up the effort and expected to amend the legislation to allow Jews in and thereby help relieve the pressure to allow them into Palestine. For example, on 3 August, Marshall assured the Iraqi government that any liberalization of those Jews currently in American camps would result in their entering the United States under a revised immigration policy being pursued by the administration. (That revision would only happen two years after the current conflict.)

In point of fact, McDonald's own recommendations could not bear close scrutiny in important respects. First, the Arab states, whatever their warlike threats, were very unlikely in any medium-term future to endanger the existence of Israel by initiating a new round of fighting. Second, the likelihood of the kind of UN-authorized Chapter VII confrontations, whether military or economic, between Israel and the Western nations that McDonald feared was nil, given domestic political realities in the United States and Europe. Third, it was clear that, under the prevailing circumstances, no amount of pressure on the Arab states could have led them, collectively or bilaterally, to negotiate a peace directly, or through UN mediation, with the Jews. Fourth, McDonald tended to exaggerate both the influence and the harm to Israel that evolving British policy was exerting in the region. After all, and notwithstanding its unchanged diplomatic goal of transferring much of the Negev to Transjordan, it *was* conscientiously — at the cost of much of its influence in the region — honoring the arms embargo imposed by the Security Council on 29 May. This hurt the Arab side inordinately as compared to the more limited impact that that embargo was having on Israel, with its surreptitious evasions and its technical flexibility in the military use of arms from various sources rather than from a single source, as was the Arab case.[21] Moreover, the British *were* restraining the most effective military force facing the IDF, Transjordan's unofficially British-commanded Arab Legion, whose orders were to avoid to the greatest extent possible confronting the IDF in areas assigned to Israel by the 29 November resolution. Those orders, in any event, were quite redundant given King Abdullah's own preference eventually to negotiate a deal with Israel, and given the very limited supply of arms and ammunition Britain was now allowing it.

However, McDonald was surely right to alert Washington that present policies were leading to a new military catastrophe and a course correction was imperative. His description of the factors that were driving Israel toward the actions he forecast was on the mark. Perhaps, as is often the case in an international conflict, no outside power could have altered the drift of events by remote control and, at best, could only have reduced the stakes involved. In the present case, the international community, as events would prove, did play that kind of role at least regarding those aspects that most concerned it: (a) keeping the fighting as minimally lethal and geographically limited as possible; (b) ameliorating the human suffering, whether Arab or Jewish[22]; and (c) protecting the prestige of the United Nations, whose role in keeping the world at peace was seen in this immediate postwar period as vital notwithstanding the obvious new hurdle being posed to the organization by the Cold War. To the extent that McDonald was able and willing to confront the State Department more candidly with a highly informed dissenting viewpoint than would likely have been the case had a career diplomat been in his position, he contributed to the development of a more realistic and effective policy as the year wore on — often at the expense of his personal relations with distrustful State Department personnel. It is important to keep in mind that literally no one in a position of influence in the U.S. government had expertise on Palestine, which had been the welcome bailiwick of the British from the start of the Zionist issue earlier in the century.

From the viewpoint of the invading Arab states, the status quo was not nearly as intolerable as it seemed for the Israelis.[23] Consider the following: (a) Arab armies were still in Palestine and still in the fight, pressing the enemy militarily, economically and diplomatically (although, as Bevin saw it, that situation still left those armies open to Israel's "mailed fist" due to the British-respected arms embargo); (b) with the passage of time, those armies could well be strengthened and better led for a renewed effort to eliminate the Jewish state[24]; (c) those armies did not by any means deplete the civilian workforce (the total population of the seven relevant Arab states was nearly 40 million) or seriously weaken the economy, unlike the situation of the Jews; and (d) even regarding the large numbers of refugees in Arab territory, the Western countries were financially moving to pick up the burden and, moreover, were using the issue as an additional source of political pressure on the Jewish state to be more accommodating in meeting Arab demands that the refugees be allowed to return to their homes. For example, Marshall on 20 August emphasized at a cabinet meeting in the White House that the Arab refugee problem was urgent in connection with the settlement of the Palestine problem; on that same day, Rusk wrote to Lovett urging him to press Epstein on the refugee problem, arguing that Israel should take back those who wished to return on the grounds that (i) a very large percentage were children, mothers, and old

Left to right: Alexander Cadogan (UK representative to the United Nations), Group Captain D.M. Somerville, and British Minister for Foreign Affairs Ernest Bevin, arriving in Berlin for the Potsdam Conference with Truman and Stalin (courtesy Truman Library, July 28, 1945; photograph taken by U.S. Army Signal Corps).

people and therefore no security threat to Israel, which was using them as bargaining chips and their property as useful assets to help meet the needs of Jewish immigrants, and (ii) in what must be seen as an eyebrow-raising proposal, Bernadotte could help the Israeli authorities ensure that, once returned, those Arabs would not be a security threat. On the other hand, in a typical dissenting comment by McDonald within a telegram sent on that same day, the special representative expressed agreement with the Israel government that it could not afford militarily to have the enemy at its back as well as in front. (As regards British policy, Bevin was pressing his UN delegation during this period to get the Security Council to "investigate [the] problem of Arab Displaced Persons and to make proposals for dealing with it"—for example, could they "return to their homes?" Bevin justified his policy in part by putting on the same footing the Arab "DPs," who were "not less than 250,000," and the "200,000 Jewish Displaced Persons in Europe," with both groups of DPs deserving identical favorable treatment.[25] In New York, the U.S. mission convinced the British not to make a formal proposal by asserting that the refugee problem was one for the General Assembly as part of its efforts for an overall peace settlement, while the Security Council was "primarily" responsible for "maintenance of peace in Palestine.")

A direct glimpse of Arab strategy designed to maximize and focus the above-cited pressure points on Israel within as *short* a period as possible may be obtained from the terms used by the Arab League in writing to the United Nations on 18 July of its members' acceptance of the 15 July Security Council call for a truce. Following is a summary of that communication from Secretary-General Azzam, as provided by the editors of the *Foreign Relations of the United States* (FRUS):

> The new truce would not achieve its purpose unless various deficiencies in the [June] four-week truce were remedied. Thus, he requested that all Jewish immigration into Palestine be stopped during the truce and that the 300,000 Arab refugees be returned home with guarantees of their lives and property. He requested also that the new truce not be indefinite but with a fixed duration to permit a last effort to reach a peaceful solution.

It might usefully be added in this context that, a few months later, on the eve of the final IDF offensive of the year, the British Foreign Office described to the American Embassy its understanding of "trends" in Egyptian policy: "(a) That Transjordan and Egypt might keep their troops in respective areas [of Palestine] on a *de facto* basis, and that this situation would gradually solidify without necessity for controversial decisions regarding sovereignty, negotiations with the PGI, etc.[26]; (b) That, while direct negotiations with Jews are impossible, [the Palestine] Conciliation Commission [just established by the United Nations] will offer the means and excuse for Arabs to work out a realistic settlement; and, (c) Extreme Arab League attitude [continues] favoring continuing hostilities."

Obviously, the late July Arab position that favored — ironically, as did Israel — placing a time limit on the existing truce would by late in 1948 be reduced only to an "extreme" position, especially after the successes of the October IDF offensive. The more prevalent trend was away from contemplating any further Arab military initiatives, or from counting on Western diplomatic pressure to force concessions from Israel, and this trend deepened after the additional successes of the December IDF offensive. This is clear from the fact that the IDF offensive was quickly followed by a series of armistice negotiations between Israel and each of its Arab enemies under the management of Ralph Bunche, the acting mediator, who won the Nobel Peace Prize for his actions in 1950. These unfavorable developments for the Arab states to a large extent were a result of their inability to effectively coordinate their military and diplomatic policies in confronting the Zionist drive for statehood in Palestine—and, even more importantly, of their unwillingness or inability to mobilize their domestic resources for a more all-out conflict involving larger numbers of fighting men. While this is not the place to deal at length with the intra–Arab factors explaining that inability, suffice it here to make the following observations:

The headquarters for the Arab League, since its establishment with British endorsement in 1945, was at Cairo, the capital of the most powerful and influential of the Arab states; an Egyptian was its secretary-general and spokesman to the world. And yet Egypt was not in a position to provide the kind of leadership expected of it in 1948. Its own domestic political situation was unstable; for example, its prime minister would be assassinated in December following a series of wavering and unsuccessful military and diplomatic initiatives starting with the days just preceding the May invasion of Palestine by the Arab states. At that time, King Farouk and his government were unsure until the final moment as to whether they were willing to join in that invasion, and this hampered meaningful coordination and unified leadership among the Arab armies.

Similar domestic instability and failure to submit to disciplined coordination and unified leadership of the Arab armies characterized the participation of the other Arab states, reflecting the traditional rivalries among them. The most important of those rivalries for the purposes of our subject was that between Egypt and Transjordan. Briefly, the Egyptians perceived Transjordan to be a British puppet, whose king and army—the Arab Legion under "Pasha" John Glubb—were, from the time that state was carved out of the Palestine Mandate after World War I, financed and led militarily as well as *de facto* diplomatically by London. The last thing that the Egyptians wanted to see come out of the war against the Jews was a British-controlled Transjordanian sovereignty over the southern part of Palestine, the Negev, so close to the Suez Canal. After all, Egypt and Britain—preceding, during, and following the 1948 war—were negotiating a revision of their 1936 treaty partly with a view to meeting Egyptian demands to eliminate the British military presence, including in the canal zone itself. (The Suez Canal issue, of course, would lead to the Anglo-French attack on Egypt of October 1956—with the active military participation of Israel and the active diplomatic opposition of the United States and the Soviet Union.)

Natural Arab diplomatic allies for Egypt in its rivalry with Transjordan-cum-Britain were Saudi Arabia and Syria. Both of these were suspicious of King Abdullah's regional ambitions, such as his dream of leadership over a "Fertile Crescent" grouping that would certainly cost Syria, and perhaps eventually even the Saudis, or so the latter feared, their sovereignty; King Ibn Saud remained fearful that the Hashemite kings at Amman and Baghdad still harbored ambitions to overthrow him and regain the holy land of the Hejaz they had lost when their father, King Hussein, the British ally against the Turks during the First World War, was evicted in 1924 by Ibn Saud from his base at Mecca. Of course, another strong base of opposition to King Abdullah and his goals in Palestine was to be found in the more nationalistic-minded among the Arab Palestinians themselves, whose most prominent leader was the ex–Mufti, Amin Hussein, head of the Arab Higher Committee (AHC), which was based in Egypt and had an accredited representative at the UN headquarters to speak for the cause of a unitary Arab state in Palestine.

Syria itself harbored territorial ambitions in Lebanon, which it saw as having been artificially taken away from it by the Christian powers, especially France, the Mandatory power over it and Syria after World War I. In 1926, France established Lebanon, with its substantial Catholic population, as a

Austin with Amir Faisal al Saud, Saudi minister of foreign affairs and head of its delegation to the United Nations, October 21, 1947 (UN photograph).

separate administrative entity, though it and Syria would remain under the Mandate into the 1940s, when France took steps to recognize them as independent republics. As for Iraq, the domestic situation was exceptionally volatile under the British-backed Hashemite rule, as exemplified by political coups against the king and by unstable government leadership; moreover, the relationship between the kings at Baghdad and Amman was marked more often than not by mutual suspicion than by brotherly love and cooperative policies.

Layered over this historical set of rivalries and conflicting ambitions were the incompatible political goals of the Arab states with specific regard to Palestine. For example, Egypt, as previously noted, was vehemently opposed to Transjordan's open ambition to absorb in his kingdom not only the Arab portions of Palestine that had been allocated in November by the United Nations to an independent Arab state there, but also the Negev, which, of course, was slated to be part of the Jewish state. Accordingly, Cairo, as a demonstration of its rejection of Mediator Bernadotte's alteration of the November resolution through his plan of June recommending Amman sovereignty over Arab Palestine, sponsored the establishment in mid–1948 of an "All-Palestine" government based at Gaza under the leadership of Amin Hussein, the arch-rival of Amman for leadership over the Palestinian Arabs, and also the uncompromising enemy of all things Jewish. (The diplomatic isolation of Transjordan on this issue was nakedly revealed by the fact that it was the only member of the Arab League not to have accorded recognition to this government.) Only by the end of 1948 would this intra–Arab competition for Arab Palestine be settled by IDF victories over the Egyptians, whose armies were largely forced out of the Negev, and by the consequent transfer of the Mufti's government from Gaza back to Cairo.

The fate of the "Gaza Strip" itself was an important factor in shaping the eventual political outcome of this first Arab-Israeli war. That small territory, never a part of Egypt proper, and whose political status would always remain uncertain, was the original home of some 150,000 Arabs but that figure soon swelled to over 300,000 due to refugees fleeing from the violence (the fighting had largely avoided the strip itself). Thus, as will be discussed later in the present study, the Gaza Strip, in addition to its strategically important location on the border of Egypt and relatively close to Jewish urban centers, inevitably became an early subject of diplomatic and political interest not only to the Arab states but to Israel as well. That is because the existence of ever-increasing numbers of refugees there (Egypt was unwilling to accept them in any significant amount) offered an opportunity in the postwar period for Israel to suggest to the parties and the United Nations that, as one way of doing its part to alleviate the plight of those refugees, it assume responsibility for Gaza as a separate territory outside Israel proper. Its motivation in doing so was to ease the strong pressure being exerted on it, especially by the United States, to allow the immediate return to Israel proper, and to areas under its military control, of large numbers of refugees even prior to a peace settlement. Needless to say, the Arab states, for their part, would not entertain such an arrangement with its accretion of Jewish-controlled land; Egypt had the additional incentive to retain it, if only to ensure it would not fall under the Amman government. Also worth noting in this context is that the Mufti's policy in general was to *oppose* any return of the refugees to any part of Palestine ruled by the Jews — a policy that undermined the Western-supported Arab demand for the immediate return home of large numbers of those refugees.

The odd man out in this Arab struggle against the Jewish state was King Abdullah's Transjordan. He not only had territorial ambitions in Arab Palestine, as noted above, but he also was in a military and diplomatic position to satisfy those ambitions. Even more than the Egyptian army, Amman's Arab Legion was the best trained, equipped and led of all the invading forces. Geographically, it was in a position to seize control of most of the Arab Palestine heartland and of East Jerusalem, including the Old City. Moreover, as suggested above, the other Arab states did not put the bulk of their armies on the field of battle, further magnifying the importance of the Arab Legion. (The actual numbers of troops facing each other during the war were fairly equal between Israel and all the Arab states combined — well less than 100,000 on each side.) In recognition of these factors, the Arab states conferred overall military leadership on Abdullah as they planned their simultaneous invasion of 15 May. But, in actuality, each army remained under separate national commands, and the original strategic plan of seeking to split the Jewish state in half at its more northern end toward Haifa was aborted, especially with Abdullah's decision to focus on winning control over the Jenin-Hebron hill area rather than on moving against the Jews. Moreover, Abdullah diverted some of his Legion units to protect Arab Jerusalem and the Old City from capture by the Jews, further weakening any Arab effort to split Israel in two. While he would be recognized by the Arabs as perhaps having saved Jerusalem from full Jewish rule, and especially for having kept under Arab control the entire Old City with its sacred Moslem sites, he also would be faulted by some in the Arab states for having initially deferred to British policy of respecting the UN decision to make Jerusalem a *corpus separatum*. This caused him and Glubb to delay their move into the city by three crucial days despite urgent appeals from the disparate Arab forces in Jerusalem who feared a takeover of the entire city by the relatively better organized and more powerful local Jewish military. Those Jewish forces were composed of both IDF and Irgun/Stern Gang units, who had been alert enough to take advantage of the military vacuum caused by an unexpected British withdrawal from the city on 14 rather than 15 May, inadvertently catching the Arab states unaware.

On the diplomatic side, it was an open secret that Abdullah had long been in discreet contact with Jewish Agency officials prior to 15 May. The Jews, recognizing that conquering all of Palestine was neither militarily feasible nor diplomatically desirable, saw in Abdullah's Transjordan a welcome negotiating partner in the likely *de facto* partition of that land, including Jerusalem, once the fighting ended. Abdullah's critics would see his brief hesitation after 15 May as responsible for the Jewish success in remaining permanently in firm control of West Jerusalem. Actually, the Jewish forces in Jerusalem were only interested — beyond their basic goal of protecting West Jerusalem and Mt. Scopus, where Hebrew University and Hadassah Hospital were located — in controlling the Jewish Quarter of the Old City; they were incapable of capturing the entire city. Moreover, the PGI would not have wished to do so, given the unacceptable diplomatic fallout such an operation would have entailed in its relations with the West and the United Nations. Still, Abdullah would bask in his role as the savior of Arab Jerusalem and the entire Old City from Jewish rule, and he would use this role to help him counter the charge of "collusion" with the Jews. That charge was based on his secret negotiations with the Jews, coupled with the outcome of the war giving him most of what he desired in Palestine from the very start (with the important exception of having failed to achieve a link to the Mediterranean coast). His very success in this regard, unique among the Arab states, opened him up to suspicion of a prearranged settlement with the Jews, although most historians today dismiss the charge as a myth. They point out that there never was a firm, let alone formal, undertaking between the two; Transjordan's military performance during the war itself consisted of hard-fought battles in the theater of operations of primary concern to the IDF up to 18 July; the tactical and strategic moves by the Arab Legion, within the diplomatic and practical limitations outlined above, were demonstratively pragmatic, unplanned responses to unforeseeable military developments; and Abdullah avoided taking major steps that could cast him in the role of betrayer of the common Arab cause against the Jewish state — as he told the Jewish Agency's secret negotiator, Golda Meir, the night of 10-11 May in Amman, "Then [November 1947] I was one, now I am five."

In summary, by the end of the Ten-Day War of July, Israel (a) had opened a corridor and serviceable road through Arab Palestine to West Jerusalem; (b) had widened the country's narrow waistline by moving into higher terrain, where it was now facing an Iraq-led army alongside Arab Legion units; (c) had moved the Egyptians further south, as compared to their most advanced positions close to Tel Aviv, though they remained in control of essentially all of the Negev as well as the land to its east up to the Hebron region, which was under Abdullah's control; and (d) had broadened its areas of control in the Galilee region by expanding its narrow link connecting the coastal plain with its allotted territory in Eastern Galilee — parts of which, however, still remained under Syrian occupation. (The Lebanese kept their forces almost exclusively in a defensive mode along its own border with Palestine; however, as the year progressed the IDF, in its northern offensives, would seize militarily useful sites within Lebanon itself, just as it would regarding Egyptian territory in its final, successful offensive of 1948 in the Negev. All such seized foreign territory, to the relief of the U.S. and other governments, would be returned to those two Arab states as a result of the armistice agreements of 1949.) As in the case of Gaza and Jerusalem, we will have occasion later in this study to develop further the way these military issues played out in their diplomatic context.

Five

American Diplomacy at the United Nations, Mid–1948

For Palestine's future, the period between June and August was also a momentous one at the United Nations itself. Certainly, U.S. efforts to resolve the issue were operationally focused on that international body. This was consistent with the view of Secretary Marshall, who, on 13 September, stated to a leading American supporter of Israel, Julius Klein, that, *for the U.S. government*, if Palestine between November 1947 and May 1948 was a Jewish political problem and an Arab military one, it now was, *for the United States*, a Jewish military problem and an Arab political one. Marshall then set out for Paris, where the UN General Assembly was beginning its third session, during which he would personally lead the American delegation for the next two months, largely in an effort to reconcile those two problems diplomatically.

Given the secretary's strategic focus on the United Nations, especially its Security Council, it was no wonder that Under-Secretary Lovett and his staff back in Washington, as noted earlier, had enthusiastically greeted, as a "return of the *Entente Cordiale*," the recent, more cooperative attitude of America's erstwhile Near East partner and fellow holder of the veto power, the United Kingdom. After all, from the State Department perspective as the summer progressed, was it not the British who in the spring had stubbornly declined American pleas to extend the mandate a bit longer to allow more time for negotiating a truce and trusteeship plan? Did they not also continue to arm the Arab states while the United States was conducting an arms embargo in the area? Were they not, in May and June, unwilling to help enforce the truce with their remaining troops in Palestine? Were they not now changing course in line with U.S. policies, especially through their active help in obtaining, and then itself faithfully implementing, the Security Council's 29 May resolution ordering such an embargo and truce? Was it not a hallmark of our next important joint success, the Security Council resolution of 15 July, that it contained a determination of the existence of a threat to the peace warranting the application of Chapter VII sanctions, not excluding the use of military force, against any future truce violators (although the British would not go so far as to specify the Arabs as the ones who had been unwilling to extend the first truce when it expired on 9 July)? And was it not the case that the two of us were now cooperating in the field on the basis of a division of labor—we, on our part, concentrating on ensuring that our Israeli friends did not undertake further military activities and, instead, agreed to accept the exchange of the Negev for the Western Galilee and possibly Jaffa, among other concessions (including return of refugees and internationalization and demilitarization of the region of Jerusalem), while the British, on their part, concentrated on pressing the Arab states to curb their goals in Palestine by accepting a compromise that (albeit at the difficult price of acquiescing to having an internationalized, UN-controlled Jerusalem and a Jewish state as their neighbor), would allow them to carve up among themselves all of the territory originally slated by the UN General Assembly's November resolution for an independent Arab Palestine state (e.g., most of the Negev and the hills from Jenin to Hebron would be given to Transjordan; the southernmost parts of the Negev, including the Gaza Strip, to Egypt; and the Negev part of the port area of Aqaba, if not to Transjordan, then perhaps to Saudi Arabia, while northeastern Palestine went to Syria)?

It was this last matter, the territorial aspects of any prospective settlement between Israel and the Arab states, that would be at the center of a deep controversy and debate at the General Assembly in Paris starting 21 September. At the center of that debate was a plan completed and released just a few days earlier by Bernadotte in his capacity as mediator, recommending far-reaching territorial changes along the lines outlined above. The resultant debate would have serious ramifications within the U.S. government and between it and American supporters of Israel. It began with Marshall's 21 September declaration supporting the plan "in its entirety." The setting for that declaration, which had been carefully coordinated with a similar declaration by Bevin, was a highly emotional and dramatic one caused by the Stern Gang's assassination of Bernadotte just four days previously while he was traveling in the Jewish-controlled section of Jerusalem.

This Anglo-American effort to obtain UN approval of the Bernadotte Plan had, as we shall see, both farcical and tragic aspects and would ultimately fail to achieve its objective; nevertheless, it would have an important permanent effect on the future of Palestine and on the evolution of the broader Arab-Israeli conflict. It would also greatly influence, for the worse, relations between McDonald and the State Department. However, before turning to this controversy in greater detail, it would be helpful to assess the state of play within the American government itself as it reshaped its policies in light of the results of the first two rounds of fighting that ended 18 July.

Recall that, on 24 August, McDonald had warned Washington of an impending crisis in its relations with Israel and of a likely renewal of the fighting, this time on an even wider scale. He was not alone in this bleak scenario: the State Department and its UN delegation based in New York also had their own sense of foreboding. In this dark mood, as summer progressed toward the September opening of the General Assembly, lines seemed to be drawn between those devoted to the department's analysis and approach to the problem and those who were certain that Truman had a different understanding of the appropriate course of action. This latter, dissenting group believed the State Department was doing its best to mislead the president as to the facts of the matter and to hide from him the extent to which it was in reality working to undermine his policies. One way to capture the mood, details and sense of urgency that characterized this internal conflict would be to draw upon a remarkable set of unsigned, private, typewritten notes (a copy of which resides in the Truman Presidential Library) obviously written by a member of the delegation who was out of sorts with the direction of America's Palestine policy at the United Nations but was not assigned to work on that question. That writer described himself (or, more likely, in the present writer's opinion, herself) as a "disinterested party of general repute," and if it wasn't Eleanor Roosevelt, it had to be someone who so closely shared her well-known views on this subject, and who had as much influence in the Democratic Party as she did, as makes no matter. (Mrs. Roosevelt's direct responsibilities on the delegation were limited to championing, and chairing the drafting committee for, the prospective UN Convention on Human Rights; however, ever since the 19 March episode, she had actively protested the trend in U.S. Palestine policy to the point of threatening to resign.)

The unsigned notes, as summarized below, provide a concise spotlight on the core issues and dovetail with all the important matters discussed so far in this study while adding flavor and insight:

Thursday, 27 May, and Friday, 28 May: I have anxiety about an impending new reversal by the United States on the Palestine question as indicated by (a) the president's [25 May press] conference; (b) the failure of the United States to reintroduce its own draft resolution citing Article 39 [of Chapter VII, determining the existence of a threat to the peace possibly requiring sanctions], thereby leaving Russia to do so; and (c) the introduction by the British of a resolution which coupled the Jews and the Arabs both as "aggressors," and which called for an arms embargo directed against both sides as well as the end of Jewish immigration into Palestine. Therefore, I asked Carl Sherman to call Jack Ewing and Ed Flynn [senior Democratic Party officials] to get to the president before he goes on tour on 3 June to have him stop the skullduggery. However, they were both out of reach until Tuesday.

Sunday, 30 May: The Security Council vote yesterday on the British draft gives the general impression that a new Anglo-American collusion has been arranged.

Tuesday, 1 June: The British intend, with American support despite the recognition of Israel, to soften up the Jews. I am urging Ewing to recommend to the president: (a) dismissal of Loy Henderson; (b) appointment of a special advisor to the State Department to replace General Hilldring [also see below] — for example, Sumner Welles or Frank P. Graham; (c) announcement of a loan right now, and that the United States would help arm the Haganah once the truce period is over; and (d) issuance of a public declaration of non-support of Ernest Bevin's policy toward Palestine.

Ewing was aware of some of the department's moves but insisted that so was the president and so it was wrong to anticipate that the worst was going to happen. He also intimated that the United States would not let Israel die after having recognized it, and that the arms embargo would be lifted. He agreed that the important thing for the United States was to get a resolution leveling the embargo specifically against the Arab states. Ewing did promise to put my suggestions to the president before he leaves on Thursday. Meanwhile, Flynn said he was disgusted and will act in his own way.

Friday, 4 June: At a Ewing-Flynn meeting in New York with other New York Democratic Party officials, Ewing said the president: (a) intended to name an ambassador to Israel; and (b) had urged Bernadotte to allow Jewish immigration into Palestine during the truce period. Ewing believes that it was this Truman request that led to Bernadotte's statement yesterday that the 29 May resolution did not affect Jewish immigration into Palestine.

Saturday, 5 June (evening), and Tuesday, 8 June (morning): I learned that the State Department had indicated that the *de jure* recognition of Israel would not be granted unless territorial concessions were made by the Jewish state. This, coupled with the report in *The Nation*, gives further proof of "collusion" with the British Foreign Office. Chester Williams of our delegation had told me on 3 June that the delegation's goal during the truce period is "to get an agreement [regarding the Jerusalem area] ... on a Vatican City to begin with, let us say ... from there we'll go on." Upon learning all this, I decided to go to Washington to secure more facts and to contact personalities known to be close to the president.

Before leaving on Tuesday, 8 June, I heard that Flynn was aghast at how the situation has developed. He said that the president should have given instructions regarding the embargo, the Haganah, and the loan when he saw Weizmann [on 25–26 May].

Tuesday, 8 June (afternoon): In Washington, where "I saw the file on the most recent State Department attitude toward Israel" and learned that (a) the State Department no longer considered itself bound to recognize *de jure* the Jewish state, "because of the present situation"; and (b) the United States no longer needs to recognize the November resolution's boundaries, because "its *de facto* recognition was based on a *de facto* situation and having no reference" to that resolution. I then went to see (a) Senator Howard McGrath, chairman of the Democratic National Committee; (b) the "liberal" Senator Harley Kilgore, who is on good personal terms with the president, and who tried for some months to secure a replacement of Secretary Forrestal as one of the chief authors of the policy of betrayal [that is, of Truman's Palestine policy]; and (c) Leslie Biffle, secretary to the Senate minority leader, "who is regarded as the person having the closest personal relations with the President and being privy to all his thinking."

McGrath came off the floor to talk with me. I said the president is being "double-crossed" by his own State Department and that the double-cross would have the effect both of destroying all his decent acts with respect to Israel and of destroying the newly revived prestige of the president himself. I then proceeded to tell him about (a) the story of the newest step of the State Department, placing responsibility at the door of Loy Henderson; (b) the "remarkable coincidence" of Henderson "asking for territorial restrictions at the same time that the British had dropped their mask and were suggesting that recognition of Israel would be forthcoming if territorial concessions were made"; (c) the machinations in the Security Council—particularly the U.S. delegation's making no effort to get it to declare the situation a threat to peace and security, as the president would have liked, per his policies; (d) the British determination to maintain sole control of the Middle East, to push the United States out of the picture, and, if necessary, to allow every Jew in Palestine to be killed and the United States to be made a mockery of (in all this, "Henderson and his clique were willing accomplices"—to which McGrath here said that "it was intended that he should be kicked out a long time ago"); and (e) the president's needing someone in the department "who would carry out the policy explicitly." Hilldring's illness was genuine in the beginning, but at the end, when he was prepared to take on the job, it was Marshall who told him he didn't want him to come—I couldn't reveal my source to McGrath, but it was Leslie Biffle, the president's friend. McGrath assured me he would go see the president when he returns on or about 17 June, and asked me to prepare a briefing memorandum for him, which I will do.

I then saw Kilgore. I added the point to him that we were opening the doors to the very thing that we said we wanted to avoid — the possibility of Russian penetration of the Middle East. He attributed the president's inability to fire Forrestal to his not being able to get the [Republican-led] Senate to confirm any decent replacements. He said he was on first-name terms with the president and can have his ear, and so would do what he could.

Then I saw Biffle. In going over these matters with him, I pointed out the coincidence of the direct retrogression on Palestine policy with Mr. Truman's absences from Washington. I told him also that the policy of discrediting the president had penetrated to the American delegation and mentioned that one member of the delegation, in response to my question as to what the next steps of the United States were, said, "That depends on the President's next non-political speech." Biffle said the matter was so important that he would relay the information to the president at once — meaning that night, when he expected to telephone him.

My net impressions of these discussions are (a) that there is no one person or persons in the president's confidence who has continuous information concerning Palestine developments, and that this is where the fault largely lies [Comment: Hence the writer's — and soon McDonald's — emphasis on replacing Hilldring with an equally senior State Department officer sympathetic to the Jewish cause — Hilldring, as will be recalled, had first served as assistant secretary of state for occupation affairs, and then as a short-term member of the U.S. delegation, fall 1947]; (b) that the State Department is consequently able to feed the president information that can hardly be trusted; (c) that there seems to be no person officially representing the Zionist movement in this country who has the ear of key people in the administration; and (d) that "a disinterested party, such as ourselves, can put across very important ideas because of our disinterest and our general repute." Our approach has to be continuous and friendly and not sporadic, and it must draw a distinction between the president and the State Department. This last "can be made only by those people who have not been parties to attacks on the President, lumping him with every American double-cross. This is of the first strategic importance." [End of summary of these anonymous notes.]

The Achilles' heel of the writer of these notes, and of like-minded officials, such as McDonald, is that their premise — that, as the notes put it, "a distinction" must be drawn between the president and the State Department — was faulty. In fact, as our chapters on the president's off-the-record conversations show, Truman largely shared the department's views and goals, certainly regarding diplomatic and national security matters. Had the dissenters been privy to the president's private conversations with State and Defense officials, they likely would have been dismayed at how often he had actively encouraged them in the very activities that were so upsetting to the dissenters. Of course, Mrs. Roosevelt and company were not so naïve as to have full confidence that Truman was with them all the way — nor, it must be said, were many of them necessarily wed to Truman being nominated as the Democratic presidential candidate at the upcoming convention, a nomination that was accorded him on 14 July. Still, given the extent of the contradictions between his personal, public stance regarding Palestine and his private instructions and informal comments to subordinates, the dissenting group (or at least those who were serving in government posts) might well have drawn in their horns a bit in expressing their opposition. Moreover, as specifically regards Eleanor Roosevelt, she conceivably could have gone even further in her protests — notwithstanding her devotion to seeing the Human Rights Convention approved by the United Nations — and acted in June on her March threat to resign from the delegation over Palestine policy. But what were those contradictions between the White House and State Department? An analysis of them, as provided in the following chapter, will bring us to the heart of American foreign — and domestic — policy toward Palestine and the Near East as a whole as the United States prepared for the fall session of the General Assembly in Paris.

Six

The Bernadotte Plan of June 1948

Territorial Issues

As the issue of territorial boundaries between the State of Israel and the Arab states was the main factor leading to the renewal of fighting in October and again in December, and as that fighting also proved to be, paradoxically, the welcome solvent the United States was seeking by purely diplomatic means to address the conundrum of a peace formula in the region, it warrants being discussed first.

By virtue of the General Assembly resolution of 14 May and the Security Council resolution of 29 May, Bernadotte wore two hats — one as UN negotiator and overseer of a cease-fire between Israel and the Arab states, the other as "mediator" in a projected negotiation for a longer-term solution to the conflict. Though without experience as a diplomat, other than that regarding ad hoc humanitarian matters, and having no past involvement in Near Eastern affairs (never having even visited the area), he favorably impressed the skeptical Ralph Bunche by pulling off the four-week cease-fire, which took effect on 11 June; Bunche, his UN "minder," had considered Bernadotte to be but the latest in a series of governmental or UN-sponsored peacemakers practicing "haughty amateurism" on the Palestine problem since 1946. Bernadotte achieved the initial lull in the fighting by strength of personality — he exuded self-confidence and goodwill toward his interlocutors — and by brash, but calculated, overstatement of the powers he was wielding by virtue of the UN resolutions. Notably, he warned both sides of the sanctions he would recommend to the United Nations were either one to reject his proposals. (Of course, even then he would not have succeeded had both warring sides not, for their own military needs, agreed to a cease-fire.)

On the basis of the cease-fire, Bernadotte was able momentarily to bask in the glow of universal admiration on all sides. In this heady atmosphere, he and his staff decided to take early advantage of the consequent momentum and prepare a set of peace proposals for consideration by the parties. The resultant

Six. The Bernadotte Plan of June 1948

document, soon dubbed the Bernadotte Plan, was completed and submitted by Mediator Bernadotte to the world, as it were, on 28 June — some eleven days prior to the expiration of the cease-fire. Unfortunately for him, the reaction from that world was almost universally negative (even that of the secretary-general), and this caused him to revise the plan during the course of the summer, as shall be described below.

The reasons for the failure were not difficult to discern. Most importantly, it was unrealistically premised on the willingness of the Arab states to acquiesce not only to the existence of a Jewish state but also to the assignment of most of the territory originally slated for the Arab state in Palestine to King Abdullah's Transjordan. Furthermore, it proposed not the internationalization of the Jerusalem-Bethlehem area in accordance with the General Assembly's partition resolution of 29 November, but rather its placement under the sole sovereignty of Abdullah, on the condition that he would allow an international role in guaranteeing access to, and protection of, the holy places. Finally, the plan proposed the "right of return" of the Arab refugees, which, of course, was anathema to the PGI and seen as unrealistic by King Abdullah, who, on 25 July, told Wells Stabler, a vice consul from Jerusalem on temporary assignment to Amman since 13 July, that "shifts of population should take place to eliminate minority problems"; also recall in this context that ex–Grand Mufti Hussein, based behind Egyptian lines, publicly rejected the notion of any Arab refugees returning to their homes so long as the Jews remained in control, a policy that the PGI welcomed as playing into its own hand of opposing pressure on it to receive back the refugees *en masse* so long as the war continued. (At the height of the war, summer 1948, Sharett wrote for staff guidance that the PGI was watching with amazement the extent of the unforced exodus from Israeli territory of so many of the Arab residents, and that the government was pleased to "get rid" of this "huge Arab minority" in this time of "storm and stress."[1])

Other aspects of the plan were similarly unacceptable to most of the parties (Amman and London being the obvious winners):

- The question of the Negev was to be resolved by granting most of it to Transjordan, although the southernmost section was to be shared with Egypt by direct negotiation.
- Israel was to be compensated for its loss of nearly all the Negev by retaining its recent military gains in the Western Galilee and some parts of central Palestine around its narrow waistline (but not its hard-won "corridor" to West Jerusalem or the coastal city of Jaffa, which was to be returned to Arab control).
- Other invading Arab states were also to receive slivers of Palestine —

for example, Syria in the northeast and possibly even Saudi Arabia at the shoreline of the Gulf of Aqaba.

- The Haifa seaport and oil refineries were to be internationalized under the United Nations, as would be the Lydda airport.
- Israel and Transjordan were to form a customs union and a political council to rule on matters of common interest, such as the extent allowable for Jewish immigration into Israel. (If the two nations proved unable to agree in the council on immigration questions, they were to look to the United Nation's Economic and Social Council for a final decision!)

That this plan did not survive its publication on 28 June was not surprising given the harsh realities in the field, making the acceptance of even the wisest and best informed of diplomatic proposals nearly impossible. But what is surprising is the shocking naiveté exhibited here by Bernadotte and, even more so, by Bunche and his UN team of experts. How to account for such a debacle? More is needed than such obvious explanations as that the group had unwisely isolated itself on a relatively distant island for half the period of the cease-fire, or that it lacked the necessary field experience and in-depth political knowledge of the conflicting parties to have developed feasible proposals, or, finally, that it naturally felt driven to fulfill its UN-assigned second task, that of peace mediator. One might also fault its *modus operandi*, which it would follow down to the preparation of a revised plan just prior to the assassination in September of Bernadotte: the practice was for Bernadotte to remain uninvolved in the initial preparation by his staff of the peace proposals; only after the details were put on paper would he then be orally "consulted" on them (Bunche's 1950 description at Harvard) before their issuance under his name. This, of course, allowed ample scope for Bunche to put his personal stamp on the final product. An important clue as to just how that UN official assessed the problem and its possible solution is discernible from his private conversations as far back as September 1947 with the staff of the U.S. Mission to the United Nations in New York. There, he made known his views on how best to handle the recommendations of UNSCOP — that while his personal preference was to accept the minority plan recommendation favoring a unitary Palestine with appropriate local autonomy for each community, he believed the best course of action for the General Assembly would be to approve the majority plan's partition proposal, as that would at least satisfy one of the parties, in contrast to the unitary proposal's satisfying neither. Bunche, however, went on to advise that even the majority plan would need to be significantly amended if partition was to offer the prospect of stability in Palestine. He said that, since the envisaged Arab state would not be viable if it tried to stand on its own, it needed to be combined with its neighbor,

Transjordan, into a single state, which, in turn, would join in a customs union with the Jewish state.[2] This is precisely the core of the Bernadotte Plan of June 1948!

The problem was that, by the time of the cease-fire of June, conditions on the ground had already profoundly changed the terms of reference for a solution that might have prevailed the previous year. First, the military balance now favored, if not a definitive "victory" by the Israelis, at least the likelihood that the Jewish state could more than hold its own even in a sustained war against the Arab states. The consensus in June by the best-informed observers was that the IDF was capable of further territorial advances were the four-week cease-fire not to be quickly extended after its expiration on 9 July. Once this consensus view proved valid during the "Ten-Day War" of 9–18 July, Bernadotte and Bunche perceived a renewed opportunity for a serious peace negotiation involving a now less militarily feisty group of Arab states and a more secure Israel. They also finally recognized that a peace negotiation could not proceed during a mere temporary cease-fire but rather would require the condition precedent of a more substantial and open-ended truce arrangement for there to be any chance of success. This is what they achieved in obtaining the fateful Security Council resolution of 15 July, whose overly optimistic premise was that the Arabs had now had enough of their fight knocked out of them, and the Israelis now were self-confident and relieved enough, for the two parties to make the concessions and compromises necessary to end the conflict. The basic deal, as far as territory was concerned, would be for the Arabs to accept the existence in Palestine of a sovereign Jewish state, and for Israel to accept modifications to its borders that would allow the neighboring Arab states, in exchange for Israel retaining some lands it conquered during the first round of fighting, to take permanent sovereignty over other parts of Palestine, notably in the Negev (even though Israel had made it clear that the Negev would not be given up).

Second, it was now recognized that intra–Arab friction precluded the kind of amicable arrangements among themselves that the members of the Arab League were being called upon to accept; it also precluded their agreeing to peaceful coexistence, formal or otherwise, with the Jewish state. The basic explanation for this obstacle to a diplomatic resolution of the Palestine problem was that the Arab League worked at the political level on the basis of consensus — in other words, the lowest common denominator. Therefore, whereas the Bernadotte Plan's fundamental premise was that Transjordan's ambitions in Arab Palestine could provide the foundation of a general peace deal with Israel, the reality was that too many of Amman's adversaries would object to such a deal, and for reasons entirely separate from their firm opposition, as a common principle, to any recognition of Israel. For example, there was no way Egypt would agree to the depositing of the loathed, British-sponsored Transjordan in the Negev, all the way to the Mediterranean Sea, just at the time that Cairo was pressing for the departure of that colonial power from all of Egypt, including a Suez Canal zone that was so strategically close to Palestine.

Third, even the headquarters staff of Bernadotte's own sponsoring organization, the United Nations, was appalled at his plan's blithe assumption that the November 1947 resolution was null and void, thus opening up Palestine to drastic alterations. In addition to the overwhelming additional administrative and supervisory burdens the plan would impose on the United Nations in such places as Haifa and Lydda, the secretary-general was long known to consider it of the highest importance to ensure the full implementation of the partition resolution as essential to the integrity of his organization. He privately expressed annoyance to colleagues and like-minded delegates that Bunche lacked the qualities to be in a leadership role and consequently failed to harness Bernadotte's overly ambitious proposals, and that the entire mediation effort was being run under undue British influence. Just as the Israeli government did, Lie strongly rejected Bernadotte's above-noted claim, during this first truce period, that he was not at all restrained by the terms of the November partition resolution, which, he argued, had been nullified by virtue of the decision in the spring to call for a special General Assembly session to revise it. However, Lie and others underlined the fact that the Assembly had specifically declined in that session to revise the resolution. We shall return to these matters in our consideration of how the revised Bernadotte Plan of September fared at the regularly scheduled General Assembly session held in Paris that fall.

Fourth, the U.S. response to the 28 June Bernadotte Plan was, at best, a mixed one, in part favorable to some aspects of it but strongly opposed regarding others. Recall that at this stage of the Palestine problem, Washington had enthusiastically welcomed back the cooperative alliance with Britain in meeting the challenges of the Near East. London's conscientious implementation of the Security Council's 29 May arms embargo (even at the expense of its treaty commitments) and its application of direct diplomatic pressure on the Arab states to accept the Council's cease-fire call of that date were seen as signs of British intentions to work closely and proactively with the United States. Nevertheless, Washington was unhappy with the British-influenced Bernadotte proposal to place the city of Jerusalem under Amman control rather than establish there a *corpus separatum* under UN control; it also informed London that it did not support the proposal by Bernadotte to create a "free port of Haifa." As early as 29 June, Lovett had McClintock "wire" Bernadotte that the United States opposed placing Haifa "on same basis as Jerusalem."[3] More positively, of course, the United States shared the mediator's hope of achieving a peace that would involve Arab recognition of, or at least acquiescence to, the Jewish state, as well as an arrangement regarding Jerusalem that would, at a minimum, guarantee protection of, and access to, the holy places. The implicit bottom line for Washington, and for the Bernadotte team, was that *any* peace agreement voluntarily entered into by Israel and the Arab states along the above lines would be most welcomed.

But the first order of business for the United States in early July was to help ensure that the expiring cease-fire was extended and replaced with a more lasting truce. A remarkable, revised analysis prepared by Deputy Permanent Representative Jessup at the American Mission to the United Nations in New York captures the new mood of this period: (a) the PGI "has dealt very effectively with recent Irgun affairs at Tel Aviv" (a reference to its handling of the *Altalena* affair of 22 June, when it used force to block an Irgun ship from landing while loaded with arms and fighters despite the then-prevailing first cease-fire period); (b) Israel militarily is "more than a match for most of Arab States put together"; (c) if Israel is "fairly treated," it "could become a force operating to our own advantage and to [the] advantage of Arab countries"; (d) "on whole, Arabs have been accustomed for so long to look upon Jews as root of all evil that it is difficult for them to see contributions for good that Jews might make ... to welfare of Arabs"; (e) the United Nations "failed to devise a peaceful settlement of issues.... Result ... was leaving a political vacuum ... partially filled by proclamation of Israel, which might be described as extra-legal act"[4]; (f) "On credit side ... Truce Commission ... appointment of mediator ... effective machinery for supervision truce"; and (g) unlike the areas of responsibility for the mediator and for diplomatic channels, the Security Council must deal with the "demilitarization of Jerusalem."

In line with this new vision of a solution to the Palestine question, the State Department, on 3 July, informed the United Kingdom that while the Bernadotte Plan could serve as the first step toward a peace agreement between Israel and the Arab states, the main goal would be the renewal of the truce and the demilitarization of Jerusalem. This line of policy was in keeping with Truman's constant refrain to the State Department that his highest priority was to avoid further fighting in the region. Therefore, the focus of the government's attention in the days following the issuance of the Bernadotte Plan was on keeping the peace. Only after having achieved that goal in mid–July, following the second round of fighting described earlier, did serious efforts restart to push the parties into a negotiated, revised settlement. For the purposes of our study, then, we need to move ahead and examine in detail the shape of diplomatic negotiations as they developed at the time U.S. Special Representative James G. McDonald prepared to take up his Tel Aviv post in August.

The American View of Territorial and Related Problems

To enter into this aspect of American policy during Israel's War of Independence means exploring the political culture within the government as it applied to the Palestine question. McDonald's personal history, and the urgent way the president sought him out and then unilaterally announced his appointment, guaranteed that all the premises, both institutional and personal, that for decades underlay State Department policy toward Palestine and the Zionist issue would come under close examination.[5] Furthermore, spotlighting this dimension of policymaking will help us understand the very human factors affecting this exceptionally emotional subject, one that became even more heated as the stakes in the area escalated in step with the rise of tensions due to Cold War issues and as domestic politics entered ever more deeply and explicitly into the picture with the approaching presidential election of 2 November.

Even had the manner of McDonald's appointment been less brutal than it was, it is clear that he would never have had a normal chief-of-mission relationship with the State Department. The two felt a deep distrust of each other: McDonald on the grounds that the department was perennially disloyal to what he perceived as President Truman's policy support of the Zionist program, and the department largely on the grounds of McDonald's well-known professional connection to that program as well as his personal role in the 1946 fiasco of Truman's reluctant rejection of the Grady Mission recommendations for solving the interconnected Jewish refugee and Palestine problems. Notwithstanding Secretary Marshall's protest from his hospital sickbed that the appointment was an infringement of normal procedures requiring advance consultations with the State Department, it is surely a fact that McDonald would never have been included in any list of nominees that the department might have submitted to the White House once it became clear that the president wouldn't buy its initial effort merely to send to Israel a middle-level career foreign service officer bearing the title of "acting special representative."

That this is so is well illustrated by the record of Lovett's effort to convince Clifford not to proceed with the McDonald appointment when it was

Six. *The Bernadotte Plan of June 1948* 91

first announced to him by phone at 4:25 on the afternoon of 22 June — a few hours before it was made public. It will be recalled from Chapter Three that Lovett, in both that conversation and (after having hastily consulted with Henderson and other staffers) a succeeding one at 4:40, resorted to a stream of charges against McDonald's record that bordered on, it must be said, character assassination even for those frenetic times (loyalty boards were established in 1947). Thus, Lovett claimed to Clifford that McDonald should be disqualified on the grounds that, aside from being "a confirmed Zionist" whose appointment would have "repercussions" on the work of the UN Truce Commission in Jerusalem, he was "a known 'fellow traveler.'" Of course, this last was absurd and presumably based not only on McDonald's vocal support for the Soviet ally during the recent world war but, more interestingly for our purposes, on his contacts with the Soviet Union when he was high commissioner for refugees from Germany in the 1930s. In that capacity, he decided to visit that new member of the League of Nations (as well as the recent beneficiary of diplomatic recognition by the United States) in the hope of obtaining its cooperation in receiving some of the refugees. His short visit to Moscow in 1935 was criticized at the time by anti-communists in the West for having given needless support to that regime. Henderson was then a junior officer at the American Embassy in Moscow and served as McDonald's greeter when he arrived for a meeting with the ambassador. There is no evidence that McDonald recalled that contact as he entered the State Department for his first meeting with Lovett on June 25, 1948, but Henderson, a fervent opponent of an overly conciliatory U.S. policy toward the Soviet Union even then, as well as during the war, evidently had it in mind as he brainstormed with Lovett on how to block the nomination. As for Lovett himself, as assistant secretary of war he had regularly made known his firm personal support for considering the Soviet Union an essential ally — for example, in a 1942 address to a bankers' association, he said he'd "rather have Russia on my side" than depend on the "complacent and illusory theory that we are bound to win."[6]

McDonald's continuing ties to the Foreign Policy Association likely was still another consideration in the State Department's canard against him. That organization was seen by those of the ultra-conservative mindset as tainted with sympathy for the communists. A stark, relevant example of this alleged taint on the FPA occurred in 1950 when Ambassador Jessup was hauled before the McCarthy Committee to justify his connection with a luncheon offered by the FPA in the 1930s to a visiting Soviet delegation; Jessup explained that he merely had acted as one member of the FPA Board of Directors.

Had McDonald been aware of this kind of personal attack on him by the State Department on 22 June, he would have been better prepared for the animosity he would confront three days later at his initial meeting with Lovett and his staff. There, just after having met with the president, he would be directly accused by Lovett of being unfit for his post given that he didn't put the interests of America first. The under-secretary then compared him unfavorably in this regard with Stanton Griffis, the U.S. ambassador to Egypt, who "refreshingly" was only concerned with forwarding his own country's interests.[7] McDonald, obviously upset, countered that Lovett's own staff must be shocked at such a charge against him, at which point Lovett assured him that his staff fully shared his point of view, and with good reason.[8] In his pre-departure courtesy call on Marshall a month later (at which only a protocol officer was present and no substantive business was discussed, a typical experience he would have in all his consultation visits to the State Department throughout his tenure), McDonald would indirectly bring up this confrontation with Lovett by pointing out that, while he had his own personal views on policy matters, so did everyone else, and he would loyally carry out government policy in the same way all the others did. Marshall assured him that his problem with the appointment was not at all personal, but only with the way it was made.

In this setting, the State Department kept McDonald's mission isolated physically and organizationally from its network of Near Eastern posts, including Jerusalem.[9] There was very little sharing of reporting between this network and McDonald due to a general assumption throughout the Foreign Service that he would pass on to the Israelis even the most confidential information he might receive from Washington; for example, as early as July 17, 1948, when Secretary Forrestal checked with Lovett as to whether he should agree to McDonald's request for a pre-departure meeting, he was told yes, but he "should not tell him anything he is not prepared to have stated to the Jewish Agency." The basic view within the government was that any elevation of the status of the Tel Aviv mission, and its pro–Israeli leader, even such a relatively trivial one as allowing McDonald and his staff to make informal visits to UN-"internationalized" Jerusalem, would do harm to efforts to placate the Arabs and move them toward a settlement, and, equally important, would tend, especially given McDonald's softness toward Israel, to weaken the pressures that the State Department was exerting on the PGI to make the concessions it saw as necessary to obtain a peace settlement.

This double motivation to isolate McDonald from the rest of the department (i.e., personal distrust coupled with a policy of reducing relations with the PGI to a minimum) would continue throughout his tenure, even after his promotion to ambassador and the raising of relations to the *de jure* level. McDonald would justifiably complain to the end of his being kept "out of the loop" and unable to provide his input on policy making or to have the benefit of his colleagues' and superiors' candid thinking about Near Eastern strategy. Examples abound: (a) his views were never elicited in any specific way prior to the declaration of support for all of the conclusions in the revised Bernadotte peace plan of September, and he certainly wasn't told of the "secret" McClintock/Troutbeck mission to Rhodes to help draw up that plan[10]; (b) even meetings in Washington between Israeli diplomats and senior officials in the State Department were not reported to him — one glaring example was his having to learn from the Israelis themselves of Eban's meetings at the department of June 14, 1949, and obtaining from them Eban's own memorandum of conversation covering those meetings; (c) to put it mildly, there was no collegiality in the field between McDonald and his American counterparts in the other Near Eastern posts — while he would himself copy them on appropriate telegrams he sent to the department, it was unusual for any of them to copy him on their telegrams; and (d) even into his final consultations in Washington in 1950, when the president had to plead with him on grounds of the national interest not to leave the government until the end of the year, when a suitable successor would become available, he found himself unable to conduct meaningful meetings with department officials, who seemed regularly to find an excuse to cut the meetings off hardly had they begun or to decline to enter into substantive discussions with him.

Nevertheless, McDonald tended unduly to belittle his impact on U.S. policy, because, in fact, his disliked messages from Tel Aviv did provoke discussion in the State Department and between it and the president; he helped ensure this result through his unhesitating practice of addressing his key messages to both the secretary and the president or his staff, especially Clifford and Niles. Thus, his early telegrams and supplementary informal letters, sent soon after his arrival at his post in August (especially the one of 24 August spelling out why the United States and Israel were facing a "crisis in the making"), led to hard thinking and in-depth meetings between Marshall and Lovett with the president.[11] Given the importance of this period — between the Security Council's success in obtaining an open-ended truce following its resolution of 15 July and the opening of the General Assembly session in Paris on 21 September — for the formulation of American policy, it would be worthwhile to devote some detailed attention to the conflict in views between McDonald and the State Department as embodied in their various messages:

McDonald's "conclusion," as stated at the end of his 24 August telegram, was that the Jewish view was "sounder than that of U.S. and UN." In support of that conclusion, McDonald assured Washington that Ben-Gurion, contrary to the view "in some Washington quarters," was perfectly serious when he asserted that Israel would in fact fight even against an American-backed UN force on the grounds that, as he told McDonald, "What we have won on the battlefield we will not sacrifice at the council table." In a simultaneous letter to Clifford, McDonald wrote that the open-ended truce "is tantamount to taking sides with the Arabs against the Jews," because it is a "death sentence to be executed at the convenience of the Arabs"; that the "burden" of war for Israel would be less than that of "continuation of the armed truce"; and that the overly close connection with the British was leading the United States to "get itself needlessly involved" in their unrealistic military machinations — "nor [should] the President" get himself "needlessly and gravely embarrassed."

Compare this point of view with Marshall's, shown in his 16 August memorandum to Truman, sent prior to McDonald's own initial telegrams from Tel Aviv, proposing "Representations to Provisional Government of Israel Regarding Maintenance of Peace in Palestine":

(a) the PGI is assuming "a more aggressive attitude in Palestine"; (b) "hostilities were resumed" after 9 July; (c) both Israel and the Arab states "accepted ... in principle" the Security Council resolution of 15 July, including "demilitarization" of Jerusalem; (d) Israel is showing now "a new and aggressive note," the IDF is making frequent "forward movements" and "firing against Arab positions," Israel is being armed from "France, Italy and Czechoslovakia" and its "military occupation of much of the Jerusalem area" is accompanied by a refusal even to discuss militarization; (e) the PGI has officially rejected our proposal that it take back some of the 300,000 "destitute" Arab refugees from "that part of Palestine now comprising the Jewish State" — it insists on hinging consideration of such an arrangement on the opening of negotiations for a "final peace settlement"; and (f) Palestine is as serious a problem as is Berlin, and the United States and United Kingdom must not "go slack" there.[12]

It is clear, then, that McDonald's 24 August analysis was diametrically opposed to that of Marshall and therefore would not, at least in the short run, fundamentally alter the direction of American policy as exemplified in the Truman-Marshall message to Ben-Gurion of 1 September (see below). Only with the demise of the Bernadotte Plan that fall in view of the successful IDF offensives of October and December in the Negev and Galilee (along with a largely unopposed March 1949 completion of its occupation of the Negev down to the port of Elath), changing the diplomatic landscape and leaving Israel in full control of what it considered its legitimate UN- authorized boundaries, would the United States and like-minded nations cease to press Tel Aviv on boundaries, though not on Jerusalem and the return of the Arab refugees.

Thus, the conclusions reached in Washington in the midst of this still very hot 1948 war were certainly not conducive to formulating the kind of policy decisions McDonald was urging. This fact is best, and most brutally, shown by the 1 September presidentially authorized message to Ben-Gurion harshly demanding basic changes in Israeli policy—specifically, approval of swapping the Negev for Western Galilee, the demilitarization of Jerusalem, and the immediate right of return of Arab refugees, who, the message charged, had fled in large part due to Israel's own policies and actions. Were either Israel or the Arab states to "resort to arms," the message threatened, then the responsible party would be subject to Chapter VII sanctions.[13] The message truly shocked McDonald. His consequent despair at the U.S. posture during the General Assembly session that fall in Paris would lead him by November to seek and obtain authorization, with White House help, to go to that city, ostensibly to serve as an expert consultant to the American delegation on the refugee problem, but in reality (and much to the annoyance of the leadership of that delegation) to press rather quixotically and irrelevantly for a more cooperative policy with Israel. Just how irrelevant McDonald's policy proposals were during this fall period is made evident by his telegram of 28 September reporting that Sharett was going to Paris "prepared acknowledge Bernie's report as basis for discussion," although he would demand changes in it, such as that Israel would insist on retaining the Negev, which otherwise would cause it to lose nearly 3/5 of its "net area," its access to the Dead Sea and to the "Orient" via the Gulf of Aqaba, and its "22 Jewish settlements" there. McDonald added his own "personal opinion" that the GOI "argument is patent" and that a resolution of the Negev problem could be an Israel-Transjordan "mutual military alliance," which would constitute the "only effective native military force in entire Middle Eastern area south of Turkey" and therefore, would give Israel the confidence to permit the establishment of a British air base in the Negev (a possibility, however, that had already been considered and rejected by the British Joint Chiefs of Staff as too improbable and too unstable an asset within the framework of Britain's overall relations with the Arab states).

It would be useful here to jump a bit ahead of our story, because the events during McDonald's stay at Paris offer an important insight into the entire relationship between him and the State Department and also between Lovett and the president: As it turned out, McDonald's main successes during his few weeks in Paris, beginning with 18 November, were the personal ones of enjoying Paris with his daughter, Barbara, who had accompanied him from Tel Aviv, and of winning from Washington an extension of his stay into December despite the predictable objections from the delegation itself.[14]

It is this latter development that well illustrates the atmosphere in Paris and the rather bizarre role McDonald played there: John Foster Dulles, as acting head of the delegation, was upset upon learning that McDonald, on his own, had sent a Palestine-related telegram on 26 November to Clifford. Therefore, he and Rusk jointly sent a particularly cutting "eyes only" telegram to Lovett on that same day requesting (a) that he "hasten" McDonald "back to Tel Aviv" and (b) that, once there, he be instructed to give Ben-Gurion a personal presidential message urging that Israel vote yes on the upcoming omnibus Assembly resolution on Palestine as a way to ensure that Israel "has no more military objectives in mind," and to help the United States obtain approval for Israel's upcoming application for UN membership. The two also wrote that McDonald was wrong both to have sent his telegram without having informed the delegation of it and to have charged it with not working in accordance with the government's instructions.

McDonald did indeed so charge: his unduly panicky message, which was perhaps his most fearless act of independence yet as special representative, had asked Clifford to urge Truman personally to call Dulles and have him "[r]esist firmly any further whittling down U.S. program." According to McDonald, the delegation was doing just that by supporting a British draft resolution in the Security Council designed to force Israel to return to the military lines of 14 October and, more basically, to "undo" the November 1947 partition resolution. (McDonald, in closing, asked Clifford to call him at the Crillon Hotel, room #211!)

Lovett, regarding Dulles' telegram, felt constrained to be rather passive on the issue of peremptorily dismissing McDonald, fearing that the State Department would be criticized by Israeli supporters and the president's political opponents on the grounds that it was needlessly squelching a useful pro-Israel voice on the delegation. Lovett did briefly think he had a legitimate reason to send McDonald quickly back to Tel Aviv on the grounds that his presence there was necessary to help Washington keep track of the impending election in Israel for a constituent assembly. But when Clifford informed him that the election had been rescheduled for early 1949 (it was finally held on 25 January), Lovett, as he put it to McClintock on 2 December, feared that if he had ordered McDonald immediately back to Tel Aviv, "that would leave us wide open" to the charge of squelching McDonald. Accordingly, Lovett decided to "wait until Griffis" arrived in Paris from Cairo to assume his new post over the Arab refugee relief program (as stated in Lovett's diary).

McDonald would only leave Paris on 10 December, on the eve of the General Assembly's passage of the omnibus resolution on Palestine. Incidentally, he was rather ignorant as to the true attitude of Dulles toward him during this period, thinking him receptive to both his request to remain in

Paris and his policy of accommodation with Israel. In later years, McDonald would become a strong critic of Secretary of State Dulles' "even-handed" approach to the Arab-Israeli conflict. As for Dulles himself, Truman had been hesitant to approve his November appointment as acting head of the U.S. delegation at Paris: Marshall wrote the president on 18 November "in appreciation" of his having changed his mind by approving Dulles as "acting chairman" upon Marshall's departure from Paris for the United States on 22 November. (Austin and Jessup during this period were battling illness, but, in early December, Jessup was able to take over as head of the delegation.) By the time of the Security Council's post–Christmas consideration and passage of a resolution castigating Israel for its renewed IDF offensive in the Negev beginning on 22 December, the U.S. delegation, along with that of Israel and most others, was reduced to a skeleton staff— in Israel's case, a junior, locally based diplomat who had to do his best with little back-up support or personal background, a reflection of the reduced priority Tel Aviv was temporarily giving to defending Israel's new military offensive at the United Nations.

Perhaps the most vivid illustration of the irrelevance of McDonald's advice at this time relates to the statement of 20 November by Jessup to the General Assembly's First (Political) Committee, which had the responsibility of preparing for the plenary the omnibus resolution on Palestine that would be approved on 11 December. In that statement (which Truman would at times cite, but not spell out as his own *publicly* stated policy), Jessup *inter alia* said that, if Israel wished for "additional territory, it must offer an appropriate exchange through negotiations."[15] Still, over time, McDonald's insights and understanding of the Israeli scene eventually helped the government to adapt to changing circumstances more realistically and with a greater chance of success. Moreover, his advice as to how to organize a more effective international refugee relief program than the one being supervised on an ad hoc basis by Bunche's staff was accepted by the president and State Department at the end of November, including his suggested appointment of Ambassador Griffis to head the new program on leave from his Cairo post. (His appointment would be announced by Lie in Paris on 4 December.)

Turning back now to the situation in mid–1948, the wariness by official Washington, including the White House, regarding all things Tel Aviv went beyond McDonald, extending to the entire mission staff and its status.[16] Personnel assigned to Israel were systematically chosen from those whose background, or planned career path, was outside the Near Eastern region and who were not line officers within the political or even economic "cone," to use a

State Department term for functional types of work; rather, those chosen were typically from the consular, commercial or cultural cones. This practice reflected the general view that a posting to Israel was a dead-end assignment in career terms, as well as a hardship post unsuitable for family life. (However, McDonald had with him until January 1950 his enthusiastic, talented, college-age daughter, Barbara, and, starting on Christmas of 1948, his wife, Ruth.[17]) Even the military attachés would end up complaining that their reports and recommendations were usually ignored or discounted at the Pentagon as biased in favor of the Israelis.

Nevertheless, armed with his presidential letter of July,[18] which he treated as an open one, McDonald expressed confidence to one and all, Americans or not, that he would demonstrate by his work that the unfriendliness of his colleagues was unwarranted, and that he could and would in good conscience conduct mission affairs in full compliance with his official instructions — even as he would not hesitate to offer, and endorse, the Israeli view when he and his staff thought appropriate. He pointed out that his unusual personal access to all the top Israeli leaders would be a great asset, not a burden, to U.S. interests in Israel and to the UN effort to promote Arab-Israeli peace.[19]

An early testing of this position occurred a month after McDonald's arrival at his post, when Bernadotte was assassinated in the Jewish-held part of Jerusalem on 17 September. Even though it was the work of underground Jewish terrorists, members of the so-called Stern Gang, opposed to his territorial recommendations, the world naturally and understandably (despite considerations to the contrary) blamed the Provisional Government of Israel for the deed. Moreover, in the succeeding weeks the British would lead a successful effort at the Security Council to imply official Israeli responsibility for the killing and to keep that government's feet to the fire with insistent demands for a timely, full accounting of the assassination. Ralph Bunche, as "acting mediator" (a temporary title he would retain until the very end of his successful, prize-winning role as manager of armistice negotiations between Israel and the Arab states), explicitly and formally faulted Tel Aviv officials for fostering a public atmosphere at press conferences so personally antagonistic toward Bernadotte in the weeks preceding the tragedy as to have been an incitement to violence against him and his team in Palestine. The American consul in Jerusalem, John J. MacDonald, fully shared this opinion regarding the responsibility of the PGI itself for the killing, as seen in his telegram of 30 September, in which he charged that there was now a "deliberate Jewish campaign to discredit" Bunche and the UNTC — a campaign that was "developing along the lines of the attack launched on Count Bernadotte." However, it should also be noted that, hours before his death, Bernadotte's car was fired upon by Arab fighters as he passed through East Jerusalem from a nearby airport on his way to the Jewish-held part of the city; in addition, days before Bernadotte's visit to Jerusalem from Rhodes, his representative there, as well as McDonald and others, had warned him and his staff that the trip would be too dangerous, given the presence of uncontrolled armed elements on both the Arab and Jewish sides of the politically unsettled borders.

In this international crisis, McDonald would use his ready access to Ben-Gurion and Sharett (formerly Shertok) to press them to take more drastic, nation-wide measures than they initially were contemplating to eliminate all underground organizations once and for all, including those operating in Jerusalem (where the IDF had actually been coordinating with them in military matters).[20] McDonald also wrote directly to Truman and Marshall to remind them of past efforts by the Israeli government to curb Jewish terrorist organizations, such as its bloody attack of 22 June on an Irgun ship, the *Altalena*; his message also urged them not to overreact to the assassination by recalling him or otherwise unduly penalizing the Israelis. His advice by and large was heeded, with Truman, on 4 October, writing McDonald that he agreed with his recommendation not to weaken his Tel Aviv mission over Bernadotte's death.

Still, the incident further blackened and exacerbated the diplomatic setting in which McDonald's mission had to operate. Even prior to it, there was the first of what would prove to be a series of harsh messages between the White House and Ben-Gurion personally. That exchange took place in early September, when, on the basis of his instructions, McDonald confronted Ben-Gurion with a series of by now familiar demands in the name of his government, the principal ones of which were as follows: agree to territorial exchanges for any newly conquered land Israel planned to retain; accept the return of hundreds of thousands of Arab refugees from those lands and from Israel proper; agree to the demilitarization of Jerusalem as a prerequisite to its internationalization; and avoid any military actions that would threaten the prevailing truce and create obstacles to peace negotiations. In reporting back to Washington on the results of his demarche, McDonald made clear his view that U.S. policy was pushing both nations to a stark confrontation, possibly even a military one, were it to allow this line to be enforced by the Security Council under its Chapter VII authority. His emphasis was on the unwillingness of the Israelis to forgo the Negev under any circumstances, regardless of the cost. Other cautionary points included the unacceptability to Israel of receiving back during wartime large numbers of refugees, whatever security guarantees were being offered to Israel in the name of the mediator; the impossibility for Israel, especially given the history of the war thus far, to place the safety of 100,000 Jews in Jerusalem into the hands of a flimsy UN police force that could easily be overwhelmed by surrounding Arab armies; and the unfair burden placed on Israel by the open-ended UN truce, which left the Arab states on territory legally allotted to Israel, whose consequent military, social and economic burden could not be borne for much longer.

McDonald purposefully informed Washington that he had made no effort, in his meetings with the Israeli government, to go beyond the words of his instructions and attempt to convince his interlocutors of the justice of the American position. His personal concerns about it had already been sent in late August to his two principals in Washington, Truman and Marshall. In that earlier message, sent less than two weeks after his 12 August arrival at his post, he focused on the untenability of the truce and the likelihood of Israel's soon resorting to force to get its enemies out of the country. In making his case, McDonald was not necessarily recommending that the United States accept Israel's entire case, but rather that a new course of action was necessary to avoid the foreseeable catastrophe in U.S.-Israeli relations. His rather meek and unrealistic recommendations to replace existing policy focused on putting a time limit on the July truce so as to apply more pressure on the Arab states to agree to direct peace negotiations with Israel; breaking the United States from what he considered its excessive dependence on a Britain not interested in a pacific settlement of the dispute if that were to come at the cost of London's primary goal — obtaining a Mediterranean outlet for Amman; organizing a major resettlement program for the Arab refugees in their places of refuge; and concentrating less on the unlikely demilitarization of Jerusalem and more on seeking to ensure the protection of, and accessibility to, the holy places within the framework of the present *de facto* partition of the city between Israel and Transjordan. Alongside these international issues, McDonald also urged Washington to undertake certain steps designed to help promote the interests of non-communist, pro-Western parties within Israel as they prepared for the upcoming October (later rescheduled to January) elections to a constituent assembly. These steps included immediate authorization of Export-Import Bank assistance to Israel and accelerated *de jure* recognition of the state.

It was this initial August telegram from McDonald that prompted the State Department to prepare a lengthy paper for Truman's consideration regarding policy toward Palestine. That paper was duly submitted to the White House and discussed between Marshall and the president, who approved the document on 1 September. This fateful step not only set in motion the blunt exchange between Washington and Ben-Gurion previously described but also emboldened the department to embark on a bizarre secret effort,

Six. The Bernadotte Plan of June 1948

together with the United Kingdom, to directly help Bernadotte and staff prepare a revised peace plan.[21] This was to be accomplished by the dispatch of Rusk's assistant, McClintock, to the island of Rhodes, where the UN team had retired in order to write the new plan. McClintock's mission was coordinated with the simultaneous arrival on 13 September at Rhodes of a senior British diplomat, John M. Troutbeck, who was based at Cairo in charge of Palestine and related policy. There was a cover story prepared, were the two-man mission (which lasted nearly three full days) to attract public attention: that they were only there specifically to discuss the humanitarian issue of the Arab refugee problem and the assistance their two countries were prepared to provide. Of course, the mission was predictably soon uncovered and the widely disbelieved cover story had to be used.[22]

It must also be sadly reported that Lovett himself resorted to double-talk amounting to prevarication when, on 24 September, he wrote to Truman (who had inquired from his campaign train as to whether press reports were true that the State Department and the British had helped Bernadotte and Bunche on Rhodes to prepare the revised peace plan for Palestine) that "there is no truth to this story"; that it was being peddled by "Dr. Silver's organization" (the American Zionist Emergency Committee—AZEC); and that "a State Department official" had been sent, along with a British official, "to Bernadotte," carrying State Department and Foreign Office views, which "Bernadotte used with a few minor changes"—but "we had no part in the preparation of Bernadotte's Report."[23] Compare this statement with an example from McClintock's report of "midnight," 15 September, sent from Cairo following his departure from Rhodes: upon arrival, we were shown Bernadotte's revised "first draft" and then helped his team to "perfect" his "conclusions" concerning Part One, which deals with such "principal matters of substance" as allowing Israel "a token salient into Negev," even though, "in strict justice," Israel, by getting "all of rich Galilee," should, despite the desire of even its "more moderate leaders" to hold on to both the Negev and Galilee, accept that the entire Negev go to the Arabs, "to whom it would ever remain a worthless desert."[24]

For his part, Bunche, while acknowledging the presence on Rhodes of the American and British diplomats, denied at the United Nations and to the press that they were there for anything more than a consultation as to how their two governments were prepared to help in easing the problem of the Arab refugees—the very cover story Marshall's memorandum to McClintock of 10 September, and the State Department's simultaneous telegram to Cairo, instructed was to be used in the event of public inquiries about the secret mission. Bunche, at one point, tragically felt so stung by the charges that arose against him for his alleged role in the affair that, in October, he publicly threatened to resign. (The reader may share the present writer's dismay at what this would have meant for the fate of the successful armistice negotiations of 1949 had Bunche not been available, with his wealth of knowledge and negotiating skills, to manage them.) Finally, it would not be irrelevant to note that Bunche, a former member of the OSS during World War II, had been in New York and Washington during most of August, leading to a surmise that he was a participant in, if not the instigator of, this entire awkward episode. Forever after, Bunche, presumably to his personal discomfort, would stick to the cover story, including in 1950 at Harvard, where, as previously discussed, he participated as a member of a scholarly panel reviewing the Palestine experience.

Just how deeply wedded the State Department and the president were to the policy of obtaining UN endorsement of the revised Bernadotte Plan at the Paris session of the fall of 1948 is made crystal clear in a closely held message of 13 October from Lovett to an openly recalcitrant McDonald.[25] The telegram was labeled "for your information only," and it said that, during Marshall's just-completed consultation in Washington, he discussed and agreed with the president on the following relevant points: (a) the Arabs are a majority in the Middle East, a threat to the peace exists, and, therefore, Israel should have "more homogeneous and well-integrated frontiers"; (b) Israel consequently should have the "rich" Galilee while most of the Negev should go to Transjordan; (c) the Arabs already have "deep resentment ... against U.S. because of our support of Israel"; (d) British have "no projects for air bases in Negev"; (e) we see no "convincing evidence" that Transjordan is ready for "direct negotiations" in the face of "Abdullah's relations with Arab League and other Arab States"; and (f) as stated by Marshall to the General Assembly on 21 September, the Bernadotte Plan's "conclusions" represent a "fair basis" for a settlement and should be accepted "in their entirety." McDonald was then (gratuitously) assured that those "conclusions" "*were reached independently by Mediator*" (emphasis added). The lack of candor demonstrated in this message by the State Department, even in its relations with its own field representative in Tel Aviv, is, it must be said, breathtaking!

We will at a later point pick up the story of how the revised Bernadotte Plan fared as the member states of the United Nations gathered in Paris for the 21 September opening of the third regular session of the General Assembly. (Paris would also be the site of Security Council meetings that fall.) In the meantime, a survey will now be offered briefly describing the other, non-boundary issues of the Palestine question as they appeared to the United States and other parties during the summer of 1948.

Non-Boundary Issues During Summer 1948

Jerusalem

While essentially all non–Moslem member states at the United Nations gave lip service to the provision in the November 1947 partition resolution establishing the Jerusalem-Bethlehem area as a separate, UN-controlled part of Palestine, facts on the ground since then had made that plan unworkable. Israel and Transjordan clearly had taken possession of the city and were increasingly cooperating in keeping it that way, at first discreetly, and then publicly, especially after the agreement of 18 July for an open-ended truce period throughout Palestine. For example, by 27 July, Israel announced that its laws would be made applicable to West Jerusalem. However, the United Nations itself was still not prepared to fully acknowledge that a new formula for Jerusalem and the holy places was needed. The reasons for this clearly unrealistic posture were to be found in the politics of the situation: (a) the Vatican and its member state supporters in the General Assembly continued to insist on implementation of the original plan; (b) the UN Secretariat, for reasons of the organization's own prestige and credibility, was still loathe to see the terms of the November resolution altered in any basic way without the agreement of the parties concerned; (c) each member of the Security Council's "P-5," for its own purposes, wished to keep the Jerusalem question open, either as an element in pressuring the Israelis and the Arab states to reach an agreed solution to the overall problem of Palestine or, in the Soviet case, as an element in its consistent policy of demanding complete and full implementation of the partition resolution as passed — thereby, of course, creating significant difficulties for the Western nations in their relations with the Arabs; and (d) there was no consensus on the part of the Arab states themselves regarding Jerusalem's fate — specifically, not only were they far from reconciled to any non–Arab control of the Old City and its environs, whether by the United Nations or the Jews, but they also strongly opposed King Abdullah's intention to keep unilateral possession of that entire region in the name of the Arab League.

The price to the international community for retaining a fictional Jerusalem policy was that its role become ever more irrelevant insofar as it sought directly to influence events in the field. For example, the three-member enforcement team based in Jerusalem, the so-called Truce Commission (UNTC), representing, since its creation in April, the three Western consulates there (the United States, Belgium and France), hardly had the stature or the implementational tools, such as an international military force, to fulfill its role.[26] Accordingly, it has been well labeled by historians as a nonexistent, or mythical, body — especially after it was pushed aside by the Bernadotte-Bunche team in any mediation effort, and after a more substantial UN team of military observers arrived throughout the summer period to take charge of the truce agreement's implementation. Still another busybody feature of the international effort, demonstrating its utter inability to implement the partition resolution, was the General Assembly's insistence that the UN Trusteeship Council continue to develop the statute for a Jerusalem region under international rule; this elaborate legal effort (under American chairmanship) was finally given up by the Council only in June 1950, when it returned the entire matter to the General Assembly with a request that, given the impracticality of planning for full internationalization of the Jerusalem area, it review its entire approach to Jerusalem.

Events in August and September 1948 further demonstrated the growing gap between official U.S. and UN policy toward Jerusalem and realities on the ground. Israel had made clear by late August that it was not prepared to see the Truce Commission (which it long saw as biased in favor of the Arabs) exercise "supreme authority" in Jerusalem; that it was unwilling to give up control of the "corridor" to West Jerusalem from the coastal plain that it had conquered in the earlier rounds of fighting; and that, in view of the abortive Bernadotte proposal of June to turn over the entire city to Amman, coupled with the failure of the UNTC to raise objections to that proposal, it no longer felt morally bound to continue to adhere to its original acceptance *en toto* of the November partition resolution's Jerusalem provision. Israel was in full control of West Jerusalem, which included Arab neighborhoods, now largely vacated by their occupants, and it made known to Amman that it would relinquish some of those neighborhoods to its jurisdiction in any peace agreement. However, it would do so only in return for Israeli control of a supply route to Mount Scopus, which, with its Hadassah Hospital and Hebrew University, was still in Jewish hands though surrounded by Arab forces. Israeli attitudes would further harden after the 12 August destruction by Arab forces of the theoretically UN-guarded Latrun water-pumping station at the far western end of the Israeli corridor to West Jerusalem; that facility and its potable water had been seen as vital for the very survival of the Jewish residents of Jerusalem (now dependent on makeshift sources of water supply). The Arabs, moreover, despite fierce fighting, had been able to retain the strategically located town of Latrun itself, looking over, as it did, the "Burma Road" Israel had managed to construct for its corridor. The meaning of this situation for Jewish security in Jerusalem was highlighted by Israeli diplomats at the United

Nations as still another argument against relinquishing its military hold over parts of the Holy City. (By November 30, 1948, Israel and Transjordan would succeed in reaching a cease-fire arrangement for Jerusalem, including truce demarcation lines, that would hold until the Six-Day War of 1967.)

The practical implications of this Jerusalem situation from the viewpoint of McDonald's Tel Aviv–based mission as the war drew to its close toward the end of 1948 are vividly demonstrated in the following harrowing account of a group Christmas trip to Bethlehem taken by members of the mission staff—but, for obvious diplomatic reasons, not including either McDonald or Knox, although they helped negotiate and organize it — plus several American journalists. The account is based on excerpts taken from an informal letter home by Curtis Barnes, the administrative officer at the mission, under the heading "Christmas Greetings from the Church of the Nativity in Bethlehem, Palestine on Christmas Eve 1948"[27]:

> Of all the Christmas services observed the world over, the most beautiful and reverent is held in Bethlehem. This year the Church authorities persuaded the Jews and the Arabs to postpone their war long enough to permit the Christians to make this pilgrimage. Although the war was resumed with renewed vigor on December 22, the agreement held and those of us who had a deeper sense of reverence than instinct of self-preservation were permitted to attend. [The letter then lists the 13 members of the American Tel Aviv mission who were in the group along with "the Governor of the Stuttgart section of American occupied Germany," plus reporters from the Associated Press, the United Press, and the *New York Times*.]
>
> We left on a clear, bright morning and proceeded over a newly finished, winding rough road still under construction that passed through wrecked Arab villages being rebuilt by immigrants just arrived from European concentration camps.... After interminable windings and climbings we circled back on to the main road to Jerusalem which has been closed because so many people are killed in transit. It runs too close to Arab lines.... All the way into the city we passed carcasses of trucks and automobiles that had been wrecked and burned during the fighting.
>
> Jerusalem itself we saw little of because we had a specified hour when we could cross no-man's land into Arab territory. Since most of the Old City is in the hands of the Arabs we didn't get to see much of it. The new part is quite beautiful.... We had a hurried lunch at the YMCA building....
>
> We assembled in caravan line up at the American Consulate General, placed American flags on our cars and set out. We received passes from the Jewish military authorities ... [who allowed] the newsreel cameramen and press to get some good pictures. Then the barriers were raised and we drove about a half block down the street to the Arab lines for clearance ... several of us got out of the cars to have a look. Mr. Burdett, the American Consul at Jerusalem, asked us not to step on the half-buried hand grenade which was right between the two car tracks....

The Arab soldiers appeared to be friendly which was indeed fortunate.... I am ashamed that I don't know where we went for we weren't wasting any time and we had a long rough road to cover before arriving at Bethlehem ... we were required to go circuitously. Some of the Pilgrims (not of our party) went the direct road ... and were killed for their lack of judgment ... about dusk ... we proceeded direct to the Normandy Hotel which was the headquarters for the Christians....

Since a fair amount of singing occurred during dinner, a good many of the party skipped the gathering for Christmas carols and strolled down the cobble-stoned crooked streets, unlighted for centuries except for the few shops that were open....

So then ... we entered the Church of the Nativity.... But we hurried into the Church of St. Catherine in order to get seats for the Mass at midnight ... the place was jammed with the greatest variety of people I have ever seen under one roof ... [including] the Crown Prince of Transjordan....

Squeezing our way out ... we then began the irritating task of gathering together the groups who were to go back immediately ... members of our party were very nearly shot because they didn't see a sentry. It was one of the closest calls I ever hope to have....

Eventually, we got started and drove as fast as we dared, for we were scheduled to cross the lines back into Jewish territory at 4 A.M. We were driving without escort, unarmed, through wild territory where our progress could be observed for miles around by our light.... As soon as we got back into Jerusalem the tenseness left and everyone became very sleepy ... the sentries on both sides cleared us quickly.... We left about noon and returned uneventfully to our very expensive and inadequate quarters which we reluctantly regard as home for the moment. Everyone wouldn't have missed the trip for the whole world, and at that particular moment wouldn't have repeated the performance for the same price.

There is a further, discrete issue regarding the Jerusalem question that needs be discussed — that relating to the size and nature of the population in the area designated by the United Nations in its partition resolution for separate treatment as an internationally controlled sector, one that was to be ruled by one or more of its member states under trusteeship agreement with the United Nations. That sector was defined as including not only Jerusalem itself but also its environs, notably Bethlehem. The implications for population measurements of this expansion of the concept of "Jerusalem" were as follows: Prior to 1948, the breakdown between Jews and Arabs in Jerusalem, according to UNSCOP figures, was, respectively, 142,000 and 68,000. As Eban would later tell the Security Council, this meant that Jerusalem was the only city in the world in which Jews were in the majority. By expanding the definition to include the city's environs, the United Nations in its partition resolution had created an enlarged Arab population and a comparatively smaller percentage of Jews. Thus, given that there was now a more equal distribution of Jews and Arabs in this planned international sector, the Trusteeship Council's recently completed draft statute for it included a municipal council comprised of 18 Jews and 18 Arabs, plus 4 others to represent non–Arab Christian institutions based in the sector. This seemed to Israel an unfair guarantee that local governmental policy would be controlled by a permanent majority of non–Jews, because the 4 non–Moslem representatives would almost certainly always support the Arab view. Consequently, the issue provided still one more reason in Tel Aviv for opposing the evolving UN manner of implementing the Jerusalem provision of its partition resolution.

The "Old City"

This aspect of the Jerusalem problem requires special focus. Even prior to the summer events just discussed, the fate of Jerusalem's Old (or Walled) City, the core religious center of the entire area, had already negatively conditioned the Israeli attitude toward allowing the 100,000 Jews of Jerusalem to be exposed to surrounding Arab armies, even if under UN guarantee of protection pursuant to the 29 November partition resolution. In the days following its proclamation as a Jewish state, Israel had found itself at a great military and diplomatic disadvantage in trying to prevent a full Arab occupation of the Old City, which included a Jewish Quarter containing a few hundred Jewish inhabitants and in need of military strengthening. The British-led Arab Legion of Transjordan had quickly moved into the region surrounding Jerusalem from all directions, except the west, and was in a position to enter the Old City even as Jewish troops stationed in West Jerusalem were hesitating to do so, in part for fear of causing damage to religious institutions of special concern to the Western powers. While there would be criticism within Israel itself for this hesitation to take advantage of the vacuum created by Britain's rather early departure from Jerusalem on 14 May (one day earlier than generally expected), there was a similar criticism within Arab League circles of the Arab Legion's own risky three-day delay, motivated in part by the British policy of respecting the international character of the Jerusalem region, before making its move on 18 May to enter the Old City and ensure that it would not fall into Israeli hands. There followed substantial fighting within the Old City and, on 28 May, the Jews were forced to capitulate under terms that guaranteed peaceful evacuation of the Jewish Quarter. While those terms were, under UN supervision, by and large faithfully implemented, and the Jewish inhabitants safely returned to Israeli-held territory, their personal and religious property was subsequently heavily ransacked by the local Arab population. The Western Wall, of course, now became inaccessible to Jews. (That the Arab Legion had acted with London's full approval is clear, given Bevin's later statement to U.S. Ambassador Douglas that he thought it entirely proper for Abdullah to have taken the Old City for the Arabs, to whom it belonged.)

Despite the heightened prestige Abdullah gained in the Arab states for having presumably saved the Old City from the Jews, he was unable to secure Arab League endorsement of his plan, noted above, to keep permanently under sole Transjordanian sovereignty, in the name of the League as a whole, the parts of Jerusalem and its environs that his troops controlled. The difficulty rested in part upon an underlying political confrontation between Transjordan and Egypt, whose troops remained until the end of 1948 just south and west of Arab Legion lines in the Hebron area. That this intra–Arab strategic stalemate would continue throughout the entire two-year period of the UN effort to internationalize Jerusalem (1948–1950) is well illustrated by a remarkable Arab League resolve, in summer 1950, passed over Transjordanian objections, "to continue to work for a *genuine* [emphasis added] internationalization ... and the putting into force of the constitution which the Trusteeship Council drew up on April 4, 1950." Thus, Egypt and like-minded opponents of the Hashemites would, at least theoretically, have preferred a UN control over Abdullah's in the Holy City.

In summary, as the General Assembly prepared to open its Paris session on 21 September, the Israeli posture regarding Jerusalem was more flexible than that of the Arab states, and this fit in well with one of its priority objectives that fall: election to the United Nations as a member state. In contrast to the Arabs, who were maintaining their opposition to any partition of Palestine, including Jerusalem, Israel put forward publicly and privately (particularly to Transjordan and the United States) a possible solution regarding the Holy City and its environs in the hope of being perceived as acting more reasonably than their adversaries — not that they realistically expected a positive response from the General Assembly that fall. This solution, which Israel would in fact have felt able to live with, centered on the internationalization, under UN control, only of the Old City, buttressed by the issuance of security guarantees by Israel and Transjordan for the protection of, and access to, the holy places and related religious institutions wherever they existed in territory those two would continue to administer. That the United States, under certain conditions, would have likely supported such a solution in a General Assembly vote that fall is suggested by Secretary Marshall's opening remarks, on 21 September, describing the American goal as obtaining the agreement of all faiths for a "*practical* [emphasis added] plan for a permanent international regime in the Jerusalem area and for the protection of, and free access to, the Holy Places." A further indication of the compatibility of U.S. and Israeli policies may be seen in McDonald's authorized statement to Ben-Gurion a few days earlier, on 6 September, to the effect that his government would agree to the existing division of Jerusalem so long as the holy places were assured of international protection.

While the handling of the issue at that fall's General Assembly will be discussed further at its proper place in this study, we might here jump forward to confirm that not only did the kind of solution just outlined not fly but the Assembly also adopted a resolution that December that hardened UN insistence on the total internationalization and demilitarization of the entire Jerusalem area in accordance with its partition resolution of 1947. (This resolution received full backing by the Soviet Union, in keeping with its basically passive policy, as previously described, of insisting in both the Assembly and the Security Council—but without resorting, in the latter body, to the use of the veto—on full implementation of the 1947 partition resolution. The Soviet practice was, in those instances when it ostensibly disliked a draft Council resolution, simply to abstain, rather than cast a veto, but also to show its apparent displeasure by having the Ukrainian representative cast a harmless negative vote in its stead.) This setback for Tel Aviv, coupled with Foreign Minister Sharett's ill-advised earlier assurance at Paris to the American delegation that Israel planned no major military initiatives against the Arab armies that year, produced a crisis of confidence between Ben-Gurion and Sharett, who promptly resigned from government, adding still one more personal drama to the diplomatic events of 1948. Sharett had acted in the belief that the UN vote on Israeli membership would take place prior to, and be facilitated by, such an assurance of Israel's military planning. Ben-Gurion had not authorized Sharett's move, and, as general policy, he strongly opposed any effort to pay a price, at the expense of Israel's sovereign rights or security requirements, merely to become a UN member. Nevertheless, the prime minister refused to accept Sharett's resignation, and he remained in his post amid deep emotional exchanges between the two long-time colleagues. Israel would gain membership only in spring 1949 after its successful armistice negotiations with the Arab states following the two successful IDF initiatives begun on 14 October and then 22 December (and a further, nearly unopposed IDF drive to the port of Elath in March 1949, thereby giving Israel full control over all the Negev in accordance with the November 1947 partition resolution). All these developments left the *de facto* partition of Jerusalem between Israel and Transjordan intact.

Arab Refugees

Of all the key issues facing the United States during the Arab-Israeli War of 1948, and during the remainder of the Truman administration, this one, regarding the fate of the Arab refugees, represented the president's clearest set of directives in his relations with the State Department. Unlike questions such as the Negev, the status of West Jerusalem, the timing for *de jure* recognition, and the arms embargo, Truman allowed no wavering based on his own doubts, or on back-door channels with the Israelis and their supporters, to confuse his subordinates' understanding of his policy toward the refugees. Therefore, there were no important inconsistencies in the State Department's implementation of that policy. Essentially, he saw it as a humanitarian issue that had to be resolved as soon as practicable through the return of hundreds of thousands of Palestinian Arabs to their homes in Israel and to territories controlled by it.

The contrast was stark between this position and that of the government in Tel Aviv, fully backed by Special Representative McDonald, to the effect that Israel could not afford to face a military threat of having an "enemy at its back as well as in front" while the war was still going on. Also rejected by the White House was Israel's view (a) that it was totally innocent of any responsibility for the Arab exodus, which was the result, in the first instance, of the aggression by the Arab states; (b) that the exodus, although obviously having certain clear and openly recognized long-term advantages domestically for the Jewish state, was almost entirely a spontaneous act by the Arabs, who were understandably frightened by the excesses at the battle front, excesses committed by both sides, and who were also convinced by the Grand Mufti, based in Egypt and, after August, in Gaza, that they would soon be able to return with the assumed early Arab victory; (c) that there was no Israeli general policy for the forceful eviction of the Arab residents in its state or elsewhere — to the contrary, the policy was a more honorable and internationally self-enlightened one of actively encouraging them to stay, even as the British, during the months prior to their departure from Palestine, were acting in the opposite direction by facilitating that exodus, including providing escorts and vehicles for it; and (d) that the economic and social burden of having to accept the immediate return of large numbers of refugees would be an impossible one for Israel to bear given the wartime circumstances and the inalterable policy of accepting Jewish immigrants.

Washington had answers and rebuttals to all these Israeli assertions, and the State Department was alert enough to utilize them to the maximum in view of Truman's wholehearted backing on this issue. This was especially

Six. The Bernadotte Plan of June 1948

important to the department given the issue's extraordinary political and moral appeal internationally in the context of the overall departmental approach to the Palestine problem. That approach, of course, was to continue the by now well-established tactic of pressuring Israel to make the concessions the State Department believed necessary — and sufficient — for the Arab states to come around and acquiesce in the existence of the Jewish state.

A succinct statement of the premises upon which the State Department based its actions regarding the Near East was contained in a telegram to London of 24 August. The purpose of that message was to ensure that both the United States and the United Kingdom, in keeping with their renewed *entente cordiale*, would be following compatible and mutually supportive policies in their respective relations with the Arab states:

> In the space of a few short years, the United States has fallen from a position of unequalled esteem, respect and honor in the attitudes of the peoples of the Arab world to one of embittered distrust and animosity.
>
> The outstanding achievements of American philanthropy over a period of nearly a century, plus a somewhat long-range admiration of America's accomplishments in peace and war, were responsible for the former, and the U.S. foreign policy vis-à-vis the Palestine problem is entirely chargeable for the latter.
>
> As of the moment, we must recognize that the Arab countries of the Near East are convinced that America alone is primarily responsible for the success which has attended the establishment of the *de facto* State of Israel in what is regarded as Arab territory. The part which other great powers have had in the past or present in bringing about that which is inimical to their interests has largely been forgotten in the wave of anger directed at the United States for her part in bringing about the present situation. Despite the role which the United Nations has played in the matter, even this international body has not taken very much of the curse off of the United States leadership and backing.
>
> The problem, therefore, which is posed is: In view of this extremely unfavorable position of U.S. prestige, what ... general principles may be established at this juncture as general guidelines to our information activities and programs as a whole in the Arab States? ...
>
> There is a widespread tendency in the Arab world to divorce American foreign policy and its baneful aspects from individual Americans and American institutions within the Arab countries.... We should refrain from comment or reporting, except with special guidance, on the activities of private American institutions and enterprises in the Arab States in order to preserve the concept that Americans and their private activities are not agents of their government, but do represent America as distinct from official American policy. The purpose of this caution is to retain existing good-will toward American institutions and enterprises in the face of general antagonism toward American policy.

As tracked so far in the present study, the State Department designed a course of action with the goal at least of minimizing this "curse" upon the United States. The aim was (a) to reduce its official visibility in Israel and play for time, partly in the expectation, widely shared in the capitals of the world, that that new nation would not long be able to withstand the military opposition of the Arab states; (b) to be seen as championing the Arab cause to the extent compatible with its inalterable burden of having voted for the partition resolution of November 1947 and then having been the first to recognize the Jewish state in May 1948; and (c) particularly after the series of Israel's military victories in the first two rounds of fighting, to pressure it to limit its territorial goals and to make diplomatic concessions. The general attitude by departmental personnel around the time of the July truce was well put by Ambassador Jessup in New York, when he expressed exasperation that, after all the support given to Israel by the American government, it should be grateful enough to be more cooperative and flexible than it had been in meeting international demands looking toward a final settlement with its Arab neighbors.

One of the more prominent demands on Israel, as noted earlier, was that it accept the return of hundreds of thousands of Arab refugees even prior to a peace settlement and, in fact, as a necessary precondition to such a settlement. This demand can best be understood in the context of the overall posture of Washington as it related to policy toward the Jewish state. The pattern becomes clear when the various points of pressure applied in 1948 on the Jewish state are shown in a bald, non-priority listing: arms embargo starting prior to the November 1947 partition resolution; freeze on the release of Jewish displaced persons of military age in American camps in Europe who were not authorized by Bernadotte to go to Palestine; cooperative efforts with the United Kingdom to interdict the arrival in Palestine of organized Jewish groups fleeing from Communist Bloc countries; *de facto* versus *de jure* recognition coupled with a low-level diplomatic title for its representative in Tel Aviv[28]; blocking the release of Export-Import Bank funds; sponsoring the open-ended feature of the Security Council's truce resolution of 15 July; increasingly strong cooperation with the United Kingdom, considered by Israel as a military enemy; and using various devices at the United Nations to cushion what would otherwise be strictly bilateral pressure on Israel (such as the UN Truce Commission in Jerusalem, Bernadotte's peace proposals, Security Council arms embargo of 29 May, General Assembly endorsement of the demilitarization of the Jerusalem area including IDF evacuation of its corridor to West Jerusalem, conditioning U.S. active endorsement of Israel's application for UN membership with demands for concessions to the Arabs, and placing the

Six. The Bernadotte Plan of June 1948

Arab refugee question on the agenda of the General Assembly's Political Committee rather than treating it as a separate humanitarian issue in the Assembly's Social Committee).

Despite appearances, the State Department's overall policy toward Palestine was not nearly as lopsidedly at Israel's expense as one might suppose from the above outline. An examination of four important issues for the Arab states yields solid reasons to understand the Arab view that, in fact, the scales were tilted against them, as follows:

a. The explicit thrust of American policy, joined after May by the British, was to create conditions on the ground designed to lead the Arabs to acquiesce to the existence of a Jewish state. The unacceptability to the Arabs of this basic fact was not at all diluted by Western and UN pressure on Israel to limit the territorial fruits of its military victory and to agree to other concessions, with a view to sweetening the bitter pill for its enemies.

b. Once the Jews escaped total military defeat in the first half of 1948 and began to receive surreptitiously major arms shipments from Czechoslovakia and other sources, the American arms embargo — and, after the passage of the Security Council resolution of 29 May, the UN one — worked, not against Israel, but, as suggested earlier in this study, against the Arab States. In large part, that was because the Arabs were tied to British-produced armaments and ammunition and therefore were limited to that source of supply even as the United Kingdom cut them off in faithful implementation of the Security Council resolution. The Israelis, for their part, were not at all limited in that way — they were able to utilize a variety of arms manufacturers as they built up their defense forces from scratch, as it were. Moreover, the small UN truce observer team was inadequate to its task, and Israel was increasingly uncontrollable as it received ever-larger shipments of armaments, including fighters and heavy artillery, from Europe. Despite strenuous State Department efforts to prevent the United States from serving as a source of arms supply, and especially of funding for Jewish purchases in Europe, it was unable to make much of a dent. For domestic political and legal purposes, the department was inhibited from pushing for a ban on the barely disguised practice of diverting alleged charity funds collected in the United States for use in the purchase of arms elsewhere.

c. The Jerusalem area was of special concern to the Arabs, who were profoundly opposed to its internationalization in the face of the firm policy of the West and the United Nations to achieve just that. The Arabs argued that the motivation for this Western policy was to ensure Christian control over the Holy City, thereby introducing an unwelcome and unhelpful religious element into the controversy over Palestine.

d. The Arab exodus from Israel, and the steadily increasing influx of Jews into it, became for the Arab states a major grievance against the West and the United Nations. They saw this process as a direct and predictable consequence of the international endorsement of the establishment of the Jewish state. Moreover, it had soon become clear that the nearly half-million Arab refugees camped on their territory, a figure that was rapidly increasing with each new round of fighting, required the kind of financial and managerial support from the international community that was not forthcoming. While the American government from the start took the lead at the United Nations in organizing and financing a relief program, the process was slow-moving and limited in scale compared to the desperate needs, which the Arab states themselves were unable (and, in some cases, openly unwilling) to meet. Only in 1950 would the more substantial UNRWA operation be put into place, assuming until today the main burden for relief and work projects. This arrangement, in the eyes of some present-day observers, was unfortunate, because, in their opinion, it guaranteed that the Arab refugees, not being an unmanageable financial or social burden on their countries of residence, would never truly be resettled and integrated into them; instead, they would remain a potent political weapon in seeking diplomatic support for their cause in the international arena. This opinion has much to recommend it and would not necessarily be rejected by the American policymakers who had originated the UNRWA system — after all, as George McGhee himself wrote in his memoirs, "We assumed that the UN relief program would not last long."[29]

A country-by-country breakdown of the numbers of Arab refugees in camps by the end of 1948 would indicate which Arab states were most directly involved in the problem: Gaza Strip (under Egyptian rule but historically not an integral part of that state), 200,000–245,000; West Bank, 160,000–220,000; Transjordan, 75,000–80,000; Syria, 100,000–110,000; Lebanon, 90,000; Egypt, 8,000; territory occupied by Israel since the war's start, 7,000; Iraq, 5,000. Total: about 750,000 — out of a total population of all the Arab states amounting to 30 million. (The U.S. Marine Corps general in charge of the UN military team in Palestine, William Riley, believed that the officially accepted number of refugees was inflated by duplicate registrations and by Arabs falsely claiming to be refugees from Palestine.)

The fate of the Gaza Strip provides insight into the politics of the refugee problem in 1948–1949. Toward the year's end, Israel was offering various proposals designed to deflect pressures on it, mainly from the American president, to allow what amounted to about half of the above total number to return. Perhaps its potentially most important proposal, one that would have impacted as much as a third of the refugees, was to itself take on responsibility for the

Gaza Strip and all its refugees (assuming international help as well). This proposal was not acceptable to Egypt, which, as the figures suggest, had a policy of keeping to a bare minimum the number of refugees on its own sovereign soil. Cairo, among other considerations, did not wish to risk the distinct possibility, were they to hand Gaza over to the Israelis, that, in the end, they not only would have to receive the bulk of the Arabs fleeing from Israeli control of the Strip but also would have lost that militarily useful buffer territory itself.

Still another Israeli proposal was its stated willingness to take in up to 25,000 refugees of non-military age, on a case-by-case basis, for family reunion purposes. Tel Aviv's motivation in making these informal proposals went beyond the refugee issue *per se*: its approach was also due to a paramount concern not to alienate Truman. The president at times lent his name to hard-line written messages to Ben-Gurion in which the refugee issue was prominently featured, coupled with a demand, as Israel's "best friend," for a more forthcoming Israeli policy. More than once, Truman bolstered his appeal with a threat to "reevaluate" the American policy of support for the Jewish state. This threat was taken with the utmost seriousness by Ben-Gurion, whose primary foreign policy goal was to ensure that the United States never resort to arms in forcing Israel to take steps against its will; he felt that, without U.S. participation, the international community could never pose a military threat to his country.

An important tangential issue related to the Arab refugee problem concerned the fate of the remnant Jewish population in Europe. It began to come up in earnest when Bevin in late July instructed his delegation at the United Nations to recommend to the Security Council that the Jewish displaced persons in Europe be offered the opportunity to go to countries outside Palestine as a counterpart to Israel's allowing the Arab "displaced persons" to return to their homes in Israel and Israel-controlled territory. The American delegation managed to squash this British initiative by arguing that the matter of Arab refugees should only be treated in the General Assembly and not in the Security Council, whose sole responsibility is maintenance of peace. Still, especially in the face of persistent Arab demands that the Jews seeking to leave Europe should find refuge outside the Arab world, Marshall and his colleagues had to continue defending the closed-door policy the United States and most of the Western countries were following. For example, in early August, he told the visiting Iraqi foreign minister that the president expected Congress in the near future to liberalize immigration legislation, opening the United States up to a larger influx of Jews in European refugee camps and thereby relieving pressure for them to go to the new Jewish state.

This assurance by Marshall was a highly optimistic forecast of a more liberal American immigration policy. That past June, the president very reluctantly had signed into law the "Displaced Persons Act of 1948," which explicitly distinguished between the "Jewish" occupants of DP camps and the non–Jews. The law set the total number of DPs to be allowed into the United States at 200,000 — of whom only those "Jews" who were already in the DP camps before December 31, 1945 would be eligible. This limitation meant that the bulk of the Jewish DPs would be disqualified, because, by 1948, most of the 1945 residents, the subject of Truman's Harrison Mission, had already managed to leave Europe — including 28,000 to the United States by authority of the so-called "Truman Directive" of December 22, 1945, allowing them to enter on the basis of unused, existing quota limitations assigned to East European countries. Therefore, the subsequent large Jewish influx into the American-run displaced persons camps in Europe had arrived largely from the Soviet Bloc area. As Truman stated in his signing statement of June 1948, this new law contained a discrimination to which he objected and would work to correct as soon as possible; however, only in 1950 would a new law be passed that did not include any discriminatory provisions against Jews. (The 1948 law also had authorized the entrance into the United States of 2,000 Czech citizens whose country, it will be recalled, had recently suffered a Communist coup d'état.)

The State Department, along with the White House, had lobbied Congress, as it was deliberating on the 1948 bill, to drop the discriminatory feature against the Jews. This was in keeping with the department's policy of diverting Jews from immigrating to Palestine, a policy that had its most explicit articulation in the draft UN trusteeship agreement its delegation had unsuccessfully floated in April–May 1948 at the special session on Palestine held by the General Assembly in New York. Under the article dealing with immigration, that agreement would have allowed "Jewish displaced persons" to enter Palestine for the first two years, but only under the supervision of a UN-appointed "Governor-General," who would establish "regulations" for the "selection" of such immigrants. After that two-year period, the Governor-General would annually determine, "in accordance with the absorptive capacity of Palestine" and "without distinction between individuals as to religion or blood," the level of any "further immigration.... Provided that not more than [here a number was to be inserted by the Assembly in its final text] persons shall be permitted to enter Palestine to establish permanent residence in any one year." This draft agreement would also have defined "citizens" of Palestine as follows: "(1) Persons resident in Palestine on July 1, 1947, who were not on that date nationals of any state outside of Palestine; (2) Persons resident in Palestine on July 1, 1947, who were nationals on that date of a state outside of Palestine, if they have filed with the Government of Palestine at any time before November 1, 1948, a declaration in such form as may be provided by the Government of Palestine, that they renounce their former nationality in favor of Palestinian citizenship; (3) Persons who have resided in Palestine for three months and who, while continuing to be residents of Palestine, file with the Government of Palestine a declaration that they renounce the nationality of any state outside of Palestine of which they may be nationals, *and take an oath of allegiance to the Government of Palestine* [emphasis added]; and (4) Children of Palestinian citizens, wherever born, provided such children have not at birth or subsequently acquired the nationality of a state outside of Palestine."

It must be said that no State Department document of this period is so revealing of a lack of reality as this one. Among its absurdities is its unstated premise that the United Kingdom would agree to continue under the United Nations its previous role under the League of Nations as the "Government of Palestine"; that the General Assembly would, so soon after its November 1947 partition resolution, approve such an about-face in policy; and that either the Jews or the Arabs would agree to the proposed arrangement.

Staffing and Policy Issues Within the U.S. Government

It would be a classic "pathetic fallacy" to assume that the relevant agencies within the government that were involved in the split on Palestine policy were themselves endowed with human emotions or characteristics as distinct from those of the incumbents who determined policy in accordance with their own judgment and values. Therefore, especially given the extraordinary role individual personalities played regarding this particular issue, an account must be taken of the views and biases of the principal actors. One way to broach this aspect would be to examine the strange episode of General William Hilldring's abortive appointment as special assistant to the secretary of state, 28 April–26 May, 1948, when he abruptly resigned. Far from being a mere personnel matter, this experience is relevant to all the internal policy clashes touched upon thus far in our study.

Hilldring was a favorite of those relatively few in government who shared Eleanor Roosevelt's strong support for a Jewish state. He initially earned his reputation as an officer sympathetic to the plight of the Jews in Europe when, as assistant secretary of state in the immediate months after the Second World War, he was responsible for policy in the American-occupied zones on that continent. His next assignment, as noted earlier, was as a member of the U.S.

delegation to the United Nations for the fateful fall 1947 session of the General Assembly, where he worked most closely with the delegation's then deputy chief, Ambassador Herschel Johnson (who himself had an earlier professional exposure to the issue of displaced Jews when, in 1934, he served as a member of the U.S. delegation to the governing board of James G. McDonald's High Commission for Refugees from Germany). In the delegation, the two men were perceived as more supportive of White House policies toward the Palestine question than the State Department would have wished. After that fall session, both men left the delegation, with Ambassador Jessup eventually replacing Johnson as second in command of the American mission. (Johnson went on in April 1948 to be ambassador to Brazil, while Hilldring retired from government service.)

By the time of McDonald's 22 June appointment, Hilldring had passed from the scene, having been told in no uncertain terms personally by Marshall in late May that his April appointment as special assistant had been imposed on the State Department by the White House and it would be best that he decline to serve in it. Hilldring's subsequent public resignation letter upset Marshall because it alluded to this frosty reception by the secretary as a factor in his decision, in addition to his health problems. Lovett, of course, was of the same view as Marshall. This was made crystal clear in a phone conversation he had in April with Forrestal, who had called to express concern at the meaning of Hilldring's appointment. Lovett, according to his diary, reassured Forrestal, who was also his close personal friend, that it was all merely political "window-dressing" and would have no bearing on the ability of both their departments to continue, within the parameters set down by the president, to determine Palestine policy without undue interference from White House staff.

As we have seen, one of McDonald's first recommendations to Truman before leaving for Tel Aviv was that he appoint a successor to Hilldring. In this, he was as one with Eleanor Roosevelt, whose public writings and columns contained her view that the president needed his own man at the State Department to ensure a balanced set of reporting and recommendations to him on Palestine. While both she and McDonald tended, perhaps purposefully, to overemphasize the extent to which Truman personally shared their policy preferences, they were surely correct to believe that the existing personnel lineup at the State Department was incapable of faithfully implementing White House directives. At the head of their list of *bêtes noires*, of course, was Loy Henderson, the head of the Near East bureau, a man, it will be recalled, with a history of pushing his dissenting personal views beyond the point of acceptability to his superiors — for example, he was peremptorily transferred out of Moscow in 1943 for having too vehemently opposed what he saw as undue American friendship toward the Soviet Union. As ambassador to Iraq until 1945, he developed a strong sense of the importance to Western defenses of having a close relationship with the Arab world. Although not an "Arabist" (not knowing Arabic and not having extensive experience in the Arab world), he nevertheless, back in Washington at the war's end, became known — in the private and approving words of Lovett on July 7, 1948 — as the Arabs' "best friend in Washington." Lovett was so impressed by the importance, in the Arab states' own eyes, of keeping Henderson in his Near East position at that particular moment as to delay announcement of his departure for an overseas, non–Arab post lest that announcement weaken Arab willingness to agree to an extension of the truce beyond 9 July. It was only after that truce expired without extension, as discussed above, that Henderson's transfer overseas — as ambassador to India — was made known publicly. (The State Department had initially tried but failed to get White House approval for Henderson to go to Turkey and thereby keep him involved in Near East affairs.) A few days after these events, McDonald told the president that replacing Henderson with his deputy, Joseph Satterthwaite, would not solve the problem that he and others were emphasizing to the White House (i.e., the need to have someone in the State Department to give Truman an informed, independent view of Palestine matters). Satterthwaite would remain as Near East chief into 1949, and no successor to Hilldring was ever appointed.

The personnel in charge of the military within the American government fully shared the judgment and policy preferences of the State Department. Admiral Leahy would not leave the White House until January, continuing to make his long-standing, sharply antagonistic views of the Jews known privately to Truman and others.[30] This was as a supplement to his official acts endorsing the consistent recommendations of the Joint Chiefs and Forrestal to avoid assigning uniformed personnel for anything more than observer duties in the Palestine region — the size of the military in active service having been reduced from thirteen million members to one and a half million by early 1948. Leahy fully shared Forrestal's conviction that Palestine policy was wrongly being made on the basis of irrelevant and sordid domestic political considerations rather than on considerations of national security. Leahy's personal attitude toward the Jews was so well known that, at the peak of the presidential campaign in September, he offered his resignation to Truman in light of newspaper criticism that he was anti–Semitic; a reading of his private diary would give many examples of the truth of that charge, including an entry from spring 1948 in which he told the president that one of the opponents to his call for a military draft, Albert Einstein, was not really a U.S.

"citizen," having been made so only in 1940. Truman wrote Leahy from his campaign train rejecting his letter of resignation, saying, "While you and I don't see eye to eye on some things, we are always frank with each other.... [We are] friends come hell or high water." Similarly, Clifford, who was a presumed source of the leaks on Leahy to the newspapers out of concern that he had become a political liability to the president, wrote him to deny any role in the stories and to reaffirm his friendship and support.

It should not, therefore, be surprising that the only pocket of officials, outside the White House itself, acting in sympathy with the Zionist cause, and in opposition to the consensus against that cause within the closely knit U.S. diplomatic and security establishment based in Washington, was a small, rotating group of delegates to the United Nations in New York. The one constant presence within this group beginning in 1947 and throughout 1948 was Eleanor Roosevelt, who, as discussed earlier, could only act as a gadfly, not having any formal responsibility whatsoever regarding the Palestine question. Two others who shared her view did, in 1947, have such a responsibility, and they were supportive of efforts leading up to the U.S. vote in favor of the partition resolution. These two, of course, were General Hilldring and his senior on the delegation, the one career diplomat in this dissident group — Ambassador Johnson. When both left the delegation after the end of the General Assembly session in December, Mrs. Roosevelt remained as the lone opposition voice at the time that the previously described "anonymous" note of May–June was written, summarizing the main points at issue between the dissenters and the State Department.

The policy conflicts that surfaced periodically in 1947–1948 between the U.S. delegation to the United Nations and its superiors in Washington regarding the Palestine question closely paralleled those fought out within the government as a whole and are therefore worth briefly characterizing here, starting with a retrospective view of the momentous events that occurred during the second session of the General Assembly in the fall of 1947. The policy debates during this period frame the issues that would have to be addressed by the government as it pragmatically worked out its policy in the face of the ever-changing circumstances of the Israeli war of independence during 1948.

Helping us to distinguish the differing points of view is the fact that each responsible State Department unit had its representative within the American delegation in New York. Thus, if Under-Secretary Lovett looked to his bureau chief for UN affairs, Rusk, to keep an eye on overall policy matters in New York, Rusk, in turn, would make use of one of his former direct subordinates, John Ross, to monitor implementation of that policy at the United Nations. Similarly, the Near East bureau would temporarily post to the delegation one of its own field ambassadors — for this second Assembly session, Ambassador Wadsworth from Baghdad — to serve as a liaison with the Arab delegations and to lobby within his own delegation for the recommendations of Henderson and company. At times, the principals themselves, Rusk and Henderson, would personally participate as advisors to, or members of, the delegation at UN meetings. There was in 1947–1948 an obvious absence of such a link between White House staff and anyone on the U.S. delegation fully devoted to serving as the president's eyes and ears in New York. Notwithstanding Truman's confidence in the head of the delegation, Ambassador Austin, the latter was not willing, as we have seen from his actions in March 1948, to buck the wishes of the State Department regarding Palestine policy. As regards Eleanor Roosevelt, who was not a confidant or even a political booster of the president, she, in that spring of 1948, had been reduced to consulting a junior member of the delegation to get a sense of the general direction of policy as the Palestine issue reached a crisis stage in late May. And, looking ahead to the fall of 1948, at the third session of the General Assembly held in Paris, the White House had to make a special request to Marshall to allow its short-term political appointee, Benjamin Cohen, to participate in delegation discussions regarding Palestine at a time when there were fresh rounds of fighting in October and December — and when Marshall was trying to conduct a policy of close association with the United Kingdom's outspoken endorsement of the Bernadotte-Bunche plan. That plan became a political football, because it flew in the face of the pro–Israel planks of both parties, and it would be only immediately after Truman won the election on 2 November that he would give Marshall the green light, just as he had before the presidential campaign heated up in October, to return to that alliance with the British at the United Nations.

But, for the moment, we will here focus on events of the fall of 1947, when the United Nations made the momentous decisions regarding Palestine, first in organizing the UNSCOP investigation of the problem, and then in its two-thirds decision of 29 November to accept the committee's majority recommendation in favor of partition. The U.S. government was a major proponent of the UNSCOP initiative in May, and — despite the qualms of the State Department's Near East bureau, clearly shared by essentially all career Foreign Service officers in the field — it felt bound for that reason, as well as for reasons of standing policy of the Truman administration, to accept in September the majority recommendation so welcomed by the Zionists. However, in doing so, the American policy at the United Nations, by the firm instructions of the president and enthusiastically endorsed by all elements in the State Department, was to avoid "carrying the banner" in the General Assembly as it wrestled with the UNSCOP report that fall; rather, the policy was to refrain from lobbying for the majority recommendation with the goal of avoiding having it appear as "the American plan" and not "the UN plan."

As is typically the case in such matters, despite having established an agreed policy within the government, this did not in itself ensure a unified effort as that policy was carried out in practice. Illustrating the old adage that where you stand depends on where you sit, the American delegation at the United Nations, initially under the close supervision in New York of Secretary Marshall until he left for other duties in October, adopted an increasingly forceful presentation of its endorsement of the majority recommendation for partition. This was an inevitable consequence of Marshall's own opening statement on 17 September to the Assembly session in which he urged favorable consideration of those recommendations. The delegation, under the pressure of ongoing events, including charges in the American press that the U.S. endorsement was merely lip service and not sincere, began in October to spell out in detail, during formal deliberations of the ad hoc committee that the General Assembly established to consider the UNSCOP report, its view of how to implement the majority recommendation for partition. The more the delegation did so, the more elements within the State Department in Washington, led by the Near East Bureau's Loy Henderson, were becoming exasperated with the departure from what they considered established policy regarding the Near East and relations with the United Kingdom.

The delegation's point men in the ad hoc committee were Ambassador Johnson and General Hilldring. They particularly earned Henderson's wrath by having touched the third rail of State Department policy in the Near East: close coordination with the British. Johnson, at a 22 November meeting of the committee, spoke out against the stand-off UK policy of non-participation in any UN effort to promote a solution to the Palestine problem. He criticized the British for being unhelpful and for having rendered the committee's task more difficult by not having "closed any of the gaps" in the planning for partition's implementation. Johnson went on to describe the British policy as disloyal to General Assembly decisions and wondered how a delegation, by abstaining, could promote cooperation between the peoples of Palestine and the member states of the United Nations. In particular, he wondered "what would happen if the United Kingdom withdrew its troops without any decision having been reached."

In a biting memorandum of 24 November to Lovett, Henderson wrote that

> the policy we are following in New York at the present time is contrary to the interests of the United States and will eventually involve us in international

difficulties of so grave a character that the reaction throughout the world, as well as in this country, will be very strong ... unless the British continue to remain a force in the Middle East, the security of the Middle East will be gravely endangered. It is impossible for the British to remain a force in the Middle East unless they retain the friendship of the Arab world. By our Palestine policy, we are not only forfeiting the friendship of the Arab world, but we are incurring long-term Arab hostility towards us.... In Mr. Johnson's speech of Saturday, the British were castigated before the whole world for not agreeing to suggestions of the Subcommittee [of the ad hoc committee] which, if followed, would certainly have ruined British relations with the Arab world and would probably have resulted in the British being forced to withdraw from the whole Middle East.... Mr. Johnson, on Saturday, indicated before the Subcommittee that if the situation in Palestine should develop into a menace to peace, the matter would naturally come before the Security Council and that the United States, along with the other four Great Powers, would be prepared to share responsibility for removing this menace ... we ought to think twice before we support any plan which would result in American troops going to Palestine. The fact that Soviet troops under our plan would be introduced into the heart of the Middle East is even more serious.

While the readers of this memorandum, which was widely distributed in Washington and within the delegation in New York, would not have found the line of attack a new one, its personal animus against Ambassador Johnson, a fellow career Foreign Service officer but one without field experience in the Near East, did represent a departure, as did the moral certitude that informed it ("the Arabs are losing confidence in the integrity of the United States and the sincerity of our many pronouncements that our foreign policies are based on the principles of the Charter of the United Nations"). Lovett wrote on his copy of the memorandum that he "read this to the President.... I explained that the Department thought the situation was serious and that he should know of the probable attempts to get us committed militarily. We are continuing to refuse."

An early glimpse of Henderson's analysis was offered when he participated, at Lovett's request, in a delegation-wide meeting in New York on 15 September under the chairmanship of Marshall. Not surprisingly, the most outspoken opponent of his analysis was Eleanor Roosevelt, who argued that the Arabs were more afraid of the Soviets than of the United States, and that, contrary to the expectations of both Marshall and Henderson, the Soviets might very well vote in favor of UNSCOP's majority recommendation. Mrs. Roosevelt went on to urge U.S. support for the majority UNSCOP recommendation for a reason entirely separate from, and "at least, or more important than," Palestine-specific issues: the need to "promote the success of the UN."

This exchange, coupled with Henderson's subsequent interventions from

Washington, defined the policy debate within the government as it continued into 1948 and the period of full-scale international warfare between Israel and the Arab states. But, before leaving our account of developments in 1947, two specific events occurred that warrant our attention, because they had a direct bearing on attitudes at the time and on subsequent perceptions of how the actions of the Truman administration influenced the shaping of American policy toward the Arab-Israeli conflict. The two events were with regard to (a) Truman's telephone call of 19 November to Johnson/Hilldring regarding the State Department's instructions for Johnson to call for a vote, in that day's deliberations of a subcommittee of the Assembly's Palestine ad hoc committee, on the American proposal to amend the UNSCOP recommendation that the Negev go to the Jewish state so that most of that area would be assigned to the Arab state; and (b) Truman's lifting the ban, just a few days before the fateful 29 November vote by the full Assembly on the UNSCOP majority recommendation for partition, against any active lobbying by the U.S. delegation in favor of that recommendation.

As for the Negev issue, although the original State Department instruction was to force a vote on the American proposal even (if necessary) in the main, ad hoc committee on Palestine, Johnson on that morning of 19 November convinced the department to alter its instruction because, were the proposal to fail to win majority support in the ad hoc committee (as was considered likely), that would so shake other delegations who were prepared to support partition as to jeopardize achieving the basic U.S. policy goal of obtaining a favorable vote on the overall UNSCOP majority recommendation itself. The most Johnson would recommend would be to call for a vote on the American proposal only in the ad hoc committee's subcommittee; were that vote to fail, as expected, then he would in the ad hoc committee itself agree to support the subcommittee's decision in favor of retaining the assignment of the Negev to the Jewish state, as UNSCOP recommended. Henderson supported this Johnson-recommended change in the department's instructions, given the reality of the lack of support for the change regarding the Negev.

When Weizmann convinced Truman during his visit of that date that the American delegation was about to push to assign the Negev to the Arabs, the president immediately after the visit made his controversial call to Johnson and Hilldring as they were about to go to the subcommittee meeting that afternoon. Hilldring took the call and confirmed that he was unhappy even with the modified State Department instruction, because it could jeopardize obtaining the necessary two-thirds support in the Assembly for partition. This led Truman to instruct Hilldring and Johnson not to do anything that might "upset the applecart." Given this instruction, Johnson decided to refrain from making any intervention at all in that day's meeting of the subcommittee; only on 22 November did he manage a territorial arrangement acceptable to the Jewish Agency representatives following the work of that body in which a few miles of the southwestern border of the Negev, adjacent to Egypt, was reassigned from the Jewish state to the Arab state. It was this arrangement that prevailed in the committee and in the final Assembly vote of 29 November in favor of partition. The oversimplified historical version of the alleged negative effect of Truman's intervention has it that, had he not made that phone call, the United States would have gone on record in the Assembly debate as being against assigning the Negev to the Jewish state, a change that, in the opinion of some, might well have won support of the Arab states and thereby have allowed for a diplomatic solution to the Palestine question in 1947. The facts of the matter do not support such an opinion, but rather indicate that the United States, even had the president not made his phone call, was not planning to force a vote on the Negev either in the ad hoc committee itself or in the final Assembly vote were it to fail in the subcommittee; moreover, the State Department's push in favor of giving the Negev to the Arabs was clearly more of a ploy to soften its image with them, and also to show solidarity with the perceived need of the British to have a friendly power on the Mediterranean coast north of Suez, than a serious expectation that its move either would win majority support at the United Nations or would alter the firm determination of the Arab states to reject any form of partition, regardless of the boundaries between the Jews and the Arabs in Palestine.

As for the last-minute authorization by Truman to lift the ban on lobbying actively for the partition resolution, once it passed on 25 November in the ad hoc committee, albeit shy of the two-thirds majority it did not require in committee but would be needed in the General Assembly, the controversy surrounding this move has ever since had an even deeper and more long-lasting effect on attitudes toward U.S. Palestine policy than did the controversy just described over the Negev issue. A main reason for this is that there was a convergence of interest, for both supporters and opponents of the Truman administration's policy of endorsing the majority UNSCOP recommendation for partition, to emphasize (whether validly or not) that the government played the key role in obtaining the two-thirds needed for Assembly approval on 29 November. Supporters of Truman's action found it useful to underline that role's alleged importance as a way to ensure continuity in Truman's personal support of the new State of Israel; opponents of the lobbying similarly gave it great importance as a way, especially in the following year, 1948, to undercut that support by spotlighting the responsibility the United States, incurred as a result of its pressure tactics — to now take the lead and rectify the violent consequences in the Near East, which allegedly were a direct consequence of that "U.S.-commandeered" vote.

The problem with this scenario is that an examination of the actual voting process does not support the view that the partition resolution would have failed in the Assembly on 29 November had the Americans not gone all out to lobby in its favor (just as many other interested delegations, on either side of the issue, had been doing for several months). Key to an understanding of why this is so is that the two-thirds requirement was not computed on the basis of the entire UN membership, or even of those members who participated in the voting, but *only of those who voted either yes or no; abstainers were not included* in the computation as to whether the two-thirds requirement was obtained or not. Thus, in the ad hoc committee's 25 November vote, which sounded the alarm bells for supporters of partition, there were 25 yes votes, 13 no, 17 abstentions, and 2 "absent." That meant, of the 38 votes that counted (25 vs. 13), 26 yes votes would have been needed for a two-thirds approval of partition (⅔ of 38, rounded to 39, eligible votes), whereas only 25 were obtained. This led to even more intensive lobbying and horse-trading efforts by all sides to either, from the pro–Arab point of view, keep support for partition shy of the two-thirds that would only now be needed in the impending Assembly vote or, from the pro–Zionist point of view, find the additional vote or two to ensure that pro-partition result.

Of the 17 abstainers and two absentees in the 25 November vote, the American focus was on Liberia and Haiti (abstainers) and the Philippines (an absentee along with Paraguay). Charges would be leveled that unethical pressure was applied by pro–Zionists in Congress and the private sector to get those three countries to vote yes in the Assembly. The State Department, with the president's backing, expressed outrage at these tactics, which it saw as outside the bounds of normal diplomatic practice and certainly as unauthorized by the executive branch of the government itself. The actions of private American citizens particularly upset the department, partly because its top two men, Marshall and Lovett, as shown by a record of their comments, had an imperfect understanding even at this late stage of the diplomatic status and internal composition of the Jewish Agency — for example, that it carried over to the United Nations from its official status in the League of Nations as an internationally recognized body whose membership at the executive level required the inclusion of private citizens outside of Palestine itself. In any event, the three "target" countries did change their votes to yes in the Assembly's historic action of 29 November.

But the question remains: Were those three yes votes really essential to

Six. The Bernadotte Plan of June 1948

the success of the partition resolution? The answer is no, for the following reason: Of the 17 abstainers of 25 November, 5 were Western nations (France, the Benelux group, and New Zealand) whose eventual yes votes in the Assembly itself was forecast by all informed observers. There was no perceived need to apply pressure on them, even if one dubiously were to grant that they would have been as susceptible to such pressure by the United States as were the aforementioned countries of Liberia, Haiti and the Philippines. Therefore, were one to assume that these three had not been pressured and had not changed their stance, the 29 November vote would have shown the following results: yes, 30; no, 13 (Greece, *despite* American pressure, changed from abstention to a *no* vote, while Paraguay moved to a yes vote). Rounding to 45 the 43 yes and no votes of 29 November (30 vs. 13), the result would have been favorable to partition, given that the 30 yes votes would have exactly met that requirement (⅔ of 45) even without the yes votes of Haiti, Liberia, and the Philippines. Moreover, even had Paraguay also remained outside the yes or no columns, that still would have left 29 yes votes as against the 13 no ones — meaning that a ⅔ vote for partition would only have required 28 votes out of the total of 42 relevant votes cast (29 vs. 13) — and partition would still, therefore, had been approved.

In summary, the second session of the General Assembly left an indelible stamp on the shape of the Palestine question as it entered a more militaristic phase in December 1947. Between then and May 15, 1948, the fighting remained within the confines of Palestine itself and thus has been usually labeled as the civil war phase. But this could be misleading because, even then, thousands of Arab "volunteers" had entered the country and formed an army led by Iraqi and Syrian officers to assist the Palestinian fighters in their struggle against Jewish forces, who themselves were being replenished with arms and men from abroad. In this chaotic situation, the State Department and the White House sought to curb the violence and to limit the diplomatic implications for the budding Cold War of the advent of a sovereign Jewish state bracing for a contest of survival in opposition to the surrounding Arab states. It is at this point that we now resume our story.

Seven

U.S. Policy During the Final Rounds of Fighting, Fall and Winter 1948

As the diplomats gathered in Paris for the third session of the General Assembly starting in September, war clouds were gathering once again in Palestine to darken the skies over both sites. The tenuous, open-ended truce established by the United Nations on 18 July was fraying at the seams as the hard-pressed, short-staffed UN Truce Supervisory Organization, under the command of General Riley, sought to keep the extensive lines of confrontation between Jewish and Arab forces — stretching over 300 miles — from reigniting into full-scale warfare. In this setting, Secretary Marshall, as head of the U.S. delegation, made his opening remarks to the Assembly on 21 September, thereby establishing the tone for what was to come during the next few months both in the Assembly and in the Security Council. Just as in his opening statement the previous year, Marshall's comments on Palestine created a bombshell: if, in 1947, it was that the United States would endorse UNSCOP's majority plan for the partition of Palestine, this year it was his endorsement "in their entirety" of the conclusions of the just-issued Bernadotte Plan. While that endorsement fully satisfied the requirements of America's partner in Near East policy, the British, it was anathema for both the Israelis and the Arabs (except for Transjordan). And it left the bulk of the UN membership in disarray, with the Soviet Bloc adhering to its policy of support (short, it will be recalled, of using the veto in the Security Council) for faithful implementation of the entire 1947 partition resolution, and with the Western and Latin American members seeking to find a middle ground that would neither undercut the Americans nor encourage further violent confrontations between Jews and Arabs.

As described earlier, the surreptitious intimacy with which the State Department had bound itself to the revised Bernadotte Plan of September guaranteed that the U.S. delegation would fight hard at the General Assembly in Paris for the endorsement by the United Nations of the plan's conclusions "in their entirety." And this, in fact, was the way things proceeded for the first few weeks. However, almost predictably, the strains of the presidential campaign in the United States began to affect the delegation's efforts, especially in October, when Dewey was deemed by the White House to have broken a tacit understanding not to make Palestine policy a political issue[1] — the Republican candidate had issued a charge that the Truman administration was failing fully and sincerely to live up to the Democratic Party plank in support of the Jewish state.[2] Truman's political strategist, Clifford, on 23 October, as noted above, told the president that this was a "serious error" by Dewey and "the best thing that happened to us to date." That was because, until then, the Democrats had felt compelled to keep the Palestine question apolitical and to allow the United Nations to work out a diplomatic solution without interference by the United States on the basis of domestic political considerations. Now, as Clifford next told Lovett, Truman believed he had no choice but to respond to Dewey's charge. Therefore, Lovett was to instruct the American delegation to take no action that might be construed as contrary to the terms of the Democratic Party plank on Palestine, one prime feature of which was to protect Israel's right to keep the Negev. Thus, there was an overnight change in the way the delegation had to behave regarding the Palestine crisis, which coincidentally was heating up at that very moment as a result of the IDF offensive of 14 October against the Egyptian forces in the Negev.

Until that military turn in the Palestine situation, the United Nations had been treating the subject as a strictly diplomatic and humanitarian matter for debate in the General Assembly's Political Committee. With the renewal of open, full-scale warfare, that debate brought in the Security Council, whose task was seen not only as stopping the fighting and getting both sides to negotiate a settlement but also as forcing the armies back to the lines held before the 14 October offensive. Of course, this meant a withdrawal primarily of Israeli forces, whose advances had gone well beyond those lines. The Security Council resolution demanding withdrawal was passed (with U.S. concurrence) on 19 October — that is, just prior to the change in the political treatment of Palestine by both U.S. presidential candidates, as outlined above. With that change, the Marshall-led delegation would no longer be able to conduct its affairs on Palestine without micro-management by the White House and the president, personally.

The sequence of events regarding the Palestine crisis between August and October is so revelatory of U.S. foreign policy toward the Near East, and so illustrative of the unusually important degree to which domestic political considerations affected the handling of a national security matter, that it warrants a brief recapitulation.

As early as 8 August, Bevin had begun to press the State Department to work with his foreign office in preventing a repeat of the fiasco resulting from Bernadotte's issuance of his June peace plan. The idea now was for the two powers to help the mediator prepare his "final proposals" before they were published. The State Department was receptive to this idea, especially given its unhappiness with aspects of the heavy-handed, British-influenced June plan that were contrary to American views, such as the assignment of Jerusalem to Transjordan and of the port city of Haifa to the United Nations. Moreover, as that month progressed without showing movement toward the opening of the serious peace talks envisaged by the Security Council resolution of 15 July, and as the fresh arrival in Tel Aviv of Special Representative McDonald had brought in its wake a series of strident personal messages to Truman and Marshall warning of an upcoming crisis not only between Israel and the United Nations but also between Israel and the United States, the urgent need for a new diplomatic initiative was becoming obvious, especially in light of the looming third session of the UN General Assembly in September.

Even as it was coordinating its next steps with Bevin, the State Department made certain that it would have its own domestic ducks in order. It did so by seeking and obtaining from the president his approval of what it was proposing to press on the Israelis in the upcoming push for a final settlement of the Palestine conflict. This was achieved in late August on the basis of a lengthy memorandum, followed up by a personal meeting on the subject between the president and Marshall, outlining the details of its policy toward Israel and the Arab states. The key result of this consultation was a joint message from the president and Secretary Marshall to McDonald on 1 September instructing him to meet with Ben-Gurion and set forth American expectations as to how Israel should help the United Nations break the present dangerous stalemate. Entirely separate from this demarche, and in an action unreported to the president, the State Department proceeded to move ahead both in its undisclosed, joint approach with the British to the mediator at Rhodes, as described earlier, and in its preparations for the course of action to be followed by the U.S. delegation at Paris.

With every subsequent query by the White House staff regarding American diplomatic activity on the Palestine question — notably, the demand that Israel give up the Negev if it wished to retain its military conquests elsewhere, such as Western Galilee, or that it accept, even prior to a peace settlement, the return of hundreds of thousands of Arab refugees, or that it support the demilitarization of Jerusalem — Marshall and Lovett would refer them back to that presidentially endorsed instruction of 1 September containing the specific policies that the State Department was now seeking to carry out. Most notably, it was Clifford — showing how haphazard was his participation in the making of foreign policy, and how distracted from international affairs in general he necessarily was by his duties on the presidential campaign — who was frequently taken aback in September and October by the stance of the delegation at Paris. He had to confess to Lovett in late September that he had been unaware that the president had approved on 1 September the course of action the department was following at the United Nations and in its relations with Israel. It would only be when the president himself intervened in late October, after Dewey's sharp introduction of the Palestine issue into the political campaign, that the White House managed to rein in the aggressive, unqualified delegation support of the Bernadotte Plan of September. But, even prior to that late October definitive shutdown by the president of any delegation action or statement whatsoever regarding the Palestine question, he began progressively to whittle down its freedom of action in the face of increasing doubt that the State Department was being totally honest with him regarding its role in the preparation of the Bernadotte Plan. Thus, on 13 October, the delegation was instructed through the Clifford-Lovett channel that "we should not carry the ball anymore" on getting approval of the Bernadotte Plan, and, on 18 October, a first-person telegram from Truman to Marshall stated: "I request that no statement be made or no action taken without obtaining specific authority from me and clearing the text of any statement." That this presidential instruction left the State Department in a state of confusion is evident in Lovett's remark on that day to an inquiring staff member (McClintock) that he didn't know if it applied only to activities in the General Assembly or also to those at the Security Council.

A further step in this progressive limitation on the Paris delegation's Palestine-related activities occurred on 21 October, when, in a most unusual action, Marshall joined with Eleanor Roosevelt to send an urgent message to the president recommending that, given the awkward situation for the delegation in view of the unspoken but universally understood role domestic politics was playing in the deliberations on Palestine, it be authorized to make a frank statement to the General Assembly urging it (and, logically, the Security Council as well) to delay its consideration of this question due to the need (a) to see how effective the Security Council's 19 October resolution demanding an end to the fighting in the Negev would be[3]; and (b) to avoid "exposing" Palestine to "partisan political pressure." This message was the product of an effort by Marshall to keep the peace within the delegation, which, as was the case in the previous General Assembly sessions, was embroiled by dissension over Palestine policy. The dissenting group's composition had only one constant member, Eleanor Roosevelt, and now, in the Paris session, she was joined by the White House–sponsored, former State Department counselor, Benjamin V. Cohen.[4] Marshall and his staff, from the start of the session, had constantly to keep a wary eye as to how far they might go without arousing public dissension within the delegation and without creating controversy between it and the overheated domestic political scene, either of which would complicate their chances for achieving their diplomatic goals in Palestine and retaining the full confidence of the president.[5] The 21 October message was the result of a last-ditch consultation, a virtual formal "negotiation," between the two American camps in the face of the crisis caused by the renewal of full-scale fighting between Israel and Egypt. However, the White House rejected this appeal as impolitic, and Marshall's revealing response was to throw up his hands and say that was fine, but now the delegation would just have to "grin and bear it" as others would continue to criticize the American stance — and as the supporters of the Arab view would continue to claim, without rebuttal, that the true motivation of the American appeal for delay was to allow the IDF to complete its conquest of the Negev. (The supporters of the Israeli side naturally took the position that it was bizarre for Tel Aviv to be accused of aggression in a territory that the United Nations itself had assigned to the Jewish state.)

Not surprisingly, then, both Marshall and Lovett were mortified by this progressive presidential clamp-down, which had a very personal, negative consequence for Lovett in his relations with the White House. Even prior to the events of October, Lovett had earned the suspicion on the part of the presidential staff that he was not being honest with them regarding departmental actions on Palestine. His above-noted outright denial to the president on 24 September that the State Department played a role in the preparation of Bernadotte's revised peace plan was rapidly losing credibility with every newspaper report confirming the presence of McClintock and Sir Troutbeck at Rhodes; moreover, Congressman Emmanuel Celler, a New York Democrat, returned from a trip to Israel and publicly charged on 22 October not only that the United States and Britain indeed had helped Bernadotte prepare his revised peace plan at Rhodes[6] but also that the U.S. consul general at Jerusalem, John MacDonald, was sharing with the Arab side secret military information he was obtaining as a member of the UN Truce Commission based in that beleaguered city. (MacDonald was quickly transferred out of Jerusalem by the State Department, leaving the consulate, and its role on the UN Truce Commission, in the hands of a quite junior Foreign Service officer for the next year.)

Earlier, in connection with Marshall's opening statement of 21 September to the General Assembly, White House staff had expressed consternation that the text of that statement had not been sent to the presidential campaign train for advance approval, a charge that Lovett denied, claiming that it was the fault of the awkward means of communication between the State Department and the campaign train. (However, Lovett had made certain that Republican Senator Vandenberg, the chairman of the Foreign Affairs Committee, would receive an advance copy of Marshall's statement by having Mrs. Vandenberg hand-carry that "top secret"–labeled document from Washington to the senator, who was back in Michigan. This was in line with Lovett's standard deferential policy, throughout his tenure, of keeping that senator closely informed of planned State Department activities.[7]) Finally, and most damaging to Lovett personally, was his "no comment" answer, at his weekly Wednesday press conference of 27 October, to a question as to whether he or Marshall had been consulted in advance regarding the president's explosive public statement of that previous Sunday, 24 October, that he did not support the conclusions of the Bernadotte Plan except as "a basis of negotiation," in contrast to the previous policy stated by Marshall of pushing for their approval "in their entirety." That answer was taken as a negative by the press, much to the discomfort of the White House. This episode particularly upset Clifford, and with good reason: Lovett's diary clearly shows that the two men had consulted on that previous Saturday regarding the president's planned statement of the next day in rebuttal to Dewey's charge of lack of support of Israel. In that consultation, Clifford accepted Lovett's advice on some of the wording for the statement (such as that, unlike candidate Dewey, Truman, as president, had to act with more responsibility in formulating foreign policy). Moreover, Lovett the next morning, Sunday, had, in fact, sent a telegram to Marshall in Paris alerting him to the presidential public statement to be issued that evening reaffirming the Democratic Party plank. Furthermore, that telegram had included the comment that Truman's statement "represents the most we could get in reference to the UN"— including that the Bernadotte Plan provided "a basis of negotiation." (For the present writer, one plausible explanation for Lovett's unwillingness at the press conference to speak more fully about his role in the preparations for Truman's 24 October public statement was that he was obeying an earlier order from the White House, on 13 October, not to talk about Palestine at his press conferences, and that, in fact, he was quite happy on 27 October to honor that order, because it put a distance between the State Department and the White House regarding the change in policy regarding that hot subject.)

Following a private meeting with Lovett soon after that Wednesday press conference, Arthur Krock, reflecting the point of view of the top echelons at the State and Defense Departments, wrote in the *New York Times* on the next day, 28 October, that "[l]ast Sunday, Lovett was shown the President's statement on Palestine, which was at variance with the position taken by Secretary of State Marshall," and was informed that "it must be issued because of what Governor Dewey had said on the subject a couple of days before." It is important to note the discrepancy between Krock/Lovett's "Sunday" dating of when he was "shown" Truman's statement and the actual date, Saturday, that (per Lovett's diary) was when that event actually occurred. Lovett was hiding from the press the fact that he had time to alert Marshall of Truman's public statement of that Sunday evening and that Lovett actually had had a hand in shaping that statement.

Krock's column also touched upon a separate issue between Lovett and the White House that further undermined relations between the State Department and the president, and that tended to weaken Truman politically as election day approached: Lovett, Krock dutifully wrote, only "recently" received a "summons to the White House where he was to hear for the first time Mr. Truman's proposal that Chief Justice Vinson be dispatched as an intermediary to Stalin." At that meeting, which was held before the press and cameras in anticipation, according to Krock and Lovett, of a public announcement of the project, Truman was questioned as to whether he intended to ascertain the views of Marshall in Paris. Thereby embarrassed into promptly doing so, he learned from the secretary that he had "fundamental and unsurmountable objections" to the project, which was immediately cancelled. (Present-day readers of Krock's columns should probably not take at face value this version of the event, if only because Lovett's diary shows that he and Clifford were in frequent contact throughout October regarding the Berlin crisis, making it hard for at least this writer to believe that, in all this time, Lovett was left unaware of the president's plan to send Vinson to Moscow.)

A third aspect of Krock's piece is also worth citing here, because it reflected the temper of the times: Lovett and Forrestal, he wrote, were "both from 'Wall Street,'" which Truman "has denounced" as "harboring 'gluttons of privilege.'" (Lovett later thanked Krock for this column.)

There were several remarkable developments in the evolution of American policy toward Palestine during this September–October period of progressively encroaching White House management over Marshall's delegation in Paris. The most public centered on the passage by the Security Council of two resolutions on 19 October, even as the president was doing his best to block any actions there that might give Dewey further ammunition for his charges of non-support by the administration of the Jewish state. One of those resolutions demanded, in effect, that the IDF give up its gains and return to its pre-offensive lines of 14 October; the other described the Israeli government as responsible for the assassination of Bernadotte and criticized it for not having done enough to investigate the crime and report back to the Council. That the U.S. delegation voted in favor of these resolutions is striking evidence of how negatively Washington viewed the role of Israel in the reopening of the war in Palestine.[8] Similarly, the State Department, in its official *Bulletin*, quoted with implicit endorsement a message from Bunche to Shertok of 17 September that described the assassination act as a "breach of the truce of utmost gravity for which the PGI must assume full responsibility ... [due in part to] prejudicial and unfounded statements concerning truce supervision attributed to you and Colonel Yadin [IDF chief of staff] ... at your press conference in Tel Aviv Thursday 16 September ... [statements that] are not the kind of statements which would be calculated to discourage reprehensible acts of this kind." (As late as July 20, 1949, Bunche, in his final report to the Security Council as acting mediator charged that the Government of Israel [GOI] had failed to give "adequate protection" to Bernadotte, and he, therefore, without "any protective force," had to leave it up to the discretion of the "local authorities to determine how much or how little protection is needed by the UN personnel.")

The GOI countered from the start of this affair that Bernadotte had turned down an IDF offer to escort him as he entered Western Jerusalem, and that Bernadotte's planned visit to Jerusalem had been publicized in that city well in advance of 17 September, allowing the Stern Gang to prepare for the assassination days before the 16 September Sharett press conference. However, Eban for a period was cold-shouldered by UN colleagues, although not by Lie, who, Eban wrote Weizmann on 24 September, was "a tower of strength to us ... even in the immediate aftermath of the Bernadotte assassination." This social isolation against Eban was most visible when he attended the funeral ceremonies for Bernadotte in Stockholm, even though the latter's widow, Estelle, a Manville heiress from New York who had accompanied her husband on his trips to the area, was making her view publicly clear that neither Eban nor the Government of Israel should be seen as responsible for the assassination.

Thus, Truman and Clifford were clearly still determined, in this period prior to the challenge from Dewey, to give the State Department a wide berth in its response to the Near East crisis, especially in the context of the explosive broader events threatening to lead to military confrontation with the Soviet Union. And, in fact, there was much to commend the terms of at least the first of the two 19 October resolutions: while demanding withdrawal back to 14 October lines, that document also, in a separate paragraph, called for the immediate start of Israeli-Egyptian negotiations looking toward a settlement beyond a mere truce. This provision was open to interpretation, and Eban privately worked out a procedure with a most cooperative Ambassador Austin, the Council's rotating president for October, in which the latter was to confirm to the Council the accuracy of an Eban statement to it that troop withdrawal was dependent upon the *simultaneous* opening of negotiations between the two sides. When Austin made this confirmation, there were no objections from the rest of the Council, who were perhaps oblivious to its implications. Eban would in the succeeding weeks make good use of this Council action in defending Israel's rejection of Bunche's demand for immediate withdrawal, pointing out that Egypt had not complied with the related Council demand that it open negotiations with Israel. Thus, while Bunche did succeed in getting the two sides to agree on 22 October to a truce, he was unable otherwise to change the situation on the ground.

After Truman's 24 October public statement reaffirming his full backing of the Democratic Party plank on Israel, there was no longer any question of the U.S. delegation actively participating, pending the results of the 2 November election, in further UN deliberations over Palestine at Paris, whether in the General Assembly's Political Committee or in the Security Council. The delegation was now told to keep totally mum, not even responding to challenges to its position up to that date — in effect, as Marshall himself put it, the Americans had to "grin and bear it" as other delegations debated the next steps to end the threat to the peace officially declared by the Security Council in its recent resolutions. Obviously, it was an open secret throughout the United Nations that the American delegation was acting out of considerations of domestic political politics. This caused such personal embarrassment to the entirety of the delegation membership that Marshall and Eleanor Roosevelt sent the previously cited joint message to Washington urging that the delegation be authorized to state frankly to the Assembly that its holding posture was due to an inability to play its part for the moment on the Palestine question pending clarification of the views of the electorate in the United States once the results of the 2 November election become known. The reaction of the White House to this delegation recommendation, which, if acted upon, could only have further embarrassed the president at home, was, as noted, a firm negative and an even stronger reaffirmation by the president of his wish that the delegation avoid active participation on the question and work to delay any UN resolutions until after the election. The priority presidential concern behind these instructions during this peak period of the election campaign was made crystal clear in an "eyes-only" telegram from Lovett to Marshall at the start of November, as follows: "President feels consequences [of] any major disunity in delegation along party lines" must be avoided.

That element in White House instructions demanding a delay in any new UN resolutions until after the election was easier said than done, especially given the relentless drive by the United Kingdom and its Chinese co-sponsor to follow up their successful push for the 19 October resolutions with a new Security Council resolution that would press Israel even harder to withdraw back to pre–14 October lines. In the face of this prospect, Truman on 30 October instructed the delegation, on a contingency basis, to be quiet and only abstain were it forced to vote before 2 November on such a new resolution.[9]

Just how hectic, tense and personally distasteful for both Marshall and Lovett this situation was can be gleaned from the following "eyes-only" Lovett telegram of 30 October to the secretary: "past experience ... is increasingly dangerous and intolerable. I can imagine what you have been through in Paris. It has been absolute hell here." In reply, Marshall wrote the next day, "Will see Dulles Monday [i.e., 1 November, Dulles having conveniently absented himself from Paris in recent days so as to avoid any possible association of Dewey with a pre-election vote on a Security Council resolution unfavorable to Israel] ... but fear this will not give time for him to consult Dewey and get his instruction before vote on Palestine resolution." As early as 2 October, Rusk reported to the State Department (a) that Dulles, having just returned from a consultation in the United States with Dewey, was absenting himself from delegation meetings on Palestine, because "of lack of bipartisan approach"; (b) that the "Jews have succeeded in playing one party leadership off against the other in contest for votes — votes which obviously cannot be delivered to both parties"; and (c) that according to Dulles, it was the Democrats who were responsible for the failure of Forrestal's effort to get both parties to agree not to compete over Palestine, and that, since the Republicans felt they were going to win, they could therefore "take broader view on this specific issue" than if the election seemed to be a closer race. Crossing with Marshall's above-cited telegram of 31 October, Truman instructed that, while the British draft resolution (i.e., the future one of 4 November) met with his own approval, if Dewey were elected, and if he disagreed with the draft, Marshall should check with him (Truman) before the vote for a final decision.

In the terminology used by Truman and Lovett in their telephone exchanges, the plan now was to suspend action under the "original program" and go back to it only if Truman were to win the election. That "original program," of course, consisted of a full backing of the British policy, including support of the conclusions of the Bernadotte Plan. That the president fully, even enthusiastically, backed this policy, were he unhindered by domestic political considerations, would become even more clear in his instructions to Lovett the day following his electoral victory: Marshall was authorized to act on the original "full program" and do "whatever he thinks best" without any need to further consult him — he would have the president's unquestioned support. This last development opened up an entire new phase of American and UN policy toward the Palestine question in the form of the Security Council resolutions of 4 and 16 November and 29 December, and also the General Assembly resolution of 11 December, and it is to this phase that we now turn.

The 4 November Security Council resolution was a landmark event: by emphasizing previous Council resolutions that cited Chapter VII, it threatened the application of the sanctions authorized under that section of the UN Charter against any side resisting implementation of the resolution's terms, as interpreted by Mediator Bunche. Its anti–Israel tone was most in evidence when it went so far as to endorse the "continuing consideration" by the General Assembly of "the future government of Palestine" pursuant to the Council resolution of April 1, 1948 — the U.S.-initiated resolution that had led to the fruitless effort at the Assembly session of April–May to block implementation of partition and establishment of the Jewish state.[10] In accordance with the Council resolutions of 19 October and 4 November, Bunche now was in Palestine demanding the return of forces to their respective lines of 14 October, the establishment of a neutral, UN-administered demilitarized zone (as distinct from the mere truce demarcation lines that Israel was insisting upon) between IDF and Egyptian forces, and the immediate easing of the Israeli siege against Faluja, where one-third of all Egyptian troops in the Negev were surrounded by the IDF. None of these orders was appealing to Israel: in Eban's sarcastic words, Bunche was being thrust into the role of commander-in-chief over all military forces in the Negev. That these various moves by the United Nations were more than mere theatrics is evident in Lovett's stern warning to Israel's special representative, Eliahu Elath (formerly Epstein), that Chapter VII was a real threat to Israel, which, if it wished to keep "Western Galilee or Jaffa," must give up most of the Negev. (It was Ben-Gurion's constant view throughout this war that the only real danger to the military success of the IDF was if the United States actually fielded its own armed forces against it, obviously a most unlikely contingency.)

The position taken by the State Department and U.S. delegation at Paris, as previously outlined, was fully in line with the remarkable presentation given to Ambassador Douglas in London by the British Imperial General Staff on 29 October and sent forward to Washington by that diplomat with his standard enthusiastic endorsement and his claim that much of the world was being kept in the dark by a purposeful "concealment" about the true dangers posed by the progress of the Zionist program.[11] The extravagant views contained therein about the threat to Western interests posed by the Palestine situation went beyond even the Pentagon Talks of the previous year in their apocalyptic and comprehensive analysis of the stakes involved. Clifford's comment of March — that, if the State Department had left anything out in its list of reasons for blocking partition, he didn't know what it might be — would seem applicable to the British assessment of the problem. Here is a brief summary of its key points:

• The "disintegration" of British-Arab relations due to the arms embargo is alarming, especially given the prospect of a "war with the U.S.S.R." in which any Western "offensive" would require a "greater emphasis" on having Middle East partners than ever, because they would provide the necessary "defense zone" from which to launch heavy bombers against the Soviet "Achilles' Heel" (i.e., the Caucasus).

• At present, the West lacks that zone due to "Arab-Jewish hatred and inter–Arab hatred" stimulated by the Russians, who (a) have established a "large Soviet mission in Tel Aviv" and an even larger one in Beirut; (b) since the end of the war, have continued to provide "assistance to thousands of Jews from Soviet satellites" seeking entrance into Palestine, and this, including the resultant terrorism, has "embarrassed" us and "was a factor in British decision to leave Palestine"; and (c) in any new war between the Jews and Egypt, could capitalize on the unique cooperation established between Jews and Arabs in the various Communist Parties by creating a "fifth column" at the expense of the British military presence in Egypt. This last point is a good illustration of the "impact of Israel on Arab political thinking," and only the upcoming election in Israel will serve as a "good index of strength" of the Communist Party and other leftist groups there.

• Soviet "connivance" in the delivery of Czech "arms and airplanes ... poisoned" British-Arab relations and increased Arab hostility toward the United States; also, Soviet approval of the UN partition resolution, with its "hourglass" shape, predictably is leading to endless Jewish-Arab "friction," exacerbated by unproven, but correct, reports of Soviet covert financing of the Mufti's activities.

• American endorsement of that resolution has unfortunately led to friction with us on Palestine strategy; moreover, the United States, having accorded only limited, "provisional recognition" to the Tel Aviv government, has given a political advantage to Moscow, which has granted Israel "full recognition" as a state.

• The Jewish-Arab conflict had led to increased financial pressures in the Arab states, which are exacerbating the problem of settling the Palestinian refugees and, therefore, hampering the economic development necessary to curb communist influence in those countries; the same is true regarding the consequences of Arab military defeats, which open the door to further Soviet penetration and possible revolutions. Also of concern is that the situation is endangering the presence in those states of the Jews, especially in Egypt and Iraq, whose departure would further damage Arab economies.

• The "vapid UN handling of Palestine problem" could turn the Arabs toward the Soviet Union as a "more purposeful" source of help.

• Romanian oil being shipped to Haifa's "oil dock and refinery" for use by the PGI poses a threat to meeting the oil requirements of the European Recovery Program.

• Even the Crusaders didn't succeed in splitting the Arab world geographically as Israel has now done in the Negev—a "feat." "If Arab world is to be bulwark against Communism, there must be some corporate sense between States as well as free communication."

McDonald's own analysis of the 4 November resolution was contained in his telegram sent soon thereafter, as follows[12]: (a) there was no way the IDF would return to the 14 October lines and give up its protection of the many Jewish settlements to the south — Egypt had been doing all it could, despite the presence of the UN Truce Observation team (UNTO), to destroy them between 14 May and October[13]; (b) Bunche wrongly described the Negev as in a state of "extreme tension"—actually, calm prevailed and Egyptian forces were, in fact, voluntarily withdrawing from some of their overly exposed positions, such as Isdud and Majdal along the coast north of Gaza; (c) it was totally unrealistic to expect Bunche to enforce the power given him by the resolution to obtain the "restoration Negev position" in the absence of a UN military force entering the area and opposing the IDF; (d) the effect of the resolution on the PGI was to make it even more tense than ever; (e) both Bunche and the UNTO confirmed that the Iraqi forces in the central theater opposite Tel Aviv were continuing their "provocations"—were Chapter VII sanctions perceived by Israel as inevitable, it might then feel that the IDF might just as well also take action against those forces, thus expanding the zones of large-scale warfare; (f) under these circumstances, the PGI was naturally looking to the Soviets as holding the key to blocking the imposition of sanctions; and (g), the United States should not play into Bevin's hands, especially given the British history of mistaken judgments.

Not surprisingly, one of the strongest negative reactions to the U.S. role in the passage of the 4 November resolution was that of Eleanor Roosevelt, whose protesting letter in Paris to Marshall and the president, vacationing in Florida, led Truman, when Lovett read it to him by phone on 8 November, to instruct Lovett to reaffirm to Marshall that "the President said use his best judgment and whatever he does will be satisfactory. Doesn't like how these people [read: the Israeli authorities] have been acting up. Doesn't want General Marshall to feel he is handicapped in any way."[14] After Lovett supportingly interjected that the United States had to ensure that Great Britain not "give stuff [military arms] to Arabs — it will blow things wide open, and we'll give to the Jews," Truman naïvely responded that the two sides should "sit down" and "negotiate a settlement"— his "main objective" was to "prevent further bloodshed." Lovett then added (in a reference to what would prove to be the future Security Council resolution of 16 November, calling for "armistice" talks without preconditions) that, "if the resolution, which you approved yesterday, passes, that will reduce tensions enormously." (As we shall see, that resolution, though accepted by Israel, was rejected by Egypt, and the IDF resumed its Negev offensive on 22 December, raising "tensions" even higher as Israeli forces now entered into Egypt proper — albeit only for immediate tactical reasons — and as Israeli Spitfires, supplied by Czechoslovakia earlier in the year, shot down five British ones that were reconnoitering over the war zone.)

Like Eleanor Roosevelt, Clifford was deeply upset by the passage of the resolution of 4 November, telling Lovett the next day by telephone from Florida, in a further demonstration of his in-and-out role in foreign affairs, that he felt the president was "double-crossed again," and that he would tell that to Truman. Lovett easily convinced Clifford that it was the president's own policy that was being followed at the United Nations (as indeed it was), and that the 4 November resolution was, in fact, favorable to Israel, for it did not apply sanctions on the Jewish state, nor did it require the IDF to withdraw immediately and without conditions back to the lines of 14 October (here, Lovett is seen to back the Eban-Austin interpretation that the opening of negotiations was to occur simultaneously with any withdrawals).

Also in this post–4 November period, Lovett defended to Epstein the American role in the Council by arguing that Israeli opposition to the resolution, even according to Henry Morgenthau (who, as head of the Jewish National Fund, had just returned from a fact-finding tour of Israel), was really all about the forthcoming elections there, and that while U.S. recognition of Israel had been based on the original partition boundaries, Israel was now seeking to change them and, therefore, the United States no longer felt bound by them. (Here is another striking example of the shiftiness in the State Department position regarding the basis for American recognition of Israel — recall Henderson's explicit statement to Epstein on 29 May that recognition was *not* based on the November partition lines.[15])

With reference to Lovett's allusion, in his 8 November telephone conversation with the president, to still another Security Council resolution in the works, one that had already been approved in draft form by Truman on 7 November, this newest initiative at the Council was a product of Bunche's increasingly urgent advice that it had to go beyond calling for a mere truce if a renewal of the fighting was to be avoided. Instead, that now most influential of UN officials was insisting, the Council should focus on getting the two sides to negotiate a full-scale armistice as a more permanent basis on which to establish a final peace settlement. This was much more than just a nuance in the way Bunche approached the Palestine problem. With the exception of the panicky period of final fighting in late December and early January, it would help usher in a relatively more realistic diplomacy at the United Nations, which would be based on (a) tacit acceptance of the military balance of power favoring Israel; (b) a consequent de-emphasis on passing grandiose Security Council edicts demanding immediate truces, troop withdrawals, and the establishment of large swaths of UN-administered neutral territory between Israeli and Egyptian armies; and (c) a more modest political goal of seeking an intermediate step — armistices — between truce and final peace settlement.

The most immediate action taken by the Security Council in adopting this more realistic approach was its resolution of 16 November. While, as Lovett put it in a conversation with Clifford right after its passage, "the situation was getting terribly confused ... multiplicity of resolutions and Mediator's orders, etc.,"[16] it was nevertheless true that the focus now was less on seeking alterations in the military balance and more on bringing Israel and Egypt to a diplomatic understanding that would stabilize that "situation" sufficiently so as to enable them to move on to an even more permanent arrangement.[17]

The 16 November resolution, while citing Chapter VII, did not, in contrast to earlier such citations, explicitly threaten disobeying parties, but only referenced it as an element of the 4 November resolution; however, in response to the subsequent IDF offensive of 22 December, the Council passed a resolution on 29 December that renewed the 4 November express threat of Chapter VII sanctions and the demand for all forces to return to the 14 October lines.

Not surprisingly, the British had, short of exercising their veto rights and thereby creating a direct confrontation in the Council with the United States and other Western members, vehemently opposed passage of the 16 November resolution, which it saw correctly as the demise of the Bernadotte Plan of September and as a fatal weakening of the demands contained in the 4 November resolution. In contrast, France and Canada openly acknowledged that the latter resolution was a mistake, given that the Council would never impose Chapter VII sanctions against Israel, which consequently might feel free to conquer *all* of Palestine. Although this revised strategy was adopted by the Security Council, the same change toward a more realistic policy was less evident in the General Assembly, which passed an omnibus resolution on 11 December that continued its insistence on the internationalization and demilitarization of the Jerusalem area under UN control and on the right of return, "as soon as practicable," by the Arab refugees. On the other hand, the Assembly did follow the Council's lead and drop any reference to the Bernadotte Plan, to the benefit of the new UN approach of no longer seeking the imposition of its own solutions to the Palestine issue irrespective of the realities on the ground (Jerusalem, as always, being a special case). The Assembly at this time created a new agency, the Palestine Conciliation Committee (PCC), to help bring Israel and all five concerned Arab states to the negotiating table. As a primary backer of this innovation, the United States joined it as one of three members, the other two being France and Turkey, thereby progressing one more step in its inevitable direct involvement in Middle East peace.[18]

The Israelis had been unsuccessful in urging the American delegation on 6 December to include a Slav on the PCC. Therefore, Ben-Gurion instructed the Israeli delegation not to pursue that goal; he also was unenthusiastic about an Australian candidacy, not seeing that country, or at least its current leadership, as a pro–Jewish counterpart to Turkey's pro–Arab stance. By 13 December, the Israelis would express displeasure to the United States for having acceded to British-sponsored membership for Turkey and France, the latter being especially interested in obtaining internationalization and demilitarization for the Jerusalem area, per the terms of the Assembly's omnibus resolution of 11 December. The vote in the Security Council and General Assembly on the composition of the PCC had taken place on 12 December and was as follows: in the Security Council, the Soviet Bloc alone abstained and, in the Assembly, the vote was 41–7–4. In light of these developments, Epstein in Washington was instructed to emphasize the need for the United States to appoint a strong personality who was friendly toward the Jews. On 5 January, Lovett told British Ambassador Frank that Israel viewed France and Turkey as biased against it, and therefore looked to the United States to be its fair-minded PCC member, and also that the United States will try to be a "true conciliator," a role that, he explained, meant it would not be able to back Bevin's goal of using the PCC to obtain U.S.-UK goals — but that Joseph Keenan, the designee as American representative on the PCC, would "comport" himself per Jessup's 20 November statement at the United Nations (i.e., the Israelis "could not have it both ways").

Bearing on these developments were the following: (a) on 11 December, French Foreign Minister Robert Schuman stated to the General Assembly that the Israelis were inflicting on the Arabs "the horrors committed against the Jews during World War Two"; and (b) according to the Israeli delegation, at the time on 13 December when the British delegation convinced the Americans to support Turkey and France, Dulles had chosen to stay out of the room. Regarding Turkey, it is also worth noting a later analysis by the British embassy in Ankara, as contained in a telegram to London dated August 15, 1950: Turkey holds "the unrealistic policies and petty armies of the Arab States in great contempt and ha[s] made no attempt to enter into military commitments with those governments"; therefore, while it voted against the UN partition resolution of November 1947, it then recognized Israel without concern over any Arab reaction.

Throughout the next year, 1949, the Truman administration, as we have had occasion earlier to report, would look to this group for policy guidance in its relations with Israel in particular, which was more often than not the sole target of pressure to make concessions deemed prerequisite to obtaining the acquiescence of the Arab states to its peaceful existence. (The PCC unfortunately came on stream at the same time that Bunche, as "acting mediator," independently was conducting armistice negotiations at Rhodes. It did not seek the benefit of his experience and insights, and it inevitably created much diplomatic confusion as to what was being urged upon the parties by these two overlapping, uncoordinated UN agencies.)

An indication of Truman's personal feelings regarding Israel during this period can be seen in his letter of November 29, 1948, in answer to one from Weizmann expressing concern over American intentions in light of the UN resolution of 4 November.[19] The president typically sought to reassure Weizmann that the United States would not take any steps to "undermine" Israel's military victories,[20] that the Democratic Party plank would be carried out, and that the United States would oppose any territorial changes from the partition resolution that were unacceptable to Israel (leaving out, as usual, the important qualification that Israel, on the other hand, must give up some of that territory in exchange for any it wished to retain beyond those original borders!). The president also assured Weizmann, whose letter had urged such favorable action, that the Export-Import Bank would provide a long-term loan; that, once Israel held its elections, the United States would extend *de jure* recognition; and that it would encourage direct negotiations with the Arab states. In sum, the contents of this letter and its warm tone could not have prepared the Israelis for Truman's vehement personal messages to Ben-Gurion of the next few months questioning Israel's claim to be a peace-loving state worthy of becoming a member of the United Nations (30 December)[21] or, in support of the *indirect* negotiating efforts of the PCC, demanding that Israel give up the Negev if it wished to keep the Western Galilee (29 April).

As early as December 14, 1948, Douglas, in reporting Bevin's demand that the PCC place its emphasis on "fixing the boundaries of Israel," endorsed and expanded on the specifics of that demand as follows: the British "interest in the problem of the Negev was mainly strategic"; Egypt and Transjordan must be in friendly hands "so that British and Allied forces could use them in an emergency" and for "defense in depth of the Canal area"; therefore, the Jewish state should be north of the vital roads of Rafah-Bethlehem-Jericho and Auja-Bethlehem-Hebron-Jericho; and Transjordan should have "a corridor to the sea" on the basis of negotiations with Egypt. Here, we see what would prove to be the final effort by Bevin to pressure both the United States and the Israelis to bend to his vision of a peace settlement based on a diminished Jewish state as compared to that outlined in the United Nations' partition resolution. As described below, this British program would lead it to an end-of-year burst of controversial military moves that, in their failure to halt the IDF drive to occupy all that the PGI saw as its rightful legal territory, and in their lack of support in the British Parliament, would, when coupled with the progressive failure of British diplomats in Egypt to retain their military presence in the canal zone or to keep that canal under international control, mark the beginning of a rapprochement with the Jewish state that would lead to London's coordination with it and France (upset over Egyptian assistance to the Algerian rebels) in the Suez War of 1956.[22]

To understand the reason for Truman's above-noted, stern 30 December personal message to Ben-Gurion, a brief recapitulation of the British reaction to the military events of that month, and its political consequences, would be in order:

Among his military moves, Bevin, in December, transferred British troops from Egypt to the Jordanian port of Aqaba, generating controversy in the United Nations, the United States, and, of course, Israel, all of whom saw it as an illegal direct involvement in the war, threatening thereby to dangerously expand it at the expense of Israel and as an invitation to Soviet infiltration. A second move creating even greater alarm was Bevin's personal order to send British fighter planes over the border war zone. IDF planes, Spitfires obtained from Czechoslovakia, shot five of them down. The anticipated diplomatic consequences of this event led to much initial despair on the part of Israel's leadership, who now feared an open war with the United Kingdom, as did Truman and the State Department. But it so happened that Richard Crossman, a former member of the 1946 Anglo-American Commission on Palestine, was visiting with Weizmann and Sharett, and, as that British M.P. would later write in his book, *A Nation Reborn*, he assured them that this actually "was 'good news' as now Prime Minister Clement Atlee would have to 'disown this madness.' And so it turned out." Within two weeks, the United Kingdom did, in fact, extend *de facto* recognition to Israel, and Crossman, with good reason, would further write that "a statue should be erected to Ernest Bevin as the real founder of the State of Israel — upside down, with his head in the sand."

Also note that (a) on August 22, 1949, Bevin would justify to King Abdullah his actions of late 1948 by stating that the United States had failed to support the Bernadotte Plan because "Jewish influence was very strong there," and that he'd sent British troops to Aqaba, where they "had checked further Jewish aggression" into "Egypt"; (b) just prior to that transfer of troops to Aqaba, where Britain had already been maintaining ships and a naval unit, Bevin on 14 December had informed Douglas of that plan, which he described as part of a "proper balance" in British policy that also included sending troops and materiel to Amman itself; and (c) Lovett informed Truman on 12 January that the State Department had expressed concern to Bevin prior to his sending those troops to Aqaba because it could lead to a widening of the war and the involvement of the Soviet Union.

Israel, on the first anniversary of the passage of the UN partition resolution of 29 November, formally applied for membership in that organization. Its foreign minister, Sharett, it is worth recalling, had taken it upon himself to privately assure Lie and the American delegation, among others, that his country planned no further military offensives pending UN consideration of its application. Sharett did so on the assumption that Israel would be accepted as a member state within a few short weeks. This assurance came back to haunt him when the Security Council on 17 December failed to approve its application, which was left hanging even as Israel was now planning to force Egypt out of most of the Negev in light of that enemy's failure to enter into armistice negotiations pursuant to the Council's 16 November resolution.[23] Sharett, it will be further recalled, had acted without the knowledge of Ben-Gurion, who, when informed of Sharett's maneuvers, opposed making any military or other concessions to obtain UN membership, writing to Sharett that he would only pay "membership fees" for that goal and Israel could wait several years outside the United Nations, to which Sharett rebutted that, if so, Israel would then have to spend years waiting for peace. The foreign minister then sent in from Paris his letter of resignation, which, however, was rejected. Nevertheless, this difference in approach between them would come to the fore during the next few years, with Ben-Gurion taking the more hawkish, unilateral route to solving security issues, while Sharett might be seen as representing the relatively more dovish and internationalist approach.[24]

Exacerbating this crisis within the Israeli government, and between it and the United Nations, was the passage of the above-described General Assembly resolution of 11 December, the creation and membership of the PCC, which was perceived by Tel Aviv as loaded against Israel, given the basically unfriendly policies of France (especially regarding Jerusalem) and Turkey and the continuing open threats of renewed warfare by the Arab states.[25] Not surprisingly, then, the IDF unleashed on 22 December what would prove to be the final round of *major* fighting between Israel and Egypt. It did so after having reached a confirming cease-fire agreement with Transjordan at the end of November regarding their two respective forces. That Arab state, and its Arab Legion, as it had done since the truce of 18 July, would remain quiet during this next round of fighting in the Negev, which ended on 7 January with Egyptian forces remaining in Palestine, the Gaza Strip aside, only in a sliver of the eastern part of the Negev.[26] But that sliver, from Israel's point of view, was very important, given that it extended down to the port of Elath and was entirely within what Tel Aviv saw as its internationally recognized sovereign territory under the partition resolution of 1947. In a barely resisted offensive of March 5–10, 1949, the IDF quickly took full control over this one final piece of enemy-held territory in the Israeli Negev by removing — with Egypt's tacit approval — Jordanian forces from that part of it lying east of Beersheba, and then by signing with Amman a cease-fire agreement on 11 March, soon expanded into an armistice agreement (3 April) covering the central front as well. (Inasmuch as Iraq, while declining to participate in the armistice negotiations, had authorized Transjordan to speak for it, the final agreement between Israel and Amman also solved the problem of removing Iraqi forces from Palestine, where they had represented a direct threat to the Israeli central coastline. Abdullah, during these negotiations, had sought American support to force Israel to return to its original partition lines of 29 November, but the United States declined and the final armistice agreement allowed Israel to retain certain territorial advantages it had gained in the fighting in the foothills east of the coastal plain — this eased Tel Aviv's security concerns and facilitated its acquiescence to Abdullah's absorbing Arab Palestine, including East Jerusalem and the Old City, despite Ben-Gurion's continuing qualms about having what he still considered a British tool remain so close to sovereign Israeli territory.)

Interestingly, because it foreshadowed a continuing tension between the United States and Israel over remaining diplomatic issues (notably territorial exchanges, return of Arab refugees and the internationalization-cum-demilitarization of Jerusalem), Washington, in the name of the PCC, instructed the U.S. Mission in Tel Aviv, on 9 March, to protest to the Government of Israel (GOI) over the ongoing Negev offensive. Knox was the one to deliver this protest and, in reporting back to the State Department, offered his own view that the Israeli action was understandable (as indeed it was, if the main goal, per President Truman, was to end the violence and create a stable international environment in which a more permanent peace might be established in Palestine).[27]

Eight

The Diplomatic Consequences of Israel's Military Victories of 1948–1949, and Final Observations

Continuing Postwar Policy Between the U.S. and Israel

There were three underlying factors that help explain Truman's receptivity to the State Department policy of pressing Israel to make concessions to the Arab states even though their armies remained in Palestine, including parts assigned by the United Nations to the Jewish state. One was the condition (emphasized in private) he attached to his frequently stated policy of opposing any change not agreed to by Israel in the original partition territory as determined by the General Assembly. What was usually left unsaid, particularly in the domestic arena of the United States, was the condition that, if Israel insisted on retaining territory it subsequently won in battle against the Arabs, it must compensate the latter by giving up some of its original territory. In practice, this mainly meant that, if Israel wished (as it did) to retain Western Galilee and Jaffa, it must give up to the Arabs (basically Transjordan and Egypt) parts of the Negev. Of course, Israel balked at this policy on the grounds that the attacks on it by the Arab states necessarily altered the territorial plans outlined in the General Assembly resolution of 1947 and required Israel now to determine its territorial reach on the basis of what was needed for defense in the face of continuing threats from the Arab side. The rebuttal to this claim by Washington and the UN mediators was that Israel was trying to have it both ways—using the 1947 borders when those suited it, while demanding additional land as the spoils of its military success.

The second factor underlying Truman's support of State Department policy concerned the status of the more than a half-million Arab refugees. The president had a natural sympathy for their welfare and backed demands from the United Nations that Israel offer immediate sanctuary on its territory to at least 250,000–300,000 of them in keeping with the "right of return as soon as practicable" for those who wished to do so.[1] As noted earlier, the Israeli government responded that, pending a definitive peace settlement, it would undermine the country's security to allow such large numbers of Arabs of doubtful loyalty back into the Jewish state. Israel also maintained that it could not handle the additional financial and social burden of absorbing the refugees in its wartime economy, especially given that Jewish immigrants were rapidly adding to its responsibilities. Finally, Israel asserted that the great majority of the Arab refugees had fled to escape the violence created by the aggression of the Arab states and not by Israel, and that many of them did so at the behest of those Arab states without any coercion by Israel. However, Israel did progressively indicate its readiness to participate to the extent that its resources allowed in any international effort to resettle the refugees in the Arab states[2]; it also, during 1949, would gradually ease its stance under American pressure and tentatively consider allowing up to 100,000 to return, initially on a case-by-case basis, particularly in the interest of family reunification. Furthermore, Israel, it will be recalled, offered to consider — if the present occupying power, Egypt, so preferred (which it did not) — taking responsibility for the "Gaza Strip," where tens of thousands of refugees were residing and which had been assigned to the Arab state of Palestine under the 1947 partition resolution.

A third underlying factor explaining Truman's willingness to pressure Israel — in this case, as much as the Arabs were pressured — concerned U.S. and UN demands that both sides agree to the internationalization of the Jerusalem area (which would extend beyond the city itself and include, for example, Bethlehem). All the Arab states rejected this demand, in keeping with their consistent rejection of the partition resolution *per se*, although Transjordan in practice was following a policy designed to ensure its continuing control over those parts of the area it already had in its possession; in line with that policy, it arranged for leading Palestinian Arabs to meet in Jericho and pass resolutions on December 1, 1948, requesting that their country come under Abdullah's rule, a move that the State Department, in a major policy decision, endorsed the following month in these terms: "Department believes that most satisfactory solution disposition greater part Arab Palestine would be incorporation in Transjordan. Therefore, Department approves principle underlying Jericho resolutions." In that same month of January, the British advised Abdullah to avoid including in his acquisition of Arab Palestine any territory allotted to the Jewish state under the United Nations' partition resolution and to make no deal with Israel over the Negev prior to the arrival of the PCC, which Britain hoped would arrange for new boundaries in Pales-

Eight. Diplomatic Consequences of Israel's Victories

tine that would limit the Jewish state to a line north of the "Gaza-Beersheba" road and would establish "Haifa and Lydda free ports," among other arrangements.[3]

The Israelis, for their part, were unwilling to give up their control of West Jerusalem, where 100,000 Jews lived. Those Jews, as noted, accounted for nearly 20 percent of the total Jewish population in Palestine and, the Israeli government constantly emphasized, survived the war only by dint of Jewish military effort, unassisted by any international force in implementation of the UN resolution. The Tel Aviv government also regularly emphasized that, while it had accepted the 1947 resolution in its entirety, including the internationalization of Jerusalem, the events of 1948 led it to change its policy toward that city. It now was unwilling to accept the original plan, because it required the demilitarization of the area as well. Were that to be carried out, Israel feared that the Arab armies still surrounding the proposed internationalized area would then be able easily to defy the United Nations and capture it, including the now-undefended Jewish part. Given the bleak experience since passage of the 1947 resolution, the Israelis reasoned that there was no prospect of a sizable international force being organized to guarantee the city's internationalization. Instead, the Israelis feared, the safety of the Jewish residents would be resting only on the good faith of the Arabs. Of course, by the end of 1948, the Israelis, for separate religious and historical reasons, were more reluctant than ever to give up their part of Jerusalem, which they hoped eventually to integrate into Israel proper as its official capital city. Since Transjordan seemed amenable to dividing the city up between the two of them, this hope had a realistic prospect of fulfillment.

These three issues would remain bones of contention between Israel and the United States notwithstanding the welcome signatures of four armistice agreements by the first half of 1949 (only Iraq declined to negotiate with Israel but did make it clear that it would abide by whatever terms Transjordan worked out in its armistice negotiations). At times, the United States pressed so hard on Israel as to leave now–Ambassador McDonald openly despondent. Perhaps the peak of that despondent period came when Truman, still seeing Israel as the main obstacle to a peaceful settlement, still intent on having Israel open its doors to a substantial number of Arab refugees, and still insisting on Israel either returning some of the land it had conquered or exchanging part of its original territory for it, wrote a stern "personal message" in May 1949 to Ben-Gurion along those lines, ending with a threat, once again, of possible revision of U.S. policy toward Israel.[4] Subsequent communications between the president and Israel's leaders smoothed things over, and (especially after Truman downgraded his original message to one he now described as merely a private and informal note) the practical consequences of the exchanges were minimal, although it cast a pall over the relationship.

Truman's premise in writing as he did was that Israeli concessions might break the existing stalemate in UN-sponsored negotiations looking beyond the armistice agreements to a permanent peace settlement. His vehicle for achieving this goal was the "Palestine Conciliation Commission" (PCC) established, as described above, through American leadership by the General Assembly in December 1948 to overlap with and then replace the mediator operation, which was to continue until the armistices were signed and sealed. Truman's appointee to the post of U.S. representative on the PCC was at the ambassadorial level, requiring Senate approval and thereby raising the incumbent's visibility and domestic political importance beyond his likely ability to deliver the hoped-for peace. (This development illustrates how the U.S. government, step by step, during the period of 1946–1949, moved from a stance of indirect involvement in the Palestine issue to one in which it became the leading diplomatic actor. This process was foreseen in 1946 by Reinhold Niebuhr, the theologian and commentator on public affairs, who understood that the great significance of the U.S. agreement to participate in the bilateral commission with Britain concerning Palestine inevitably meant that it would henceforth be directly involved in Near Eastern political and strategic issues. Thus, especially with the failure to keep Britain directly active in Palestine starting in 1947, the United States saw itself diplomatically drawn in, most significantly, as a member of the Jerusalem-based UN Truce Commission and then as a member of the PCC.)

The outlook from the start was inauspicious for a successful outcome to the PCC operation, which began badly from the U.S. side when Truman had to dismiss his initial appointee, the previously mentioned Joseph Keenan, a lawyer from the private sector with previous experience in Japan for the government, who proved to be an alcoholic. Jessup recounts that, at a meeting with Truman and Lovett soon after this event, the president said, "Those so-and-so's [Jessup here opined, 'presumably his advisers,' Keenan being 'a political figure'] told me that he had gotten all over this. He is a nice fellow and he's a very able fellow and I knew he had some trouble like this with the bottle years ago, but they assured me that he'd completely gotten over this and so I appointed him.... You [Lovett] go ahead and pick out the proper person for this job.... I'll appoint him immediately. I'll have [Keenan's] resignation by tonight."[5]

Truman next chose a newspaper publisher, Mark Ethridge, without a drinking problem but with a similar lack of sustained diplomatic or Near Eastern experience.[6] The net result was that the State Department retained full policy control over the situation, including the nature of the advice the White House would be receiving from its PCC ambassador throughout 1949 regarding the reasons for the continuing lack of progress in Arab-Israeli peace negotiations.[7] Those reasons were the familiar ones of Arab unwillingness to negotiate with Israel on political matters except as a group and only indirectly through the PCC and Israel's unwillingness to make the major concessions that the PCC was soon demanding of it, whether regarding the return of Arab refugees, the internationalization and demilitarization of Jerusalem, or territorial adjustments. Israel, moreover, not considering the three-member makeup of the PCC as truly unbiased, naturally preferred to work directly, if usually surreptitiously, with its willing partner, King Abdullah's Jordan, which had now officially absorbed the "West Bank" of Palestine and established itself as a permanent neighbor of Israel in a *de facto* partition with which both sides felt temporarily comfortable.[8]

Even the United States gradually became adjusted to, and reconciled with, the realities of the evolving Palestine situation and began to lessen its emphasis on finding a permanent solution. It also eased its stance on Jerusalem, giving internationalization largely just lip service and focusing more on an arrangement allowing Israel and Jordan to keep control there alongside a UN "supervisory" presence in the Old City and the holy places to ensure their protection and accessibility. This was a formula that Israel, more than Jordan, could live with, because almost all UN duties would take place in the Jordanian sector, not Israel's. In a word, U.S. policy toward Israel would become more to the liking of McDonald as 1949 progressed. First, in the spring, Israel had been accepted as a member of the United Nations with by now strong American endorsement both in the Security Council and in the General Assembly,[9] and, as in the successful culmination of a game of solitaire, other countries had begun to recognize the State of Israel and establish diplomatic missions there — even including the United Kingdom, in May.[10] Thus, 1949 eventually proved to be a year that, after its difficult start, might well be labeled Israel's diplomatic *annus mirabilis*.

Even the less-than-admiring first British minister to Israel, Sir Knox Helm, would write in his 1950 summary report on events of 1949 that "Israel may well be proud of its record in 1949 ... it is very much a going concern. And this fact has important implications for the whole of this part of the world." Helm similarly softened his initial disdain for McDonald, whom he described in 1949 as a buffoonish, egotistical, boastful, wife-dominating, British-hating person, regarding him by 1950, as one who could be asked for the use of his influence with the leaders of the GOI to obtain a long-sought-after private meeting with them.[11]

The year 1949 also witnessed the release of all remaining Jewish displaced persons in the camps of Western Europe and Cyprus[12] and the approval of a $100 million loan by the U.S. Export-Import Bank.[13]

Lovett Diary and Final Conversations with Truman, July–December 1948

As in the case of Chapter Three, we will draw on Lovett's "diary" as a way to recapitulate in "real time" some of the key events of this time period and to focus specifically on the off-the-record views of President Truman and his White House staff in their telephone conversations with Lovett regarding the Palestine question:

Context

By the end of this final period in Lovett's tenure, military events in the field would sweep away the bulk of the UN agenda on the Palestine question. Gone was the U.S.-UK-sponsored Bernadotte peace plan of September, which had replaced the universally rejected one of June; in its place, a relatively more realistic program was progressively developed by December that focused on stabilizing the situation as it actually was rather than demanding a return to the frontlines that had existed prior to the various rounds of fighting. There were three such major rounds, each of which preoccupied the American government, which had taken the lead by now in orchestrating the UN response to the crisis. The fighting in July had been initiated by the Arab states, which had rejected the first truce ending on 9 July; this resulted in a so-called "Ten-Day War," in which the Israel Defense Forces (IDF) demonstrated its clear military superiority over the Arabs, at least in the short run. The second and third rounds of 14 October and 22 December were initiated by Israel and succeeded not only in driving the Egyptians out of most of the Negev but also in occupying the Western Galilee, up to the Lebanon border, even though it had been assigned to the Arab state under the partition resolution.

By the start of the eventually successful armistice negotiations of the early months of 1949, chaired by Ralph Bunche, who had taken on the mediator role when Bernadotte was assassinated (on 17 September in Jerusalem by the Jewish terrorist group known as the Stern Gang), Israel felt finally in a position to hold elections (25 January) and establish a permanent government. This met the preconditions set by the United States for giving *de jure* recognition to that country (in March); the United States also helped Israel win UN membership soon thereafter, despite still another Israeli military offensive in March to force the Egyptians out of the remaining parts of the Jewish-

Eight. Diplomatic Consequences of Israel's Victories   155

allotted Negev, up to and including the valuable port of Elath on the Gulf of Aqaba. However, there would remain major issues between Israel and its supporters in the West, notably over (a) creating a UN-governed separate zone in the entire Jerusalem area, as envisaged in the November 1947 partition resolution, and (b) either returning the Arab refugees back to their homes in Israel (or in Israel-controlled territory) or, for those choosing not to return, helping them to resettle permanently in the Arab states. In the midst of all these developments, the American government had to conduct a presidential election that would bring explicitly to the fore the important role domestic politics would play (as it had always played since the Palestine question developed into an urgent international crisis in 1945) in determining particular diplomatic policies and maneuvers. No one felt more upset about this than Marshall, Forrestal and Lovett, who all considered it a harmful and irrelevant intrusion into national security issues. Lovett would attribute Forrestal's deteriorating mental condition and eventual suicide in March to his preoccupation with this lack of a constructive bipartisan policy.

8 July

Tells a staffer that the Democratic plank on Palestine is "absolutely terrifying ... de jure recognition, guarantee of boundaries, etc." Later, he tells Clifford that the truce is ending and "we are going ahead with plans for evacuation [of] American personnel." [On the previous day, he had Navy Secretary Sullivan keep the fleet in the area, because, if war spread outside Palestine, that would increase demands on it, including evacuation of up to 7,000 U.S. citizens in Palestine.]

9 July

[When the Arab states decline to extend the truce and instead renew the war, Lovett tells Clifford that] Rusk by phone from New York advises that "the British for the first time on our side supporting Israel." [But the British would not go so far as supporting a U.S. proposal that the Security Council cite the Arab states by name for a breach of the peace under Chapter VII of the Charter.]

10 July

Tells Marshall's executive secretary, "White House wanted President [to] make statement he favored lifting arms embargo now that truce is over — finally got that one cured."

12 July

Tells Clifford that Democratic plank regarding "State of Israel" is "ok," but technically no country has a "right" to buy arms in the United States as it is a "privilege" only.

17 July

McDonald is in Washington for pre-departure briefings, and Lovett tells Forrestal to agree to see him, but he "should not tell him anything he is not prepared to have stated to the Jewish Agency." [Actually, that agency had been replaced by the provisional government upon the proclamation of the State of Israel, and its delegation at the United Nations replaced by the new government's own delegation, thereby eliminating the burden to the Tel Aviv authorities (and specifically to their UN ambassador, Abba Eban) of having to share power in New York with the Silver-led "American Section" of the Jewish Agency.]

21 July

Along with various staff members, Lovett sees McDonald for less than an hour [in a very contentious meeting, during which Lovett makes clear his distaste for having an out-and-out Zionist representing the United States in Tel Aviv; at a later meeting with Marshall, McDonald alluded to this personal attack, and the secretary assured him he did not share this attitude.]

18 August

Tells the U.S. Export-Import Bank the State Department wishes to delay approving Israel's request for a $100 million loan on grounds of political instability and wartime conditions there, but says president doesn't want to "give flat turn-down."

1 September

Advises Democratic vice-presidential candidate, Senator Alben Barkley, not "go to Tel Aviv since it is a very tumultuous country. Senator said he didn't think he would go." [He didn't.]

16 September

Discourages Clifford from the idea of Truman announcing *de jure* recognition now, even before Israel holds an election for a constituent assembly and establishes a permanent government; says "we could do it, if we want to take the consequences, which would be serious.... Israel itself" is holding up recognition by postponing the election, and "it is not our doing."

17 September

[With Bernadotte's assassination this day in Jerusalem by the Stern Gang, the Department and the British agree to accelerate pressing the United Nations to approve his just-released revised peace plan, which includes the Negev-to-the-Arabs proposal. The General Assembly is now starting its third regular session, which is being held in Paris.]

22 September

Lovett defends against White House criticism, from the presidential campaign train, that he had failed to clear with them Marshall's Monday statement in Paris of his full endorsement of the recommendations in the Bernadotte Plan, saying that he had sent it to them as a "top secret" message on Saturday. [As a result of this confusion, procedures for communicating with the train were revised.]

29 September

Clifford calls from campaign train: "Re: Palestine and President's proposed telegram to Secretary Marshall indicating a reversal of program." Lovett: "If the President, in view of past history in this matter, does anything that shows the slightest vacillation, it'll mean we have breached our agreement with the British, our name will be mud in all the Arab countries, and it'll affect our prestige. It could even be disastrous to the Berlin [Blockade] negotiations. Discussed a proposed statement for the President to make." [The basic change was to water down Marshall's stated approval of the entire set of recommendations in the Bernadotte Plan to one that describes those recommendations as "a basis for discussion."]

6 October

In response to Clifford's request, Lovett says, "I'll call Mr. [William McChesney] Martin of Export-Import Bank to see if they could get it [the loan to Israel] moving again." [Marshall, in connection with health problems, comes to Washington and holds consultations with the president and Lovett on 9–11 October.]

11 October

Former Treasury secretary Henry Morgenthau, currently chairman of the United Jewish Appeal, visits, following which Lovett calls CIA's Hillenkoetter: "Morgenthau going to Tel Aviv and does not want to be asked to be a spy; he will find out everything he can, however, and report to us."

13 October

Lovett by phone to Rusk in Paris: "we shouldn't carry the ball on this [the Bernadotte Plan] anymore. Mr. Rusk said, if Mr. Lovett would make the bench, he'd sit on it." [This instruction was based on Truman's new order, issued under pressure of campaign needs, no longer to press in favor of that plan.]

19 October

Rusk calls: "prospects of getting postponement of Mediator's report, etc., very good." [This was the post–17 October goal of the delegation in light of Truman's secret, eyes-only telegram via Lovett to Marshall (cited earlier) that further clamped down on the delegation's room for maneuver regarding Palestine: "I request that no statement be made or no action taken without obtaining specific authority from me and clearing the text of any statement." When this late Sunday night telegram was famously and quickly leaked to the press by an unknown source, it inevitably cast suspicion on the State Department itself as that source, contributing to the atmosphere of distrust between some members of the White House staff and Lovett personally — a distrust that would become even more personal and public when Lovett, as described below, left an impression with the press on 27 October that Truman's public policy statements on Palestine favoring Israel's case at the United Nations were not being cleared with Marshall.]

23 October (Saturday)

Clifford calls: "Dewey's reaffirming Republican plank, and president therefore would have do 'same thing'"; Lovett: "I'll get in touch" with Marshall "right away." Later, the two work out agreed language for a presidential statement, including Clifford's acceptance of Lovett's suggestion that the president say that "he is more than candidate and therefore has to be more responsible."

25 October

[The press begins to wonder about a split on Palestine between Truman and Marshall, given Truman's 24 October (a Sunday evening) statement taking a hard line in favor of Israel's position and implying rejection of Bernadotte's recommendations. The situation becomes exacerbated for Lovett personally in his relations with the White House when, at his weekly press conference on 27 October, he says, according to the *New York Times* the next day, that the White House had notified him of the planned statement on Sunday afternoon, at which time he notified Marshall.[14] The situation becomes even further complicated by leaks to the press of an "eyes only, midnight" telegram of 28–29 October, sent by the president via Lovett, ordering Marshall to keep the delegation totally silent on Palestine until after the 2 November election.

29 October

Lovett tries to convince Clifford that the leaks came from a "New York" source, to which Clifford responds, "inconceivable," because only Truman, Clifford, Lovett and Marshall knew of it.[15] Lovett by phone then tells Rusk to "sit tight," except if it's to deny that there is "a split or anything like that" between Marshall and Truman; Lovett adds, "time is the important element." [In fact, with the help of a procedural device arranged by the Canadian delegation, the Security Council, despite the renewal of war by an Israeli offensive against the Egyptians in the Negev starting on 14 October, did drop the Palestine issue until right after the election. Meanwhile, the delegation sat uncomfortably mum in the General Assembly's Political Committee discussions on the Bernadotte Plan.]

1 November

Marshall instructed by president via Lovett to try to avoid Security Council action on Palestine until 3 November, but, if he cannot, then "abstain"; "thereafter, would proceed on the previous understanding." [The 4 November Council resolution created still more public questions as to whether Marshall had approved it without Truman's input, because it demanded, *inter alia*, that the Israeli forces return to their pre-offensive lines. In fact, Clifford and Lovett had that day, 4 November, "discussed changes in draft Security Council resolution" prior to the delegation approving it in the Council.]

8 November

Truman, by phone from Florida [having his dander up in reaction to a letter from Eleanor Roosevelt protesting the 4 November resolution, and its threat of "sanctions" against Israel, and expressing doubt that the president had been told of the true situation[16]], had Lovett "tell General Marshall President said use his best judgment and whatever he does will be satisfactory. Doesn't like how these people have been acting up. Doesn't want General Marshall to feel he is handicapped in any way." Lovett: we must get the British not to "give [military] stuff to the Arabs — it will blow things wide open, and we'll give to the Jews." President: they should "sit down ... negotiate a settlement ... my main objective is [to] prevent further bloodshed." Lovett: if the resolution that the president approved the day before passes, it "will reduce tension enormously." [The new resolution would be passed by the Security Council on 16 November and did water down the 4 November one, especially by calling for the opening — implicitly without preconditions, such as troop withdrawals — of "armistice agreements" as a basis for peace negotiations. But this did not immediately "reduce tension enormously": the Israelis resumed their offensive on 22 December, made an incursion into Egypt proper, and shot down five British warplanes that were observing the situation in that war zone.[17] All of this, as noted earlier in this study, prompted a strong protest from Truman to Ben-Gurion[18]; nevertheless, it did help lead to the Bunche-conducted armistice negotiations of the early months of 1949 and to relative stability in the area until the 1956 Suez war. These developments in the field led the United Nations, both in the General Assembly and in the Security Council, to drop any and all further references to Bernadotte's peace plan of September.]

12–13 November

[President overrules Lovett, who] tells the Justice Department "President want us to issue visa" to Irgun leader Menahem Begin. [On 9 December, Lovett declines to see Begin.]

16 November

Tells Clifford the Security Council resolution was passed, but "situation getting terribly confused ... multiplicity of resolutions and Mediator orders [i.e., from Bunche to both sides to establish stable demarcation lines], etc."

17 November

Reads to Arthur Krock of the *New York Times*, who'd called about the "frosty" reports from Florida about Lovett, "the text of his press conference of 27 October relating to Palestine, which was what really started the trouble." [Lovett the next day thanks Krock for his resulting column.]

4 December

Tells Clifford that he will "pick up" Goldmann's passport [as a naturalized citizen since May 1946], "since he is representing a foreign government [Israel] in another country [the United Kingdom], and since our regulations provide that he cannot be there on an American passport." Clifford: "ok as far as I knew."

7 December

Marshall has operation on kidney, "two cysts ... the size of tennis balls."

3 January

[Along with Marshall, Lovett sends the president his letter of resignation, to which Truman responds]: "Dear Bob ... heartfelt regret ... effective January 20." [Truman's simultaneous letter to the secretary characteristically opened with a respectful and formal "Dear General Marshall."]

3 — Beyond the Armistice Agreements

If, in 1949, events within the Near East itself were conducive to a relative normalization of relations between the United States and Israel, those of 1950 outside that area served to accelerate and confirm that trend. In particular, the Berlin Blockade and the June 1950 start of the Korean War shifted America's focus both geographically and diplomatically, because, especially regarding Korea, it now applied the litmus test of support for its UN-authorized leadership against North Korea (and the Soviets) as the basis for the determination of its policy toward any given country. In this situation, Israel recognized that it would have to choose between holding to its policy of political neutrality (and thereby keeping open the hope of receiving Jewish immigrants from behind the Iron Curtain) or coming out on the American side and avoiding the loss of the kind of diplomatic and financial support it required from the

West to survive and grow. Its decision was a foregone conclusion, and within days of the war's start, Israel at the United Nations had not only voted in favor of the steps to counter the invasion of South Korea but also responded to Secretary-General Lie's call for concrete help by offering to send medical supplies to the front. As the year progressed, the United States would also promote selection of Israel as a member of various General Assembly committees coordinating the war effort.

Helping this normalization process along between the United States and Israel was the fact that the Arab-Israeli conflict was quiescent even as it remained potentially volatile. To help ensure that it would not boil up again, the United States and its two principal Western allies, the United Kingdom and France, decided to issue on May 25, 1950, a "Tripartite Declaration Regarding Security in the Near East" pronouncing their determination to guarantee "the peace and stability of Arab States and Israel"; to prevent the "development of an arms race" by limiting "the supply of arms"; and to prevent any "violation" of existing "frontiers or armistice lines" by taking immediate action, *whether within or outside the UN framework*, if any one of the parties was seen to be "preparing" an "aggression" against another.[19] Obviously, this declaration, although it proved to be short-lived once the Soviets broke up the arms supply monopoly of these three Western powers, was a most welcome one (in a sense paradoxically) by both the Israelis and many of the Arabs— especially Jordan and Lebanon, each of whom feared encroachments from its neighbors, Lebanon from Syria and Jordan from the latter as well as from Egypt. (Ibn Saud, too, expressed his deep concern privately to the American government that he still felt threatened by his long-time enemies, the Hashemite rulers of Jordan and Iraq.) As for Israel, Ben-Gurion stated, "We should prize the Charter of the UN and respect the [Big Three] Declaration [of 1950].... [But] Israel stood up by its own strength and will stand firmly only if it trusts first and foremost in itself as a power of growing greatness."[20]

When McDonald left his post for good in December 1950, he was full of hope that a permanent peace in the area would not be far off. The situation had been so unthreatening that he had spent more time in that last year writing his book on his mission in Israel, published the very next year, and visiting the United States for several weeks in mid-year (with the forlorn hope that Truman would allow him to resign then and there) than he did on official business in Israel. He also would pridefully write that he had indulged in an "extracurricular" activity by obtaining the president's confidential permission to enlist General Riley, the American in charge of supervising what was now called the UN military armistice commissions, in his secret effort to ease the Vatican stance on the internationalization of the Jerusalem area. While Riley accepted the proposal and did have a private audience with the pope, nothing came of it in practical terms. (In one of his own audiences with the pope, McDonald learned that the Vatican was unhappy that, whereas McDonald had been initially designated as the "*U.S.* special representative" to Israel, Myron Taylor was only the president's "*personal* representative" to the Vatican.)

As we now know, McDonald's rosy outlook rested on very shaky grounds. Moderate Arab governments would fall to leaders less amenable to peace, the Arab refugee problem would fester and grow, the Soviets would gain that feared foothold in the Near East, and the Moslem world in its entirety would increasingly pose a diplomatic problem for both Israel and its principal supporter, the United States; McDonald went so far as to predict in his book that he did "not anticipate the much-talked of 'second round' between Israel and the Arab States." What the American diplomat, Evan Wilson, wrote in his memorandum to Henderson and company of April 1, 1946, captures a truism of U.S.-Arab relations that remains valid even in the present day: The Arabs fully recognize "that there is real sympathy for Zionism — on any definition — in our country"; therefore, the State Department's policy of telling them that we are "even-handed" does no good and may give them the idea that we are "trying to conceal" the true situation in the United States; consequently, the Arabs see no value in our assurance of "consultations."

Wilson was writing from Lausanne as a staff member of the Anglo-American Committee of Inquiry on Palestine. His reference to "consultations" was with regard to presidential assurances by Roosevelt and then Truman, although it surely applies to other aspects of American policy, most notably its offer of "good offices," and so forth. Bearing this out, even decades later, note that, on August 21, 2010, the American envoy for Arab-Israeli peace talks, George Mitchell, was quoted in the *New York Times* as saying, "We will be active and sustained partners, although we recognize that this is a bilateral negotiation.... And we have indicated to both parties that, as necessary and appropriate, we will offer bridging proposals" (of course, his mission was unsuccessful). Also note the observation of J.C. Hurewitz, as stated in his previously cited comments at Harvard in 1950, that, although France and Turkey sought U.S. guidance as members of the PCC, American policy remained "ambivalent," alternately sympathetic to Israel or to the Arab states, "instead of following an independent and consistent policy," and that the United States appointed four successive representatives on the PCC "in less than a year," and only the fourth was a "career diplomat," which was needed to ensure "no further turnover." Hurewitz, a former UN official assigned to the Palestine question, assessed the PCC's errors as follows: (a) it "embarked upon its activities before it had an opportunity of profiting from Bunche's productive experience with armistice negotiations"; (b) "it had no real comprehension of its assignment: for the longest time, the Committee regarded its primary function as that of good offices ... instead of conciliation — that is, not only of bringing the parties together but of taking an active part in the actual negotiations"; and (c) it was "timid when it should have been bold, and obdurate when it should have been flexible."

It was only after the "Yom Kippur" war of 1973 that the United States developed a more consistent policy toward the Arab states, when Kissinger made it clear to them, and most specifically to President Anwar Sadat of Egypt, that while the United States would always work to protect the national security of Israel, it would, within that limitation, do all it could to further the interests of the Arabs. Of course, from the Israeli point of view, the U.S. role as an even-handed mediator would remain marred, notwithstanding the end of the Cold War, so long as it continued to be dependent on Middle East oil and, therefore, continued to be at least as concerned with its own overriding national security interest not to antagonize the Arab states as with its necessarily more objective role as mediator.[21]

4 — Final Observations

Perhaps the postwar history of the Palestine question offers one of the best demonstrations of the political truth of Proust's observation: "The human plagiarism which it is most difficult to avoid, for individuals (and even for nations, which persevere in their faults and continue to aggravate them) is the plagiarism of ourselves." An overview of the current state of play of American policy toward the Palestine question, as compared to the original features of that policy, usefully sheds light on that Proustian truth.

A listing of the major features and desiderata of U.S. policy during the 1948 war would surely include the following: an arms embargo on the combatants; the internationalization and demilitarization of the Jerusalem area, including international versus Israeli control of the "corridor" between the coastal plain and West Jerusalem; cooperation with the United Kingdom in the form of a division of labor in which the British would focus on aligning the Arab states with Anglo-American policies, while the Americans would do the same regarding Israel; avoiding direct involvement in the military aspects of the conflict while using the United Nations to the greatest extent possible as the stalking-horse for achieving diplomatic goals and for limiting the geographical scope of the conflict to Palestine itself; buttressing this indirect approach with appropriate bilateral pressure on Israel, such as maintaining only a limited and low-level official presence in the country and holding out the bait to it of *de jure* recognition, financial assistance through the Export-Import Bank, membership in the United Nations, and so on, as a reward for cooperation on the key issues of territorial exchange, return of refugees, the status of Jerusalem and the holy sites, and flexibility in the conduct of direct or indirect negotiations with the Arab states without resort to military offensives or military ultimatums; banning Israeli ties with the Soviet Bloc either officially or through the underground Jewish organizations operating in Palestine; and, finally, more at the purely "stick" end of the policy, (a) resorting to periodic presidential threats of reconsideration of the self-described American policy of being Israel's "best friend," (b) pushing for harsh UN resolutions that tended to curb IDF gains on the battlefield and to portray the PGI as the "non-peace-loving," key obstacle to a resolution of the conflict, and (c) blocking its own diplomatic officials in Israel from involvement in the formulation of American policy, while publicly announcing that policy without prior consultation with either those officials or the PGI.

Merely listing these policy characteristics serves to illustrate how deep was the change in the American stance, by war's end, in consequence of the signature in 1949 of the armistice agreements, and especially by the summer of 1950. Gone now were the diplomatically abnormal (indeed, punitive) limitations on relations between the United States and Israel, the ban on arms imports into the region as a whole, the hold on Export-Import Bank assistance to Israel and other regional countries, the intense focus on UN resolutions (especially those of the Security Council) dealing with Palestine, and the profound impact on foreign policy of domestic political pressures associated with a presidential election campaign.

Nevertheless, much of the underlying concerns and themes of that policy remain, even to the present day, including the very terms in which the Arab-Israeli conflict is couched in international and domestic discourse. Are we not still focused on territorial swaps, right of return of refugees, amount and quality of arms shipments to the region, extent of the U.S. commitment to Israeli security, and the political fate of Jerusalem? Are we not still debating, within the American body politic and in the conduct of our diplomatic relations, whether the ongoing Israeli-Palestinian conflict remains the cause of the continuing instability in the region, and whether its resolution would end that instability? Are we not still uncertain regarding the extent to which domestic public opinion, whether organized as "lobbies" or inchoate but demonstrable, has a legitimate role to play in the formation and execution of foreign policy? Is it not true that, although Cold War concerns of Soviet intervention are gone, they have been replaced by concerns over other, non–Arab threats to the stability of the region? Are not those threats now fortified by perhaps even deeper and more global ideological and religious underpinnings and by technological advances that make military weapons more destructive than ever? Is not Dean Acheson's frank criticism, in his memoirs, of the Truman administration's method of addressing the Palestine question still valid — that "this idea that the United Nations was and should be something different from its members and could assume responsibility without power has been a curiously persistent one"?[22]

As regards the performance of the United Nations during this war over Palestine, probably the most able defense of it was offered by the British ambassador to that organization throughout this period, Alexander Cadogan, who obviously would not have agreed with the conclusion of his military colleagues in London that the UN performance by the end of 1948 was "vapid." Below is a summary of Cadogan's assessment (apology, if you will) of April 20, 1949, regarding the United Nations' 1948 performance.[23] Some of its judgments, as the reader will see, must have astonished and shocked the Foreign Office and others in the London establishment for their frank criticisms of the Arab position and their implicit agreement with the case that the Israelis were trying to make at the United Nations.

> The Jewish state's existence "vindicated" the General Assembly's "recognition" of this basic fact; the Assembly acted wisely by rejecting the minority recommendations of the UNSCOP report given the Arab states' "behavior"— the Assembly thereby showed "political realism and sense of historical judgment"; the United States faced Arab defiance with "a policy of vacillation and retreat"; the Soviet policy was one of strong, pro-partition support; the Security Council's resolution of 15 July gave to the "aggressor" [read: the Arab states] the advantage by accepting "the presence of Arab forces in various parts of Palestine," including parts of Israel and Jerusalem, where they "had no international business to be"; that resolution's open-endedness fulfilled the Council's Chapter VII responsibilities; Israel, through its October and December military offensives, called Bunche's "private" policy of "bluffing the parties into relative submission" and, instead, got him to lead the Security Council into passage of the 16 November resolution and the parties into armistice negotiations."

In conclusion, Cadogan wrote, "This, I submit, is not a bad record for the world organization," which does not "profess to be a world government." More debatable, as this study has tried to show (at least as regards the Palestine question), was Cadogan's additional assertion that the Security Council is not authorized by the Charter to order political solutions.

Of course, for the author of the present study, the obvious commentary on Cadogan's assessment is that, while what he says is all well and good, in the final analysis, the United Nations had little impact on the events in the field, which, as J.C. Hurewitz and other historians point out, could only have been redirected if the member states (notably the United States and United Kingdom) had put their own military resources to work and actually *prevented* the creation of an independent Jewish state, among other positive as well as negative steps, such as the demilitarization and internationalization of the Jerusalem area. Since such a true intervention was not in the cards, the United Nations basically remained irrelevant as a serious impediment to the evolution of the Palestine question in 1948. But Hurewitz, in his Harvard presentation cited earlier, did grant the United Nations such "accomplishments" (as he put it) as the establishment of a Jewish state, the extrication of the United Kingdom, the limitation of the area of combat, and the leadership toward agreements on a "truce and then to a binding armistice." Finally, there is merit to Eban's frequent description of the UN role as having been that of an issuer of Israel's birth certificate rather than its parent. Ben-Gurion's statement during the height of the war is of a similar ilk: the only event that would intimidate him would be if the United States sent its own military force against Israel. Much of this study provides evidence for this narrower assessment of the "accomplishments" of the United Nations as compared to that of Cadogan and even Hurewitz. Moreover, in this light, the present writer would side with those who see Truman's various, but basically only verbal, actions in support of the Zionist cause from November 1947 onward as having a more important long-term impact on events in the Middle East, and on the role therein of the United States, than as seriously influencing the final outcome of the 1948 war.

In sum, given the fact that the Arab-Israeli conflict has not been resolved and remains a central element in the overall tensions within the Middle East, it seems obvious that it would be fruitless to try here to draw up a set of more-or-less definitive "conclusions" on the basis of the findings of the present study. Nevertheless, some final summary observations are in order with a view to highlighting the tenacity of the original roots of the conflict in the hope that a deeper understanding of those roots will contribute to providing an answer to the key question: Why has this conflict been so resistant of solution, so intractable down to its subsidiary issues? The pat answer, of course, has been that the two sides themselves have stubbornly held to their positions, the one determined to safeguard its national security from the continuing menace so obviously surrounding it, and the other equally determined to reduce and, if possible, totally eliminate the presence in its midst of an alien, distrusted and even hated foreign people.

This answer does not wholly satisfy: The Arab-Israeli conflict, had it been able to work itself out in a more traditional, "parochial" manner (to use Hans Kohn's term cited the beginning of this study), would by now surely have been more or less resolved. That Israel has made a formal peace with its principal Arab enemy, Egypt, is a manifestation of this premise and a belated, if only tentative and partial, proof of the validity of Bernadotte and Bunche's candid working premise that the two sides would first have to have the fight taken out of them before real progress toward a final settlement would be possible. Instead, and despite that peace treaty with Israel's most formidable Arab enemy, the conflict has continued as a festering humanitarian sore, a constant, ever-widening international crisis, a sustained and dangerous issue maintained at fever pitch, and a perennial threat to world peace and comity. This cannot be attributed merely to the tenacity, or inflexibility, with which the two sides have confronted the conflict. Rather, from its start, the Palestine question has been plagued by its being intertwined with broad international issues, whether related to traditional diplomatic and military considerations or to profound religious and other essentially ideological considerations. This has had the consequence, looking at the problem from a Western point of view starting in 1947, of allowing a variety of outside actors to put "their two cents in" (often in an unfortunately frivolous, uninformed way due to their not having to risk or invest important assets of their own or not *really* believing that there was any danger of a world war over Palestine, or that the West would suffer the loss of its oil supplies, or that its cultural facilities would be immediately shut down, or that its embassies would be sacked and lives endangered); these individuals subsequently found themselves not only authorized, but indeed required, to play a role, especially at the United Nations.[24] Even the U.S. government, as described in this study, at times took less than a responsible view regarding how to react to the crisis; its officials apparently saw the situation as one allowing them to let their imagination influence their activities more than was warranted by the facts of the matter[25] (for example, Rusk, as late into the issue as October 1948, believed wrongly that there was a large Arab population in the southern part of the Negev, and this, therefore, "would cause a new refugee problem for Israel" were it to succeed in replacing the Egyptians there[26]). Also relevant to an explanation of this behavior is the fact that the agencies and officials responsible for handling the Palestine issue were under intense *domestically* derived pressure — because of the matter's unusual importance for the American body politic, not least of which included the president in his role as head of a political party — to take actions purely to ease that pressure in the full knowledge that they were inefficacious. (This same phenomenon applied to the situation of many other member states of the United Nations and helps account for the remarkable number of fluctuating or contradictory votes recorded there on the Palestine question in 1947–1948, as various domestic constituencies took turns applying political pressure on foreign ministries, France being an outstanding example.[27])

Notwithstanding the above considerations, the Palestine question obviously was universally recognized as a serious problem containing the germs of a longstanding threat to international peace and specifically to Western interests in the Middle East. While desire often, in this early period of the crisis, took precedence over reality in the formulation of policy, the American officials responsible for the area fully recognized that they were playing a holding game[28] and that, at some time in the near future, the United States would have to invest more substantively in order to meet the challenge. That is why, as early wishes as to how the Israeli-Arab conflict should be resolved went up in smoke, policy accordingly began by and large to better match field realities, especially as compared to the policy followed at the time of Israel's War of Independence.

Chapter Notes

Chapter One

1. William Leahy, *Diary*, Library of Congress (microfilm).

2. This information is based on an examination of all telegrams sent out by the State Department in 1948 as contained in that year's volumes of *Foreign Relations of the United States* (Washington, DC: Department of State) (henceforth *FRUS*). The department practice is to place the name of the secretary or the acting secretary at the end of each telegram as the nominal authority for it. The only times when neither the name of Marshall nor that of Lovett appeared on those telegrams were on 19 March and the immediately surrounding days, when the name of Willard Thorp, assistant secretary of state for economic affairs, appeared as the nominal authority.

3. Ibid., 728–31. (Unless otherwise stated, all *FRUS* citations are from 1948, volume V, part 2, *The Near East, South Asia, and Africa*.)

4. According to the Israeli government's *Political and Diplomatic Documents: Preliminary Volume, December 1947–May 1948*, Israel State Archives, 714, 2 May, the Jewish Agency in New York passed on a report that "Lovett said recently that had he been available, that speech [of 19 March by Austin] would never have been made." But it is hard to reconcile this alleged claim by Lovett with his having, before leaving for Florida on 15 March, approved the 16 March instruction to Austin. Moreover, Lovett had known at least since January that Marshall was scheduled to go to California for a few days starting 18 March (according to the records of the George C. Marshall library) and could easily have scheduled his vacation for some other period in keeping with their standard practice of always having at least one of them on seat "to mind the store," as Lovett put it in his oral history at Columbia University. Perhaps, and more credibly, he meant that, had he been at the department, he would have ensured that the president expressly cleared that instruction. Supporting this latter possibility, as will be discussed below, is the fact that, from Florida, Lovett on 18 March instructed the department (which subsequently failed to follow his directive) to clear with the White House a proposed telegram to Austin that was connected to the planned 19 March statement and that therefore would have alerted the president to that planned event, something the State Department was determined to avoid at all costs.

Note: Each volume of *Political and Diplomatic Documents* (henceforth *PDC*) contains a "companion volume" that provides English-language summaries of selective, Hebrew-language documents contained in the respective main volume. Unless stated specifically as coming from the companion volume, the citations in the notes are from the basic volumes.

5. *FRUS*, 645.

6. Ibid., 728–31.

7. March was a crisis period in U.S.–Soviet relations. Truman addressed a joint session of Congress on 17 March and, for the first time, identified the Soviet Union as the "one nation" blocking peace. The triggering event was the Communist coup in Czecho-

slovakia of 24 February. See, for example, James Forrestal, *Forrestal Diaries*, edited by Walter Millis (New York: Viking, 1951), Chapter X, "The March Crisis." It is one of the ironies of the matters dealt with in the present chapter that, while Marshall left the management of the Palestine problem to Lovett, it was he who felt so strongly as to be the one, at least in this instance, more prepared to take drastic action at the president's expense.

8. Leahy, *Diary*, October 8, 1947: (a) On 13 October, there will be a British-American conference "on general strategy in the Near East." (b) At the 10 October "special meeting" of the Joint Chiefs of Staff, [Leahy] will tell the Secretary of Defense of "the military implications involved in taking any side" in the Jewish-Arab contest in Palestine. The Joint Chiefs "are clearly of the opinion that involvement of the US to any degree in the Palestine controversy is disadvantageous to our national security."

Also, on January 7, 1948, Leahy denied to the press that he had any "knowledge" of "staff conversations ... by the American and British staff officers ... at the present time."

9. For a bald statement that the president's Palestine policy was threatening to upend the entire strategic edifice of U.S. Middle East policy, see George Kennan's memorandum of February 24, 1948, in *FRUS*, 655–57. See also Leahy, *Diary*, November 3, 1947: Ibn Saud's 30 October message to Truman "is in the same sense as an oral statement made by Ibn Saud to President Roosevelt in the Suez Canal February 14, 1945."

10. During this period, the general meaning of "Near East," as distinct from "Middle East," was that the former's "core" was "the Arab world and Israel," while excluding Iran and Turkey, whereas the latter term included those two countries. See N. Frye, *The Near East and the Great Powers* (Cambridge, MA: Harvard University Press, 1951), v.

11. See *FRUS*, 1947, vol. 5, *Near East*, 485–626, including editorial note on page 602.

12. *FRUS*, 593–94. For the 1946 abortive London agreement, see Chapter Two in this book.

13. For a brief analysis of the Pentagon Talks from the British point of view, see Uri Milstein's *History of the War of Independence*, vol. 1: *A Nation Girds for War* (Lanham, MD: University Press of America, 1996), 136–41.

14. *FRUS*, 1947, 563.

15. Leahy, *Diary*: (a) February 27, 1947: [I] don't understand why Marshall wants to help save Greek and Turkish governments "in view of his present attitude toward the Government of China," whose stability" is of much more importance to America than the Mediterranean States." (b) March 7, 1947: Under-Secretary Dean Acheson told the president that if the Communist Party takes over Greece, it would "result in complete Communist control of Western Europe and the Middle East."

Leahy, in his entry of January 8, 1947, regrets that Truman chose Marshall over his own recommendation (Forrestal) to replace Secretary of State James Byrnes — Marshall was Leahy's second choice. On February 8, 1948, he agrees with his frequent companion, William Bullitt, that Marshall "is determined to cause the collapse of Chiang Kai-Shek's central government" by failing to give it a sufficient level of arms.

16. See *Forrestal Diaries*, 342, where Foreign Secretary Bevin told the State Department's Loy Henderson that "the fall of the Middle East would virtually mean the end of England as a power."

17. Ironically, by 1949, "Aramco had cut back production" because "the price of crude oil had fallen" and Saudi Arabia's financial situation had become "darker" due to the royal family's "extravagance" (*British Documents on Foreign Affairs*, Part IV, Series B, *Near and Middle East*, 1950), xx.

18. Czechoslovakia's foreign minister, Jan Masaryk, reportedly told his "personal friend," Sharett, that "I don't know very much about oil pipelines, but I know of another pipe through which Jewish blood has been flowing for many long generations" (see Arnold Krammer's *The Forgotten Friendship: Israel and the Soviet Bloc, 1947–1953* [Chicago: University of Illinois Press, 1974], 67–68).

19. See *FRUS*, 1099–1101, where, on June 6, 1948, Henderson opined to visiting British

diplomats that, were the United States to lift its arms embargo and the Jews able to receive arms as well as Jewish immigrants of military age, "it was quite likely that the Jews would win. Extremists might push on to Transjordan (raids have already occurred into Transjordan)."

20. Ibid., 573 and 579–80. For a harsher judgment on the historical damage to Western interests in the Middle East done by the Jewish demand for, and British issuance of, the Balfour Declaration itself, see Kennan's memorandum to Lovett, January 29, 1948.

21. *FRUS*, vol. 5, part 1, 6, and part 2, 546ff.

22. Were the British unable to retain either Egypt or Palestine, then Cyrenaica would meet the military need to "be able to fight from the Middle East in war," especially given their loss of India "as a base for ... deployment of force," but, ideally, they would have "Palestine as a screen for the defense of Egypt" (see Peter Grose's "The President versus the Diplomats" in Louis and Stookey's *End of the Palestine Mandate*, 15–16).

23. Ralph Bunche, the UN acting mediator for Palestine following Bernadotte's death in September 1948, reported at a Harvard conference in 1950 that "never once in the course of our negotiations with Arabs and Israelis was any mention made of oil to Bernadotte or to myself," nor did religion "really figure" in the conflict — these were "happy circumstances," along with the fact that there was no East-West division on Palestine (Frye, *The Near East and the Great Powers*, 114–18). Note that oil flow to the West during this first Arab-Israeli conflict was unaffected except for the Iraq-Haifa pipeline interruption. The situation as a result of the Suez War of 1956 was a "different kettle of fish," as a former head of Aramco put it (Thomas C. Barger, "Middle East Oil Since the Second World War," *Annals of the American Academy of Political and Social Science* 401 (1961), 40).

24. Leahy, *Diary*: (a) January 14, 1948: [I] attended a Forrestal lunch for the Canadian Minister of Defense: "subject ... generally confined to the partition of Palestine which both the Canadian and American guests considered wrong and dangerous to the future defense of Western Civilization." (b) There is a report of "Paul Robeson leading a Black America attack on US." (c) January 17: Reports show that the partition resolution "has already produced a dangerous condition of rioting that approaches a general civil war that can be quieted only by the use of superior military force.... The great dangers ... are a world-wide war between Moslems and Christians, or an occupation Eastern Mediterranean countries by Soviet troops resulting eventually in American withdrawal from the oil-rich Middle East, or an expulsion of the Soviets there by an American-Soviet world war ... [this is] a difficulty in which we have injected ourselves ... [militarily, our position] in Palestine appears very dangerous." Also, per Krammer's *Forgotten Friendship*, 43, General Lucius Clay, military governor in Germany, in March 1948 predicted to Washington "an imminent war. with the Russians."

25. *FRUS*, 1948, 621–23 (editorial note), and 841. Truman, along with the National Security Council, approved in writing the conclusions of the Pentagon Talks on November 24, 1947.

26. See, for example, Chaim Weizmann's *Trial and Error* (Philadelphia: Jewish Publication Society of America, 1949), 457–59.

27. *FRUS*, 1947, 1290ff.

28. J.C. Hurewitz, a UN official during that period, in speaking at the 1950 Harvard conference, said about the members of the UNPC that "the five lonely pilgrims," never having gotten to Palestine or even left Lake Success, worked there until 17 April only with the Jewish Agency to develop "plans ... for the formation of a Provisional Government" ("The United Nations and Palestine," in Frye, *The Near East and the Great Powers*, 91–105).

29. See *FRUS*, 1110, where it is stated that the embargo had been in effect against the Arab states and Palestine since November 14, 1947; also see *PDC*, 103, for a report of December 23, 1947, that Marshall had decided on the embargo "months before it was announced." In addition, on December 30, 1948, Lovett told British ambassador Oliver Frank that "our own arms embargo ... as the Ambassador knew, had been imposed by us

unilaterally even before the Security Council took action" on May 29, 1948 (see Robert Lovett, *Diary*, New York Historical Society Library).

30. *FRUS*, 629 and 688 (Clifford's 6 March memorandum); *Documents on Israeli-Soviet Relations*, Part I (ISA/WZO/ Russian Federal Archives; London: Frank Cass, 2000), 254; and *PDC*, 103 and 155–58, where U.S. Consul General William Porter (Jerusalem) reportedly was urging (January 1948) the State Department to drop the embargo as being unfair to the Jews.

31. As late as February 21, 1948, Lovett found it necessary, at a meeting with Shertok, to ask him "to enlighten me" regarding "whom did the Jewish Agency represent and under what authority" (Lovett, *Diary*).

32. *FRUS*, 882–86, 1008, 1016, and 1010. See also *PDC*, 171–73, for Shertok's message to UNPC of January 15, 1948, stating that, if there will be no international force, the Jewish state will be "insistent" on its legitimate need for arms assistance.

33. *FRUS*, 1948, 552, 554, and 593–94.

34. *Yearbook of the United Nations, 1947–1948*, Chapter 3; see also *Documents on Israeli-Soviet Relations*, 277.

35. *PDC*, 186–87. Michael J. Cohen's article, "Truman and the State Department," *Jewish Social Studies* 43, no. 2 (Spring 1981), 165–78, errs in stating that the Zionists "inexplicably ... failed to perceive that Austin's speech [of 24 February] was the first public indication of preparations to bury partition."

36. *FRUS*, 546ff. For Clifford's "If anything has been omitted that could help kill partition, I do not know what it would be," see *FRUS*, 695.

37. In a wonderful example of diplomatic flexibility, the State Department in 1950 promoted in the General Assembly the "Uniting for Peace" resolution, which allowed that forum to consider matters, most notably the UN role in the Korean War, unhindered by the Soviet veto power in the Security Council. The State Department in 1948 would surely have denied that the UN Charter gave that authority to the Assembly. See also former U.S. delegation member Philip Jessup's *The Birth of Nations* (New York: Columbia University Press, 1974), 62–64, for the view that "most" Assembly resolutions, like that of 29 November, are a "recommendation" and not "legislation." It is instructive to compare this view with that expressed by John Foster Dulles to a General Assembly committee on October 9, 1950: "The same instrument ['the Charter'] which placed on the Security Council the 'primary' responsibility for the maintenance of international peace and security ... also by articles 10, 11, and 14, gave the General Assembly power to recommend even as to matters that might be vetoed.... [Article 10 gives the Assembly the] right to recommend as to 'any matters within the scope of the Charter.' ... [This right] to recommend to members is not the equivalent of Security Council 'action' ... [but] recommendations, if made to a responsive membership, can be equally effective.... The United States delegation does not accept the view that 'responsibility' is a monopoly of the few and of the great.... If ⅔ of the General Assembly [recommends an action], then its recommendations will evoke a response ... for in these matters, moral judgments are our only reliable dependency" (emphasis added; State Department's *Bulletin*).

38. *FRUS*, 556–62. For rebuttals to Rusk, see Henderson's and Kennan's memoranda, 579–80 and 600–603. For example, Henderson argued that there was a "new" situation since passage of the November resolution, such as the actuality of a violent situation, whereas earlier that was only a "hypothetical" possibility. (Marshall would at times throughout this period claim rather lamely that the State Department had been purposely misled by the Jews, who had assured it that the resolution could be implemented without resort to force.)

39. See ibid., 756–57, 797–98 and 833, for examples of the general expectation in the Department of such a "slaughter." See also *PDC*, 528–31, where Henderson on March 26, 1948, tells Epstein that without a UN trusteeship, the Jews would be "massacred and face certain annihilation."

40. See *FRUS*, 648–51, and Jessup's *Birth of Nations*, 262–64, for the view that it is

legally correct to say that the Security Council cannot enforce a "political settlement."

41. *FRUS*, 701–2: The UN legal staff on 3 February had affirmed "the legal authority of the Security Council to partition Palestine by force." See also Trygve Lie, *In the Cause of Peace* (New York: Harper & Row, 1954), 167.

42. *FRUS*, 588 and 617–18.

43. Ibid, 806 and 908–9.

44. Ibid, 645.

45. Ibid., 745–46 and 749, and Robert Donovan, *Conflict and Crisis* (Columbia: University of Missouri Press, 1977), 373.

46. For example, *FRUS*, 705 (9 March instruction to Consulate General in Jerusalem) and 717 (the Jewish Agency representative, Moshe Shertok [later Sharett], tells the five permanent Security Council powers that "a pernicious doctrine was being spread in the Middle East that the UN will not follow through … the Arabs have nothing to worry about").

47. *Yearbook*, 406. That this was a change in the U.S. line from the one articulated on the eve of the vote for partition in 1947 is vividly demonstrated by Ambassador Herschel Johnson's statement of 25 November to the Assembly's ad hoc committee on Palestine in favor of approving a provision in the draft partition resolution that would request the Security Council "to act" if a "threat to the peace" were to arise in Palestine: "The General Assembly was acting [to solve the overall Palestine problem] upon a request of the Mandatory Power, and some machinery had to be devised for the action to be taken. Recommendations of the General Assembly were made to all Members of the UN and, once accepted by two-thirds of the Members, reached a position close to law" (emphasis added). No wonder Johnson left the delegation by April 1948 and was replaced as second in command by Jessup, who was more sympathetic to the changed U.S. line.

48. Ibid., 407.

49. Ibid., 406–7 and 410.

50. See Lie's *In the Cause of Peace*, 169–72, where he quotes a refrain by reporters at the United Nations: "We must do nothing — but at once."

51. *FRUS*, 697, 749 and 815.

52. *PDC*, 383 and 407. Eban saw this resolution as a first step toward implementation of the partition resolution of November; he even urged other delegations to support the U.S. resolution.

53. *Yearbook*, 404.

54. Ibid., 407–9. On 5 May, Ambassador Austin testified misleadingly, and in part falsely, before the House Foreign Affairs Committee, as follows: (a) regarding the 5 March vote: "On the motion of the U.S. to accept the request of the General Assembly to implement the plan, only five votes could be obtained in support of it"; and (b) regarding the 19 March vote: all five permanent members "found and reported that the partition plan could not be implemented by peaceful means, and they were unable to make the finding of a threat to international peace" — therefore, the Council decided upon a "Special Session" (*Bulletin*). As stated in Arnold Offner's *Another Such Victory* (Stanford, CA: Stanford University Press, 2002), 299, "even if they [State Department officials] did not intend to deceive Truman with their March 1948 trusteeship proposal, it contravened his order against 'recession' from partition."

55. Donovan's *Conflict and Crisis*, 375, labeled the reaction a "firestorm."

56. *FRUS*, 744; Lie, *In the Cause of Peace*, 172; and Allis Radosh and Ronald Radosh, *Safe Haven* (New York: HarperCollins, 2009), 306.

57. See, for example, *PDC*, 189–90. The Jewish Agency saw as unhelpful Truman's public statement of 15 January that no U.S. military forces would be sent to Palestine, although he allowed that there might be participation in a UN police force there; the agency also reported to Tel Aviv that the UN secretariat believed this was a setback for the organization's prestige, which it saw as tied to implementation of the partition resolution.

58. *FRUS*, 747.

59. Cohen's "Truman and the State Department" misunderstands Thorp's merely nominal role in all this: "Thorp was in charge of the Palestine desk during Lovett's holiday in Florida."

60. *FRUS*, 751–52.

61. Ibid., 759–60 and 774.

62. Ibid, 616. As early as April 1, 1946, Evan Wilson, a State Department official on the staff of the American section of the Anglo-American Committee of Inquiry on Palestine, wrote back from Lausanne, where the committee was putting together its report, "A compromise solution ... will require even more force to implement it, since both Arabs and Jews will oppose it vigorously" (Wilson, *Decision on Palestine: How the U.S. Came to Recognize Israel* [Stanford, CA: Hoover Institution Press, 1979], 66). In a similar vein, J.C. D'Arcy, the general officer commanding the British forces in Palestine, stated to that committee that "he thought the Haganah would be able with out difficulty to hold any area allotted to the Jews under partition, whereas larger British contingents would be required to police any solution which involved the suppression of the Haganah" (Herbert Feis *Birth of Israel* [New York: W.W. Norton, 1964], 64). That statement "was struck from the record as too secret," Richard Crossman would wryly report in *A Nation Reborn* (New York: Atheneum, 1960).

63. Clark Clifford, *Counselor to the President* (New York: Random House, 1991), 13–15.

64. *FRUS*, 750.

65. Weizmann, *Trial and Error*, 472. It is highly unlikely that Truman would have agreed even to meet Weizmann on 18 March had he been aware of what Austin was about to tell the Security Council. Cohen, in his "Truman and the State Department," ignores the fact that Marshall had put himself beyond easy reach when he writes that, had Truman "bothered to inform his Secretary of State of his meeting with Weizmann the day before ... it is hardly likely that Marshall would have issued the said instructions [of two days prior to the Weizmann meeting!] to Austin when he did." Cohen repeats this faulty chronology in *Palestine to Israel* (London: Frank Cass, 1988), 212.

66. Harry S Truman, *Memoirs*, vol. 2: *Years of Trial and Hope* (Garden City, NY: Doubleday, 1956), 163; Margaret Truman, *Harry S Truman* (New York: Morrow, 1973), 387–89.

67. Communication to the author from the Truman Library's archivist.

68. *FRUS*, 748–49; *New York Times*, "Marshall Upholds Shift on Palestine," March 21, 1948.

69. Leahy, *Diary*, March 20, 1948: "The press this morning announced a complete change in the UN of the policy of the U.S. in regard to the partition of Palestine. The President told me that this change was made without obtaining his permission and without his knowledge." John Snetsinger's still influential *Truman, the Jewish Vote, and the Creation of Israel* (Stanford, CA: Hoover Institution Press, 1974), 86–88, tries to make the following case: "A myth has existed since the time of the [19 March] event itself that the State Department acted independently in regard to the reversal.... But the truth is that Truman directly and knowingly approved the shift in Palestine policy of the United States." On that basis, Snetsinger asserts that Truman's recognition of Israel was "yet another major reversal of America's Palestine policy" (108–9).

70. *FRUS*, 759–60.

71. *Bulletin*.

72. Since Clifford for weeks prior to 12 May had been working directly with department officials, Marshall's outdated view of him is further evidence of how uninvolved he was in the details of the Palestine issue. Other examples include the following: he believed that the American delegation was active in the Security Council on 14 May, whereas it was at the podium of the General Assembly, and, as late as 12 May, he had never heard of David Ben-Gurion (*FRUS*, 974; Clifford, *Counselor to the President*, 6). Also see *PDC*, 509–21, for a Jewish Agency view of Marshall's limited interest in the subject's details. Incidentally, Lovett, for his part, showed a remarkable lack of historical knowledge of basic facts regarding the Palestine issue (e.g., recall his having to ask Shertok in February about the legal basis for the role of the Jewish Agency at the United Nations).

73. In his *Memoirs*, vol. 2, 164–65, Truman wrote, "I am sorry to say that there were some among them [i.e., 'some of our diplomats, and especially the gentlemen on

the Near Eastern desks'] who were also inclined to be anti–Semitic." In this regard, note the following:

(a) Offner's *Another Such Victory*, 536, n. 10, challenges H.W. Brands' claim, in his *Inside the Cold War* (New York: Oxford University Press, 1991), that Henderson evidently was not anti–Semitic, although he occasionally, per Brands, "lapsed into stereotypes regarding Jews." Offner observes that Henderson "treated the Zionist cause and Zionists, such as Epstein, with contempt; that he went beyond the call of duty to defeat partition; that he was given to questionable, if not mean-spirited, arguments, such as that the 'overwhelming majority' of non–Jewish Americans who knew anything about the Middle East opposed a Jewish — or 'theocratic racist state,' or that the 'thinking peoples of Asia are convinced that the Zionists, with the aid of certain Western countries, have been engaged for years in a slow process of aggression against the Arabs of Palestine,' Henderson Memorandum for Marshall [May 25, 1948, in *FRUS*, 1044–45], on Truman and Israel's boundaries." (b) Wilson, in *Decision on Palestine*, cites and endorses Henderson's memorandum to the U.S. delegation at the United Nations, dated September 23, 1947, which urged no "advocacy" of the partition proposal, because its "execution" would "arise to plague every session of the General Assembly ... [and] we shall be the target for bitter attacks by both Arabs and Jews." Henderson then went on to make the unwarranted claim that a Jewish state would be based on "the principle of a theocratic racial state," which in turn would lead to an increase of "feelings among both Jews and Gentiles in the United States and elsewhere that Jewish citizens are not the same as other citizens." Wilson, who had been a career diplomat in Henderson's office, elaborates on this theme, asserting that American Jews, uniquely among U.S. citizens, would inevitably become guilty of a double loyalty (*Decision on Palestine*, 116–23). (c) Leahy, *Diary*, January 19, 1948: A group of Americans denouncing universal military training includes "Albert Einstein and some known pink professors.... I told the President ... being attacked by such a thoroughly established American as the German Jew Einstein, who acquired citizenship in 1940 ... is a high compliment.... [We] should yield to him ... on any question of relativity, but on no question of National Defense." On September 20, 1948, Leahy offered to resign given that "some of" Truman's "political advisers" (concerned over some "newspaper criticism" of his attitude toward Jews) considered him a disadvantage for his "political prospects." The president's handwritten response from his campaign train included this statement: "While you and I don't see eye to eye on some things, we are always frank with each other ... and are "friends ... come hell or high water."

74. For example, see Brands' *Inside The Cold War*, 183: Loy Henderson's "hope that the American-backed majority [partition] plan would fail indicated, if not active sabotage, at least latent subversive tendencies."

75. *FRUS*, 722.

76. (a) Wilson, *Decision on Palestine*, 132: Meir raised $50 million in "six weeks" during her first swing through the United States. (b) On May 10, 1948, Lovett asked the Treasury Department to look into "so-called Jewish charities" that were used for "ships, etc." He noted that one was now "loading commies in Bulgaria"; that, therefore, the "basic question" was again raised" regarding "this whole racket"; and that "Jewish Joint Relief" was offering the Romanian government "$25 for every young active Jew released." Treasury Under-Secretary Archibald Wiggins: We'll check out the "tax exemption on contributions to this outfit"; "looks like we withdraw the tax exemption" (Lovett, *Diary*). In fact, Lovett never succeeded in obtaining his goal of eliminating these exemptions, in important part due to domestic political restraints for such an action, as best illustrated in a resumption of the Lovett-Wiggins conversation, as follows: On 13 May, Wiggins called to say that he had written to "these people" that, since they have not shown that they actually, as required by law, used the funds "abroad ... exclusively for educational or charitable purposes," the tax exemption "is withdrawn." Lovett: "did not expect Wig-

gins to go that far"; had only wanted "find out what requirements were for tax exemption ... and what Wiggins' previous investigation had disclosed." Wiggins: "proper use of funds in this country but that considerable funds were transmitted to Switzerland and they didn't know what happened to them." Lovett: Will, with him and Treasury Secretary Snyder, consult "sometime" at the White House to see if we should ask "these people" to justify their use of funds.

77. Milstein, *History of the War*, 141.

78. It was during this peak period of unwarranted optimism that Lovett, as he put it to Forrestal on 29 March, had his "own great idea: we ought to make permanent base of Haifa." (Actually, before Lovett assumed his State Department position, the British military chiefs had made clear to the Pentagon that a key goal in Palestine was to retain control of Haifa [see Louis and Stookey's *End of the Palestine Mandate*, 15–16].) Forrestal's response to Lovett was favorable, but he added that Lovett needed to solve the problem with the president over our "present lack of troops." Lovett then said he'd already "talked with president this morning" about this, and he wanted him now to discuss it with Senator Vandenberg. Forrestal, in agreeing, added that he did have "one division capable of moving as a unit" to Haifa. Later, after being told by Vandenberg that such military matters could only be decided by Truman, Lovett informed Forrestal that his response to Vandenberg included the following: "Jews do not particularly want a truce now; if it goes on a little longer they can say they are being exploited, would appeal to the UN and, if they are turned down, would then appeal to Russia, which would amount to blackmail" (Lovett, *Diary*).

The attraction of Haifa for Lovett and Forrestal was its oil port and related pipeline feed from Iraq and Kuwait. In any event, Haifa was the port by which the last British troops left Palestine (30 June); by September 1948, the Israelis were able to reopen and operate the Haifa oil port and refineries mainly using Socony and Shell oil supplied to it from the Persian Gulf by sea.

79. See *FRUS*, 952–53, and *PDC*, 643–46, where Lovett on 16 April privately told Charles Fahy that the United States would not do any "unusual" lobbying for the resolution it was planning to propose at the special session of the General Assembly.

80. See *British Documents on Foreign Affairs*, 186–89, for the British Embassy in Washington's summary assessment of 24 May that "the President himself has always supported partition ... his personal sincerity [is beyond doubt] ... most Americans tend to see the partisans of a Jewish state as following in the footsteps of the U.S. founding fathers and the Arabs as the modern equivalent of George the Third."

81. *FRUS*, 959.

82. Clifford, *Counselor to the President*, 21. This contrasts with Wilson's *Decision on Palestine*, 233: Lovett got Marshall to "come around to support recognition." In fact, Marshall clearly never did in any explicit way.

83. The language of that circular telegram, such as the statement that recognition will be given "within the next few hours," along with other evidence, suggests that it had already been sent out by this time; it is hard to accept that Lovett and Rusk, merely in deference to Clifford, would have sat on their knowledge for hours without sending out the alert in view of the dangers they anticipated to American personnel and property once the recognition was announced.

84. *FRUS*, 1005–8. In his 17 May memorandum to Lovett recounting his meeting that same day with the president, Marshall reported that his unspoken thought as the two were going over the events at the United Nations of 14 May was "It's a Mess!" He also noted in that memorandum that Truman did not know of those events until that meeting. See also Clifford, *Counselor to the President*, 18–24.

Consistent with, and indirectly supporting, this study's thesis that Austin knew of the American recognition of Israel hours prior to Rusk's phone call to him a few minutes to 6:00 and, furthermore, that the public sequence of events at the United Nations had been planned in advance between Austin and Rusk, is Rusk's statement to Kati Marton in the 1980s that "Austin just went home. He thought that would make clear we hadn't deliberately hoodwinked the UN delegates by not preparing them for this. I thought that was a wise move" (Marton, *A Death in Jerusalem* [New York: Pantheon, 1994], 21).

In his 1974 oral history at Columbia University, Jessup recounted that "it was a question of the vote in the 1948 elections. I am sure that that had an influence on him [Truman]. On the other hand, I think he was impressed by Weizmann, and he had his old friend Eddie, who I don't think was really so terribly influential except in arranging that one meeting [of March 18, 1948].... I think so decidedly [that Truman gave recognition] immediately and not further exploring the trusteeship possibility [Comment: No wonder Lovett found Jessup's promotion to number two on the UN delegation in April 1948 a happy turn of events].... Truman very much a political person, and the vote was very important, particularly in the cities — New York especially — and I think he was very much influenced by that.... I was broken-hearted, I felt very badly about it [i.e., that he, per the interviewer, 'hadn't been informed']; we were operating under instructions.... [Other delegations hit us with the charge that we were] just cheating [them] all the way along. It just knocks the pins out from under you.... [It did] damage to our prestige, [but] the bad effects on others who needed us didn't last very long."

85. *FRUS*, 1007.

86. Clifford, *Counselor to the President*, 17–19.

87. See Brands, *Inside the Cold War*, 183, where the author rather surprisingly goes on to say that Henderson would never have done so without Marshall's authorization.

88. Bizarrely, but also symbolically as evidence of their common support for a Jewish state, both the Soviet and American missions would, in their earliest period, be housed at the same hotel in Tel Aviv — thus, the Stars and Stripes were flown side-by-side with the Hammer and Sickle for a few weeks.

89. For a contradictory view by the State Department's legal counsel, Ernest Gross, see *FRUS*, 1052–53. Also see pages 1118–19 for Henderson's acknowledgment to Clifford that there was no "technical difficulty about exchanging full diplomatic representatives."

90. On June 21, 1948, Lovett explained to Clifford that, at the time of Charles Knox's selection as "acting representative to Israel," there was "uncertainty whether the truce would stick; therefore, had to get man who could be ordered in and ordered out quickly." Later that same day, Lovett called Forrestal to ask him to "try and think of anyone [we] can get for special representative to Israel." Forrestal, early the next morning, 22 June, called Lovett: "O'Conner of Red Cross"; Lovett: no good, "need someone with intelligence background" or a senior reserve naval officer; Forrestal: "Strauss"; Lovett: "out as a Jew" (Lovett, *Diary*).

91. *FRUS*, 1131–32 and 1140. Also, per Lovett's diary, at 4:25 on 22 June, Clifford called Lovett: "President wants to appoint" McDonald today. Lovett: Has the president "considered the fact that Mr. McDonald is a confirmed Zionist (he thinks), and the repercussions this would have" on UN efforts in Palestine? Clifford: "sure the President has considered it." Later, at 4:40, after having met with Henderson, Lovett calls Clifford and asks: Does the president "realize that McDonald is a known 'fellow traveller'?" Clifford: "imagined the President knew of it." (The appointment was announced that night.)

92. *PDC*, vol. 1, May–September 1948, 94–95.

93. Henderson's point was that the United States was not bound by the territorial recommendations contained in the resolution.

94. An insight into what Henderson had in mind regarding modifications in Israel's boundaries can be obtained from the State Department's circular telegram of June 25, 1948, providing general guidance for U.S. Middle East policy: (a) the reestablishment with the United Kingdom of the *entente cordiale* (following the passage, with British approval, of the Security Council resolution of 29 May ordering an arms embargo for the region and threatening sanctions under the Charter's Chapter VII against violators of the prospective truce) is most welcome

regarding "this onerous Palestine problem"; (b) in view of U.S. recognition of Israel, our goal now is to "redraw Israel's frontiers" to be more "compact and homogeneous" — therefore, we would support transfers of population and the assignment of the intended Arab state to Transjordan; (c) Jerusalem should be internationalized with "free access to outside world"; and (d) Israel and Transjordan should establish an "economic union" (*FRUS*, 1142ff).

95. Note that, in contrast, the United States had accorded *de jure* recognition to France and India, although those two only had provisional governments; the United States had done so regarding India in 1946, even prior to its political independence. The point here is that the decision on the level of recognition is in large part a discretionary one.

96. At Epstein's (later Elath) above-noted 29 May meeting with Lovett and Henderson, he was told by Lovett that "only Special Representative would have diplomatic immunity" (Lovett, *Diary*).

97. Radosh and Radosh, *Safe Haven*, 342–43, erroneously labels Knox, who was not a specialist in the Middle East, as an "Arabist." The authors also give Alfred Lillienthal that name, by which they apparently mean pro–Arab. Perhaps they based their error regarding Knox on the identical error made in Cohen's *Truman and Israel* (Berkley: University of California Press, 1990), 230, where Charles Knox is confused with another U.S. diplomat, M. Gordon Knox, a quite junior member of the U.S. delegation to the United Nations.

98. *FRUS*, 959. See Bayard Dodge's "Must There Be War in the Middle East?" in the *Reader's Digest* issue of April 1948 for the rationale regarding this concern over Soviet penetration of the Middle East, among other issues regarding Palestine policy during the spring of 1948. As Kaplan's *The Arabists* (New York: The Free Press, 1993) accurately puts it (79), that article by the former president of the American University at Beirut "is the definitive statement of American Arabists on the birth of Israel." That this was no mere coincidence is clear to the writer of this book, given the timing of the article and the overlap between it and Henderson-led activities on such specific subjects as the sponsored visit to America by Magnes, the role of Eddy's military analysis, and the emphasis on the alleged influence of anti–Zionist American Jews — all of which and more are cited in Dodge's article and surely reflect a coordinated campaign between the State Department and American missionary and oil company interests. See also Kermit Roosevelt's "The Partition of Palestine: A Lesson in Pressure Politics," *Middle East Journal* 2, no. 1 (January 1948) for a praise of Magnes similar to that contained in Dodge's article — neither writer notes that no influential Arab voice matched that of Magnes.

99. George Kennan, now counselor in the State Department, in a radio address of August 22, 1949, observed that the "present time" in the Middle East "marks a turning point. Why? Because there has recently emerged in that area a new, vigorous state — the State of Israel.... It has solved some problems, but it has created others. It is too early to tell what the final effect will be" (*Bulletin*).

Chapter Two

1. All sources in this chapter, unless specified otherwise, are from the James G. McDonald Papers at Columbia University.

2. James McDonald, *My Mission in Israel* (New York: Simon and Schuster, 1951).

3. Edward Sheehan, "How Kissinger Did It," *Foreign Policy* 12, no. 2 (Spring 1976), 40.

4. According to Louis and Stookey's *End of the Palestine Mandate*, 40–41, "The State Department succeeded in vetoing Morgenthau's pro–Zionist candidate [read: McDonald] for this mission and nominated instead ... Harrison." They also write that the mission's recommendations "defined the issue [for Truman] for three years to come" and that Truman, who disliked Morgenthau, didn't know that it was he who had first urged the State Department to consider the idea of investigating the DP camps.

5. McDonald's travel costs and expenses,

as well as a supplemental to his salary while serving as a high commissioner with the League of Nations, were financed in part by members of various Jewish organizations; see, for example, McDonald, *Advocate for the Doomed: The Diaries and Papers of James G. McDonald, 1932–1935*, edited by Richard Breitman et al. (Bloomington: Indiana University Press, 2007), 7.

6. In fact, all six members of the American section of the Anglo-American Committee had urged the president and State Department to drop the Grady Group's plan. As Richard Crossman, a British MP and member of the British section of the Anglo-American Committee, aptly writes, "[That group] knew virtually nothing of Palestine and were singularly ill-equipped to face the real experts of the British Colonial Office," with the result that there were "tragicomic proceedings," ending with "a typical piece of constitution making, which solved none of the underlying problems and reserved the keys of power in British hands." As Crossman notes, the State Department approved the plan, because its priority was to maintain the U.K.–U.S. alliance against the Soviet Union (*Palestine Mission* [New York: Harper, 1947], 196–97).

See also Leahy, *Diary*: (a) May 27, 1946 (in the United Kingdom): "The general opinion of the British with whom I talk seems to be that [Bevin] is an honest fumbler working without experience, that his results will be very bad for Empire defense, and not good for Egypt." (b) Earlier, the diary had recorded that on 23 May Bevin told him that "much time will be necessary in reaching a satisfactory solution to the Jewish problem there [Palestine].... He assumes that America's interest in that matter is the result of our determination to not be flooded by Jewish refugees from Europe, our desire to hold for the Administration the votes of Jews in New York State." Leahy then adds that Bevin's "misuse" of his H's "naturally displeases the upper educated classes — the only ones I meet." (c) On July 31, 1946, when back in the United States: "The President is worried by pressure applied by Jews."

7. In Lovett's case, too, it was an unexpected phone call to his home, in mid–1947, that brought him back to the federal government. In his case, it was the president who called. When Lovett's wife, Adele, told him the president was on the line, Lovett did not believe her. Incidentally, in explaining why he accepted the job, Lovett, in his oral history at Columbia University, said that he had a "very deep affection" for Truman and for Marshall (who had insisted that Lovett be his deputy), that he "absolutely loved" Bess Truman, and that, unlike Franklin D. Roosevelt's family, Truman's had a "sense of unity." Also relevant was the fact that Lovett (unlike McDonald, who was a registered Democrat) was a Republican but, as he said in that oral history presentation, he "always" voted the "Democratic ticket," because it had "better men or a better idea of what was going on."

8. In his search for a senior position with the Truman administration in 1945–1946, McDonald consulted his FPA representative in Washington, DC, for advice and was told that he should harp on his excellent relations with the Jews, because Truman was depending on their financial and political support not only in connection with the prospective 1948 election but also with his campaign for the Democratic nomination itself, given continuing doubts in that party as to whether he should, in fact, be its presidential candidate.

9. William Phillips, *Ventures in Diplomacy* (Boston: Beacon Press, 1953), 446–48

Chapter Three

1. Lovett, *Oral History*, Harry S Truman Library, 1971.

2. The diary, as stated in the notes for Chapter One, is located at the New York Historical Society in the "Brown Harriman" file.

3. William Quandt, "The Uses and Abuses of History," *Middle East Journal* 62, no. 4 (Autumn 2008), 706–7.

4. For example, what can one make of the following exchange in 1948 between the U.S. Mission to the United Nations in New York (USUN) and the State Department? USUN,

July 13, asked: Is our understanding correct that "U.S. recognition of State of Israel is unqualified, that is, *de jure*," and recognition of its provisional government is *de facto*? The department's July 15 answer was that it agreed with USUN's understanding; it went on to explain that "in case of recognition of new states as distinguished from new governments, no question of *de facto* as against *de jure* recognition is involved" (*FRUS*, 1206–7 and 1215–16). As will be noted below, the State Department to the present day dates the establishment of "diplomatic relations" with Israel only from March 1949.

Chapter Four

1. See Chapter One for the events of 1946. The CIA, in one of its earliest reports issued for the president, delivered to Truman on November 28, 1947, an analysis on Palestine that, according to Thomas Lippman's "The View from 1947: The CIA and the Partition of Palestine," *Middle East Journal* 61, no. 1 (Winter 2007), "reflect[ed] the collective judgment of" the U.S. government in predicting that the Jews would "fight bravely but eventually the Arabs would win." Lippman, in describing this as a "monumental miscalculation," wrote that the report was based on the views of the "best informed specialists," including William A. Eddy, who was the State Department's senior intelligence official at the time the paper was written and had toured the Middle East capitals that October, during which time he assured U.S. military officials that the Arabs would "throw the Jews out" easily. It is worth noting that Eddy, born in Lebanon of American missionaries, was the American minister to Saudi Arabia at the time that Franklin D. Roosevelt met Ibn Saud on his way home from the Yalta Conference, and that he served as the president's translator and note-taker at that meeting, where no other American was present. By 1948, he was working for Aramco. Copies of his original memorandum of that meeting were later made by Eddy himself and by the State Department, and they were clearly altered. This has led to confusion and controversy as to what commitments Roosevelt had actually made to Ibn Saud regarding U.S. policy in Palestine, especially Eddy's contention that the president stated "he would do nothing to help the Jews against the Arabs"—this was allegedly in addition to his assurances that the United States, so long as he was president, would undertake no hostile act against the Arab people and would consult with them before taking any decisions on the issue (see Eddy's 1954 pamphlet, *FDR Meets Ibn Saud*, and Wilson's *Decision on Palestine*, especially 50–51 and Appendix K, for his self-contradictory analysis and documentation on that aspect of the conversation). Not so incidentally, Eddy's pamphlet includes a congratulatory letter of September 17, 1953, from Admiral Leahy that, notwithstanding the fact that Leahy was absent from that meeting (although on board the ship where it was held), confirmed the accuracy of the memorandum and, in an ungracious slap at Truman, went on to offer "congratulations on all your efforts on behalf of the friendly Arabs wherever they were at that time. If Franklin Roosevelt had been permitted to remain with us longer, your success would have been greater."

A final comment on Lippman's article: He makes his own "monumental error" in writing that "in early 1948 ... the United States briefly supported a UN trusteeship for the entire territory, only to back down quickly in the face of Zionist outrage." This is a gross distortion of why the trusteeship effort failed and who was responsible for that failure; it also reveals an overly ideological and narrow understanding of the Palestine question as a whole.

2. Bartley Crum, *Behind the Silken Curtain* (New London: Milah Press, 1996 [c. 1947]), 225.

3. David Tal, *War in Palestine 1948* (London: Routledge, 2004), 42. Tal further correctly notes that another fortunate fact for Israel was that it was British policy to demand that no Arab state intervene during the mandate period.

4. On 10 July, Epstein confirmed to Lovett that Tel Aviv still would agree to truce extension (Lovett, *Diary*).

5. Kirkbride, the British ambassador in Amman, in his end-of-year round-up report on 1948, stated that the Arab refusal to renew the truce in July led to a "disaster" for the "Arab cause generally" (*British Documents on Foreign Affairs*, volume for 1948–1949, *Jordan*, 99–103).

6. U.S. Mission/New York telegrams to the State Department of July 9–13 express doubt that citing the Arabs as subject to Chapter VII in the face of threats by the Arabs to retaliate against the United States would actually be acted upon, given the Arabs states' national interests "from long-run point of view." On July 13, 1948, Jessup in the Security Council charged the Arab states with responsibility for having ended the truce; the British blocked a consequent U.S. effort to threaten the Arab states with Chapter VII sanctions (*FRUS*, 1206–7 and 1215–16).

The mission also observed that, in any event, given the "strong bipartisan support of Israel in this country, this [action] will have to be faced up to sooner or later." The editors of the *FRUS* note here that, although the mission had urged a White House statement, no action was taken.

7. The American argument at the Security Council on June 30, 1950, that an abstention by a P-5 member was not a veto included among its past examples the Soviet abstention on this Council resolution of July 15, 1948, which *inter alia* mandated the open-ended nature of the truce (*Bulletin*). It was Soviet policy throughout the period covered by the present study never to exercise its veto power on the Palestine question.

8. Arthur Koestler, *Promise and Fulfillment* (New York: Macmillan, 1949), 223. As regards the IDF offensive of 22 December that led to an urgent message from Truman to Ben-Gurion requiring an overnight McDonald dash by car to Tiberia, where the Israeli leader was staying, the United States demanded that the IDF immediately leave those parts of Egyptian territory it had occupied as part of the offensive, or else face a reevaluation of American policy toward Israel. McDonald's 1 January report concluded, much to the State Department's chagrin and understandable disagreement, "U.S.A. has now most certainly incurred serious responsibility if such withdrawal again jeopardizes Israeli forces in Negev." That telegram also reported Ben-Gurion's question of what the difference was between IDF's occupation of El Arish, which was Egypt's "forward base" for attacking Israel, and the "repeated bombings in Tel Aviv" and elsewhere in Israel by Egyptians. The difference, McDonald further reported, was stated to him by Weizmann in the following terms: while the IDF occupation was battle-related, the Egyptian attacks were for the "purpose of destroying Israel." (See McDonald, *My Mission in Israel*, 122–24, and *FRUS*, 1949, 595–606.)

9. Israeli Mission Officer Goss's telegram to Tel Aviv, July 3, 1948 (*PDC*): the truce has led to decreased interest in the nation at large and therefore to decreased "pressure" on the U.S. government "to be a friend of Israel."

10. Papers of Charles F. Knox, Harry S Truman Library.

11. At this time, there were 310 miles of twisted front and no-man's lands.

12. Amitzar Ilan, *Bernadotte in Palestine* (London: Macmillan, 1989), 161.

13. Lovett, *Diary*.

14. See *PDC*, 390–91.

15. A good example of the basis for American policy — and of the gap between Washington's views and those that would soon be expressed by McDonald in his stream of telegrams — can be found in the above-cited CIA report of 4 August, which reflected an inter-agency consensus and information from the field as of 1 July. That report contained such assessments as the following: (a) Israel and the Arab states, "or at least Transjordan," could "feel constrained to accept a Jewish state exclusive of the Negev"; (b) the Irgun and Stern Gang goal is also to capture Transjordan — the two groups are "pro–Soviet" and supported from Moscow; (c) the British goal is to reach a stalemate leading to an Israeli-Transjordanian agreement; (d) were the United States to arm Israel, that would lead to a break by the Arab states in their relations with us — we are already, despite our controls, the

main source of Zionist funding for arms elsewhere (*FRUS*, 1279–86).

This analysis was in line with what Lovett on 8 July had told Epstein (i.e., that the State Department had intelligence reports that, due to their "high classification," he could not show him but that showed up "penetration of the dissident groups in Israel," and that all Epstein had to do was to listen to the dissidents' "broadcasts") (*FRUS*, 1198). Also note memoranda by Joseph Satterthwaite, Henderson's former deputy and now successor as head of the Near East Bureau: (a) on 14 July: lifting the arms embargo "unilaterally" outside the framework of the United Nations would "constitute punitive action by the United States against the Arab States"; and (b) on 1 October: secures from Lovett authorization for a telegram to London that concurs with the British on the desirability of moving the Palestine question quickly up the UN General Assembly agenda in order to head off IDF offensives and reduce the opportunity for increased Jewish influence at the White House. However, Satterthwaite continues, the United States will not accede to British proposals for it to join with them (i) to inform the Arab governments that the United States favors Transjordan's having Arab Palestine or (ii) to endorse treaties between the United Kingdom and the Arab states containing defensive clauses against Israel (*FRUS*, 1217 and 1445–46).

16. During its October offensive, the PGI overruled Colonel Moshe Dayan's proposal from Jerusalem that the IDF take all of that city — Tel Aviv feared that such an action would harm long-term relations with Transjordan, which had remained out of the fight during this period. The PGI also wished to avoid creating unnecessary friction with the United Nations and the West; even the Soviets would have been upset, given their policy of backing the enforcement of a strict, literal interpretation of the partition resolution, including the internationalization of Jerusalem. (See *PDC*, vol. 2, October 1948–April 1949, 87.)

17. For the period of 1949–1952, official USAID statistics show that $82.6 million was provided, of which $63.7 was in the form of financial aid and $22.7 of agricultural commodities.

18. That this was in full keeping with Truman's current stance is clear from his admission to Lovett on 16 August that he felt constrained by his domestic political requirements and his wariness about Marshall's point of view: Don't give a flat turndown to the Israeli request for the moment, because "this situation has all sorts of implications.... I'd like to have a conversation with you on the subject ... about which I do not want to talk with the Secretary because of their political implications" (Lovett, *Diary*).

19. *FRUS*, 1149. The U.S. military also was instructed to alert Bernadotte's Haifa office "of any group movement" arranged by the ongoing large-scale surreptitious operation being conducted by the PGI to bring Jewish DPs from Europe to Palestine by ship, so as to prevent their uncontrolled landing.

20. This particular date was chosen in deference to the terms of the original appeal by Truman in 1945 to allow 100,000 Jews then in U.S. camps in Germany to enter Palestine immediately. By 1948, very few of those original camp residents were still there; therefore, the 1948 legislation effectively barred any significant numbers of Jews from entering the United States under the 200,000 quota. While there were well over 200,000 Jews in the camps in 1948, they were almost all recent arrivals from Eastern Europe and thus less attractive to congressional legislators for traditional, ethnic-based reasons and out of fear of their alleged contamination with communism due to having lived under Soviet rule. Those fears paradoxically were being reinforced by State Department statements and policies, even though they clearly undermined the department's simultaneous effort on the Hill, as Lovett put it to Attorney General Tom Clark, to block the bill, "because we said it was discriminating" against the Jews (Lovett, *Diary*, October 1, 1948). It is ironic that, during this period, the Soviet spy Donald McLean was serving in the British embassy in Washington as supervisor of the scare tactics alleging a Communist Party role in the unending illegal

Jewish immigration from Eastern Europe into Palestine (and subsequently Israel). Also note that the PGI sought to alleviate such concerns by underlining that it was screening arriving Jews to ensure their authentic status as refugees and their loyalty to the "Jewish State."

21. On August 22, 1949, shortly after the Security Council had lifted the arms embargo, Bevin sought to excuse himself for having supported it by telling a visiting King Abdullah that British cooperation in the embargo had been to please the Americans, but it was the United Kingdom that helped end it in accordance with the long-desired wishes of the Arab states (*British Documents on Foreign Affairs*, 1949 volume, *Jordan*, 103ff).

22. One writer has summarized the human cost to Israel of its war of independence as follows: number serving in the IDF: 116,184 out of a total Jewish population of 713,000; total deaths: 5,682, or 1 percent of the population (of that total, 1,162 were civilians, including 362 women); number of Jewish displaced persons due to the fighting: 72,000; number of killed in Tel Aviv: 172 (plus 321 injured). See Moshe Naor, "Israel's 1948 War of Independence," *Journal of Contemporary History* 43, no. 2 (April 2008): 241–57.

23. As put after the war by J.C. Hurewitz, "Dissatisfaction with the truce lines was stronger among the Israelis than among the Arabs" ("The United Nations and Palestine," 91–105).

24. This perceived permanent threat was one reason why the Israeli government was unhappy with the Security Council's decision in mid-1950 to cancel its arms embargo on the area.

25. *FRUS*, 1249–50, July 28, 1948.
26. Ibid., 1686.

Chapter Six

1. *PDC*, letter written over the period of July 20–August 22, 1948. This letter was written shortly before Sharett left for the Paris meeting of the UN General Assembly, having been specifically encouraged by Lie to attend the meeting, where, the secretary-general assured him, he would be accorded the same honors as those given to foreign ministers of other non-member states. Also during that mid-summer period, the PGI made publicly clear its position that it no longer felt bound by the UN resolution internationalizing Jerusalem in view of the fact that Bernadotte's June plan repudiated that resolution by assigning the entire city to Transjordan, that only Israel fought against total Arab rule, and that neither the Christian world nor the UNTC repudiated Bernadotte's proposal. However, the PGI went on to state that it was still open to an international solution, which, as the months went by, would focus on the possibility of leaving East and West Jerusalem under the respective rule of Amman and Israel while allowing the United Nations a supervisory and protective role over the Old City, or at least over the holy places. The United States was increasingly receptive to this type of solution. In contrast, an encyclical from the Vatican on 24 October reiterated the demand for the internationalization of the area in line with the November partition resolution — a position the General Assembly itself would continue to hold, with American *pro forma* endorsement, even in future Assembly sessions. For their part, the Arab states charged (with blatant hypocrisy) that this harping on the holy places had introduced undue religious motivations into the diplomatic dispute.

2. Records at the U.S. Mission to the United Nations. Archives: Palestine, 1946–1953, file # 42.

3. Lovett, *Diary*.

4. *FRUS*, 1185. Here, the lawyer Jessup would be strongly opposed by the State Department's legal advisor, Ernest Gross, who, as discussed earlier, saw as perfectly legal the establishment of the Jewish state once the General Assembly ended its special session of spring 1948 without altering its November partition resolution. As for the succeeding comments by Jessup regarding the "credit side" of the UN performance, many observers, including the writer of this book, would strongly disagree with just about all

of them, especially his positive assessment of the UNTC, which in reality was toothless, disrespected by both Jews and Arabs, and seen as a one-sided, overly aggressive tool of the U.S. government. As will be presented toward the end of the present study, a more reasoned, retrospective assessment of the UN performance regarding Palestine, one that made the most of what could plausibly be said of the positive achievements of that organization, would be written on April 20, 1949, in a round-up of events of 1948 sent back to the Foreign Office by the long-term British ambassador in New York, Alexander Cadogan. Jessup, in his oral history, described Cadogan as "extremely skillful, very wise, very smart."

5. See my *Reluctant Ally: United States Foreign Policy Toward the Jews from Wilson to Roosevelt* (Westport, CT: Greenwood Press, 1991).

6. *New York Times*, "Lovett Address to Bankers," September 24, 1942.

7. Stanton Griffis, a career diplomat specializing in Latin America, had recently replaced S. Pinckney Tuck, who had retired from government to take on the position of head of the Suez Canal Authority.

8. As McDonald would later write, "My background ... will help to explain the State Department's attitude toward me" (*My Mission in Israel*, xii–xiii). That he fully reciprocated this attitude even in retirement is clear from his published comments (ibid., 199–201) about his counterparts during a chiefs-of-mission conference in Istanbul in late 1949: "in comparison with Wadsworth, the Mufti is a Zionist"; James Keeley is an "outspoken apologist" for the Arabs; William C. Burdett, Jr., "showed himself the Crusader" in a post (Jerusalem) that demanded "exceptional poise"; and Assistant Secretary of State George McGhee misconstrued British policy when he claimed that it was in complete accord with that of the United States — the true policy of Britain was not, as in the American case, to seek an Arab-Israeli peace, but rather (so McDonald wrote in 1951) to keep the region in a state of war so as to have Egypt's focus remain on Israel and not on forcing the United Kingdom out of Egypt and the Suez Canal.

That McDonald's poor relations with his American colleagues was less due to his "personal background" and more to an institutional posture in the State Department is made quite clear in the following description offered years later by a senior department official regarding a similar conference of regional ambassadors held in the late 1950s in Damascus: The U.S. ambassador to Israel, a non–"Arabist" career diplomat named Edward B. Lawson, was treated by his fellow ambassadors as though he "was the enemy, pure and simple. That he was indeed an *American* ambassador seemed less relevant than the fact that he was assigned to Israel" (Kaplan, *The Arabists*, 128). According to Kaplan, this attitude began to change in the State Department as a consequence of the Six-Day War of 1967, when staffing of the Near East Bureau and its field posts began to open up more to non–Arabists.

The mutual animosity between McDonald and the State Department personnel did not end with his death. For example, in his 1974 oral history at Columbia University, Jessup referred to McDonald as "El Dopo" and as an indiscreet leaker to the Israelis. (This calumny is somewhat surprising, given the evidence in McDonald's papers at Columbia that shows Jessup, as a lawyer in the 1920s working on a project with the FPA, appreciatively seeking and taking advice from McDonald.) It perhaps would not be irrelevant to note here that Jessup, in his oral history, reported that his "grandfather was a missionary in Beirut for fifty-odd years"; that his father was born there along with "many members" of his missionary family, who remained in the Arab region; and that once during the 1948 General Assembly session in Paris, "I made a statement" in support of an "Israeli argument," and the Syrian representative came up to me "in a friendly way and said, 'Your grandfather would roll over in his grave if he'd hear you say that — he had played tennis with my grandfather.'" (Jonathan Randal's *Going All the Way* [New York: Viking, 1983], 45, refers to Henry H. Jessup as an American missionary in Lebanon who wrote shortly after the turn of the century that that country was "the best governed, the most prosperous, peaceful and contented country in the Near East.")

9. As late as the start of the Korean War, McDonald had to wait three weeks to see Ben-Gurion, because he was at his official residence in Jerusalem during all that period. The British, of course, in 1948, not having recognized Israel in any form whatsoever, went even further than the United States in its restricting all official contact with the PGI to its previously established consulate at Haifa, whose officers could only address its communications with the government to "the Jewish authorities" via the mayor of that port city — as a consequence, these British communications were left unread by the PGI. Similarly, on advice from the Foreign Office, McDonald, whose relations with Bevin and the British generally could not have been worse due to mutual abhorrence over Palestine policy, was only able to communicate with the British government through that Haifa consulate. McDonald had a contentious meeting with Bevin in July on his way to Tel Aviv and afterward privately expressed harsh feelings about the American ambassador, Lewis D. Douglas, who was present at the meeting and apparently failed to defend the United States against Bevin's standard charges of various American errors regarding Palestine, such as paying undue deference to the domestic political influence of American Jewry and, more specifically, failing to live up to its commitments to the British ever since the cancellation of the 1946 understanding reached in London by the Grady Group.

In the view of the present writer, there is much merit in McDonald's criticism of Douglas, a political appointee who consistently endorsed and amplified throughout his tenure the most extreme views of the Foreign Office regarding the dangers being created by Zionist, and later Israeli, policies for the most basic Western interests in the Middle East. Perhaps most notoriously, especially given his choice of language, Douglas, after Bernadotte's assassination on September 17, 1948, sent a telegram that stated, "If we should become the prey to Zionist forces ... this will only prolong that dangerous sore in Palestine and possibly spread the area of infection" (*FRUS*, 1411). Douglas, during the period covered by this study, also spent substantial time in Washington on leave and was in regular direct contact with the White House and the State Department, where he did his best to publicize the need to overcome the conspiracy of silence in the press and government that he claimed existed regarding the true implications for the United States of its support for Israel.

10. On September 10, 1948, Marshall instructed McClintock as follows: "You are directed ... proceed ... consult ... Bernadotte." That memorandum cited Truman's approval of the State Department's below-discussed telegram to McDonald dated 1 September (setting forth, for use in McDonald's direct personal demarche with regard to Ben-Gurion, the official terms of American policy toward the Palestine question) as authorization for the present instruction to McClintock. Marshall also sent a telegram to embassy/Cairo laying out the cover story of what to say if McClintock's presence at Rhodes became known publicly (i.e., that he was there with a British colleague merely to discuss how the two countries could assist in the Arab refugee relief program) (*FRUS*, 1387). Also note that Bunche, at the above-mentioned 1950 conference at Harvard, used the very same cover story (see Frye's *The Near East and the Great Powers*, 117) in the following artfully worded statement: "[O]n Monday the 13th [of September], two visitors landed ... without prior announcement to Count Bernadotte.... They came officially for the purpose, and they had papers to show it, of discussing with Count Bernadotte proposals dealing with the problem of Arab refugees." Obviously, there is room here to leave open the possibility that Bunche, unlike Bernadotte, did have prior knowledge of the upcoming McClintock visit, and that, unlike the "official" purpose of the visit, the actual purpose was precisely to help shape the basic conclusions of the revised Bernadotte Plan.

11. *FRUS*, 1337–40.

12. *FRUS*, 1313–16. As for the seriousness of the Berlin problem, see Leahy, *Diary*: (a)

31 March: first word of a Berlin blockade; (b) 4 April: President has me instruct the Joint Chiefs to draw up a plan to counter, but without use of the A-bomb, a Soviet attack, whether on the United States itself or only in Germany.

13. *FRUS*, 1364–70. Also see 1387 for the State Department's policy of preferring that the Gaza Strip go to Transjordan instead of Egypt so as to give Amman "essential" access "to the sea."

14. *FRUS*, 1628–30; Lovett, *Diary*; and McDonald's *My Mission in Israel*, 100–112.

15. The statement was pursuant to a State Department instruction of 18 November. Ironically, though it was Israel that was the most opposed to such a territorial exchange, the British also criticized its formulation on the grounds that, rather than "negotiations" between Israel and the Arab states, insistence on "acquiescence" by Israel to the recommendations of the Bernadotte Plan should have been the approach for the United Nations to take. Of course, this disagreement was a further example of the temporary distancing between the United States and the United Kingdom following the adoption of the less imperious, more "good offices" tone of the Security Council's resolution of 16 November.

16. Eban wrote Weizmann on 10 July that the State Department was "dishonest" and exploited Truman's "ignorance," and that McDonald and Epstein "are not given the title or immunities of regular envoys" (*PDC*, 313–17).

17. Charles Knox wrote home in August that, unlike the newly arrived McDonald, he was not prepared to invite family members to visit or live with him in what was still a dangerous place. McDonald, a few months later, would boast that his daughter "Bobby" was now "the fourth lady of the land," along with the wives of Weizmann, Ben-Gurion and Sharett. (In fact, these four women did have frequent, warm, highly informal relations.)

18. As discussed in Chapter Two.

19. Hebrew University eventually established a "James G. McDonald Professor of American History" chair.

20. By 21 November, Israel had assured the United States that Jerusalem "is no longer bothered by IZL (i.e., Irgun) or Stern Units" (*FRUS*, 1619). See also Ilan, *Bernadotte in Palestine*, 223ff.

21. On 30 August, Marshall wrote a memorandum to Truman regarding strategy at the United Nations that included his plan to "coordinate" with the British and Bernadotte on a revised peace plan for Palestine. This memorandum was a further step in the process starting with the failed Bernadotte Plan of June that would lead to the Rhodes affair of September, including the dissembling by the State Department to the president and the public at large regarding the true purpose of the McClintock-Troutbeck mission there (*FRUS*, 1360–63). William Louis' *British Empire in the Middle East, 1945–1951* (New York: Oxford University Press, 1984), 533, reports that "Sir John Troutbeck, the fervently anti–Zionist head of the British Middle East Office in Cairo, wrote in June 1948 that in his judgement the new Jewish state would be run 'by an utterly unscrupulous set of leaders.' ... It would now be up to the British to convince the Arabs to accept the existence of no less than a gangster state."

It must be noted that Louis himself holds strongly critical views of U.S. policy regarding the Palestine question. Better versed in British documents than American ones, he is prone to factual errors that undermine his judgments. One such error, a particularly egregious and important one that well illustrates this point, is the following: On pages 559–61, he recounts an exchange of letters between Weizmann and Truman in November 1948. Truman's letter of the 29th states, "Since your letter written [on the 5th], we have announced in the General Assembly our firm intention to oppose any territorial changes" in the partition resolution "not acceptable" to Israel. Louis then wrongly explains that "Truman referred to the American statement in the General Assembly on the 20th of September." Clearly, Truman could only have been referring to Jessup's statement to the General Assembly's Political Committee of 20 November; moreover, the General Assembly had not even convened in Paris until 21 September. More significantly from a substantive point of view, Truman was here warning Weizmann and the Israeli government that U.S. policy, as Jessup explicitly stated in his 20 November statement, continued to favor strongly Israel's giving up the Negev if it wished to retain its military conquest of the Western Galilee. Louis, however, uses this gross misinterpretation of the letter exchange to accuse the American government of going back on its commitment to the British to press for assigning the Negev to Transjordan while compensating Israel with the retention of all the Galilee.

22. The State Department alerted the field that the *New York Times* would be publishing on 17 October the story of McClintock and Troutbeck's mission to Rhodes, and that the response should be that they were there only to survey Arab refugee needs (*FRUS*, 1485–86).

23. *FRUS*, 1420.

24. *FRUS*, 1398–40. Note that, as early as 8 August, Ambassador Douglas was endorsing Bevin's demand that the two governments advise Bernadotte of their views prior to publication of his "final proposals"; that, on 22 September, Epstein was given private confirmation that, according to McDonald, the new Bernadotte Plan had been written with the full cooperation of the United States and the United Kingdom (*PDC*, 623); and that, in New York, when Eban told U.S. delegate John Ross that he was astonished at Marshall's 21 September endorsement of Bernadotte's proposal "in its entirety," the American justified it by claiming that Israel's acceptance of it would help the new country become a member of the United Nations and would also, by giving Arab Palestine to Abdullah, "head off Arab League versus Transjordan" (ibid.).

25. *FRUS*, 1472–74.

26. Illustrative of the unrealistic thinking in the United Nations and the United States is the remarkable assumption, stated in the State Department telegram of October 6, 1948, to its Paris delegation, that the financing of any UN force in Palestine would come from a "special scale" with the "Big Five bearing major share" (*FRUS*, 1460–61), despite its simultaneous statement in that same message that the Soviet Bloc should be barred from participating in that force (in line with standard American policy from the start of the Palestine question to exclude the Soviets from each and every UN presence in that region). As would be particularly demonstrated in the Congo crisis of the 1960s, the Soviets would not agree to join in any special assessment designed to help the United Nations finance an activity that it opposed (in the Congo case, a military force to keep the country united under the pro–Western government based at Leopoldville, later Kinshasa) and it would hold to this stance even to the extent of risking the loss of its voting rights in the organization due to the provision of Article 19 of the Charter requiring that penalty for members who were more than two years in arrears in paying its overall assessments authorized by the General Assembly. The resultant crisis in the United Nations nearly destroyed the organization and only ended with U.S. capitulation on the issue, saying that, henceforth, the United States would also pick and choose which assessed contributions to the organization it would agree to pay.

27. See the Papers of Charles F. Knox. The only member of the party who could be considered part of McDonald's personal entourage was Harriet Clark, his long-term secretary whom he brought with him to the mission.

28. Bevin's views on the level of eventual British recognition of Israel were expressed to Douglas on 27 August in the following terms: "in principle he did not like the 'halfway house' of *de facto* recognition," because that gave the Arabs an opening to try and "change the attitude of HMG" by getting it to be more supportive of their cause in light of the ambiguous nature of the recognition (*FRUS*, 1352–57).

29. George McGhee, *On the Frontline in the Cold War* (Westport, CT: Praeger, 1997), 37. McGhee here also underlined that his short-term, dominating goal was to prevent the refugee problem from so roiling the domestic situation of the Arab states as to open the door for Soviet penetration.

30. On December 9, 1948, Epstein reported that Leahy planned to resign after the 20 January presidential inauguration —"[he has] been our capital opponent throughout his service at the White House" (*PDC*, 281).

Chapter Seven

1. The Israelis did not welcome this political understanding, because they saw it as diminishing their opportunities to influence American policy domestically by playing off one party against the other.
2. That plank stated, "We pledge full recognition of Israel.... We approve the claims of the State of Israel to the boundaries" of the UN partition resolution "and consider that modifications thereof should be made only if fully acceptable to the State of Israel"; we also support its early "admission" to the United Nations, "appropriate aid" to its economy, and "revisions" in UN resolutions, including those regarding the "arms embargo," the "internationalization" of Jerusalem and the "protection" of the holy places. Note that, in publicly reaffirming his support for that plank, Truman on 25 October typically made no reference to his qualification that any additional territory retained by Israel beyond the partition boundaries must be accompanied by appropriate territorial compensation to the Arabs.
3. *FRUS*, 1502–3. On 26 October, both sides did accept the demand for a cease-fire.
4. McDonald would only arrive in Paris in November and not as an official, accredited member of the delegation.
5. A further complicating factor was that Dulles, representing the interests of Dewey, joined the dissenting group in strongly opposing any support for a UN resolution that would threaten Chapter VII sanctions against Israel. Also note McDonald's 1 November telegram, which, in anticipation of a clash between the United Nations and Israel with American endorsement, urged that the president "avoid possibility ... withdraw head Mission as a preliminary sanction" (*FRUS*, 1536, addressed to Clifford).

6. Even prior to the 22nd, the *New York Times* reported on 20 October that "Celler says State Department and Britain intervened — untrue, Bunche asserts." In addition, Robert Silverberg wrongly leaves open the possibility that Bunche was telling the truth (*If I Forget Thee O Jerusalem* [New York: Morrow, 1970], 438).
7. For a harsh criticism of Lovett's alleged undue policy deference to Congress, and especially to Vandenberg, see Kennan's *Memoirs*, 403–7.
8. Marton's *A Death in Jerusalem*, x–xii and passim. Remarkably, at a private meeting with members of the U.S. delegation to the United Nations on September 23, 1948, Eban said that Bernadotte was a better friend to Israel than it had realized, going on to argue that the country, in fact, could afford to give up all of the southernmost parts of the Negev at the demarcation line he had proposed. Eban, less remarkably, also said that the main problems regarding Jerusalem included the need for ensured IDF access to the Jewish population there without resort to corridors having separate UN–supervised entities, as Bernadotte had proposed, and that while the city's demilitarization would be an unacceptable risk to the Jewish population there under any circumstances, and while internationalization without a significant UN police force would also be impossible, internationalization limited to the Arab-held Old City would be acceptable to Israel (Records at the U.S. Mission to the United Nations, op. cit., file # 37). In this connection, the reader might recall that McDonald's 28 September telegram, cited earlier in the text, reported that Shertok was heading to Paris, where he would oppose Bernadotte's plan to exchange the Negev for the Western Galilee, a position at variance with Eban's private statements to the American delegation.
9. *FRUS*, 1527 and 1535.
10. In the days preceding the 4 November vote, Rusk opined to Marshall that the Soviets were likely to veto it — a surprising expectation given that, as previously noted, Moscow, throughout 1948, had never once exercised its veto of a Palestine-related res-

olution. In this instance, the Soviet Union typically left it to the Ukraine to harmlessly vote against the resolution while it abstained. However, more helpful to Israel was Soviet resistance to the British effort to have the Council expand the resolution's reach to include curbing IDF's simultaneous, successful offensive to complete its occupation of the Western Galilee up to the Lebanese border.

11. *FRUS*, 1530–32. There was an even more direct coordinating link during this period between the Imperial General Staff and the U.S. government: Secretary Marshall, who had traveled to London from Paris for consultations during his stay in Paris. As for Douglas' constant refrain of a "concealment" regarding Zionism's dangers for the West, it is hard to credit this charge, given that the Palestine question was surely one of the most closely examined issues of the period, both in the press and at the United Nations, and that each and every angle regarding it was under microscopic examination. As for the frantic statement by the British Imperial Staff, one cannot dismiss the possibility that an unstated motivation for the British in making the most drastic case possible in favor of the importance of the Arab world to Western security interests, and which interests indeed were in danger, was to rehabilitate the intimate British military role in American strategic planning. That role had been precipitately dropped right after the end of the Second World War with Washington's abrupt unilateral termination of the U.S.–UK coordinating mechanism under the chairmanship of Admiral Leahy. The major factor underlying this action by the Truman administration, one so upsetting to the British, was Washington's determination (a) not to be overly tied to what it foresaw as London's upcoming policy of holding on to what it could of the British Empire, and (b) to be free to deal with Moscow without the encumbrance of that formerly close military and diplomatic tie to the United Kingdom. Obviously, as shown in the present study, the British did succeed in some measure in returning Washington to their treasured *entente cordiale* with it during key periods in the Israeli War of Independence.

12. *FRUS*, 1554ff.

13. At a meeting called by Jessup with Sharett and Eban on November 26, 1948, he protested that the Israeli unwillingness to ease its siege of a large number of Egyptian troops trapped by the IDF at Faluja, northeast of Gaza, "was blocking progress toward peace through armistice." The Israelis rebutted that "for three months the Egyptians would not let food go through to peaceful [Jewish] settlements," and that only if there was a prior agreement to enter into armistice negotiations would they lift the siege. Jessup countered that the Israelis were a "lion" fearing that letting the "mouse" out of the trap would be "suicidal" for them, and that the consequent bad "atmosphere" Israel was creating for itself in the General Assembly and Security Council was making it hard for the United States to "help Israel" there in such matters as its application for membership in the United Nations. Jessup further argued that Israel's "military risk" seemed to be insignificant compared to the "political risk" of staying with its present policy (*FRUS*, 1631). (A few days later, Israel did ease its Faluja siege to the extent of allowing in food convoys.)

14. Roosevelt had gone even further in her criticism of U.S. support of the 4 November resolution, when, on 7 November, she reportedly told Eban (a) that Truman's authorization for that support had been based on "false presentation effects resolution"; (b) that her delegation (specifically John Ross) had lied to her in rejecting her proposal to push for a further delay in the Council vote by claiming that a quick vote was necessary in order to head off a planned Drew Pearson column that would demand an even harsher resolution at Israel's expense—the opposite was true, or so Roosevelt told Eban, adding that the real delegation fear was that once Truman was back in Washington on 5 November from Kansas City, he would be subject to pro–Israel influence, leading to a typical change in his stance; and (c) that Lovett was the State Department's main misleader of the president on Palestine matters (*PDC*, volume for October 1948–April 1949, 148–50, and its companion volume, 134–35).

15. The standard State Department position in 1948 was that *de jure* recognition could not be given to Israel so long as its boundaries remained uncertain. This doubtful assertion brings to mind the fact that "the American nation, when it was established, lacked even a name of its own which would point to its territory or ancestry" (Kohn, *Age of Nationalism*, 14). Henderson and Lovett were presumably aware of this history, suggesting, therefore, that they took their line merely as a debating point to justify their policy, which was based on other considerations, as outlined earlier in this study.

16. Lovett, *Diary*.

17. See David Brook's *Preface to Peace* (Washington, DC: Public Affairs Press, 1964) for a scholarly discussion of the role of Chapter VII in the 1948 handling of the Palestine question. For example, he writes on page 9, "The Security Council ended the fighting through the use of Chapter Seven" beginning with the resolution of 29 May, then through the important transitional call on 19 October for "intermediation," or direct negotiations, replacing the prior "imposed Truce" approach.

18. For this and the following two paragraphs, see Lovett, *Diary*; *PDC*; and *British Documents on Foreign Affairs*. As stated in the text, France's main interest was to support Vatican policy regarding Jerusalem; in this regard, note the comment by its representative on the PCC, Claude de Boisanger, to an Israeli official in April 1950: France was not particularly concerned with the refugee issue, which was "an American pet subject." The PCC would be bypassed by events and disappear from the scene with its final report of September 26, 1950—a rather unusual phenomenon at the United Nations, where it is said that once you start a ball rolling, it keeps on rolling, even uphill; this very disappearance in a way proves a point made by the United Nations' Andrew Cordier (to be further discussed below) that the PCC was not really a UN agency but rather a group run by three of its member states.

19. In that letter, Weizmann, after congratulating Truman on his election victory, wrote that he was sorry to see the United States support the "U.K." resolution, which continued a "vacillating attitude" at the United Nations resulting in demands for truces that were "becoming an instrument of war"; the "Arab States ... were sent against us by the British almost like a pack of hired assassins"; the British were now "rearming" the Arabs, while the American delegation in Paris lacked "directions in line with your views"; and Israel could not afford to give up the Negev.

20. Compare this bold assertion with the more judicious observation by Hans Morgenthau that U.S.–supported decisions of the Security Council during this war "prevented Israel from exploiting its military superiority to the limit" (*Politics Among Nations* [New York: Knopf, 1955], 424).

21. In his formal rebuttal of 3 January, Ben-Gurion argued that since Egypt participated in the May 1948 "invasion" of Palestine, one that "the U.S. did not find itself able to halt," it was clear that Egypt was not a "peace-loving" nation, and yet it had just been voted in as a member of the Security Council, while Israel was being accused in Truman's message of acting in a way to perhaps "place in jeopardy the peace of the Middle East" (*FRUS, Near East*, 1949, 601ff).

22. See Crossman, *A Nation Reborn*, 83–86); *FRUS*, 1670 (for Douglas' telegram reporting on British intentions); and Lovett, *Diary*, end of December to early January entries. A final point: On January 19, 1949, the American delegation in New York reported that Bunche wished to avoid seeing the planes incident or the British troop landings at Aqaba raised at the Rhodes armistice negotiations — therefore, he urged they not be brought up at the Security Council, where there would then be "debates leading to recriminatory exchanges between Egyptians and Israelis which might have unfavorable repercussions in Rhodes"; that Lie felt he needed first to have "full information ... carefully appraised" before he could charge at the Council that the "landings" were a "breach of truce"; and, finally, that, given these considerations, the Security Council president had decided not to request that the matter be placed on the Council agenda,

while "personally deploring [the] incidents" (*FRUS*, 1949, 687).

23. Following the passage of the 16 November Security Council resolution, the United States lobbied, albeit rather moderately, in favor of Israel's membership. As Marshall told Sharett on 13 November, Israel's membership depended on its policy toward Security Council resolutions. (He might also have had in mind a point he had made in his opening speech of September to the General Assembly, when he stated that Israel's membership was linked with Transjordan's — a neat way for the United States to freeze the entire membership problem, given that Marshall knew full well that the Soviets would veto any move in the Security Council to accept Transjordan as a member!) The Security Council vote of 17 December failed to obtain the required affirmative votes, with only five in favor of Israel's application (Argentina, Colombia, Ukraine, the United States, and the Soviet Union) and five against (Belgium, Canada, China, France, and the United Kingdom) and one abstention (Syria). It is probable that this result helped decide Ben-Gurion on the timing of his 22 December IDF offensive against Egypt; for example, Sharett told Jessup shortly after the Council vote that his personal guarantee of no new IDF offensive was no longer valid. Also note that (a) Dulles, as acting head of the American delegation, had backed the yes vote, according to Eban, on the grounds that quick Israeli membership would block Israel from getting too close to the Soviets (*PDC*, 293); (b) the British and French delegates made it clear at the Council that, despite their negative votes, their governments fully accepted the reality of Israel as a state; (c) Canada, as early as 24 December, would accord *de facto* recognition to Israel; and (d) as early as August 1948, Lie was personally urging Truman and Marshall to back Israel's membership.

24. Michael Brecher has written that, whereas Sharett in May 1949 saw membership in the United Nations as playing a "creative role" toward recognition by the international community in Israel's road to statehood, Ben-Gurion typically saw it only in its "declaratory or subjective view of recognition," and "Not without reason is Eban regarded as Sharett's successor" (*The Foreign Policy System of Israel* [New Haven: Yale University Press, 1972], 265). Note that Jessup, in his statement at the Security Council on December 2, 1948, urging approval of Israel's application for membership, pointed out that according membership was not the same as "recognition" and, therefore, members could approve the former without necessarily taking the latter, purely bilateral step (*Bulletin*). Paradoxically, Canada, as reported above, took the opposite step, according recognition on 24 December, just a few days after having voted in the Council against the Israeli application.

25. On December 21, 1948, Epstein told Lovett, as noted earlier, that France and Turkey "were considered to be pro–Arab"; therefore, a "good" American should be appointed as a way to increase PGI's "confidence" in the PCC. Lovett answered that he had sent a list of ten or fifteen names to the White House and felt that a man of "profound legal knowledge would be appointed, one who would study the situation and take a direct line" (*PDC*, 312, and companion volume, 167). Douglas's 22 December message reported Bevin's expectations regarding the PCC: give it ninety days to secure a firm boundary in the Negev and a final peace agreement. Without that, Bevin would hold back any recognition of Israel, especially given his fear that the country could go communist within five years in view of the sizable immigration from the Soviet Bloc, where Jews were exposed to the philosophy of the Communist Party. If that fear was borne out, Bevin planned to take out an "insurance policy" to prevent a neutral or unfriendly Israel from controlling the Negev (*FRUS*, editorial comment, 1690ff, including that Douglas, now back in Washington, met at the end of December with Lovett and agreed that "the Department would not be able to go along with Mr. Bevin on the position the latter wished to see adopted," given the president's policy of leaving the matter up to the PCC and to the prospective

direct or indirect Jewish-Arab negotiations on boundaries, etc.).

26. The IDF had entered the Sinai during the December offensive and left it by 9 January. The Egyptian agreement to enter into a negotiation with Israel by that date was partly due to Cairo's "adamant refusal" to invoke its 1936 treaty with the United Kingdom, plus the murder on 29 December of its prime minister, al-Nugrashi (Hurewitz, "The United Nations and Palestine," 91–105). Also note that Bunche on 28 December gave to the Security Council his finding that Israel was responsible for the Negev fighting and for entering Egypt, and that it was "intransigent" in its insistence on keeping its tight siege on Faluja, where, as noted above, Egyptian troops had been trapped since October.

27. On 8 March, Ben-Gurion in the Knesset had acknowledged, "Our international position [at the United Nations], though seemingly impressive, could be reversed overnight if Truman became alienated."

Chapter Eight

1. The State Department figures for Arab refugees and their new locations as of the end of 1948 were as follows: 160,000–220,000— northern Palestine (mainly the West Bank); 200,000–245,000— southern Palestine (mainly the Gaza Strip); 75,000–80,000— Transjordan; 100,000–110,000— Syria; 90,000— Lebanon; 8,000— Egypt; 7,000— Israeli-controlled territory; 5,000— Iraq. *Grand Total*: approximately 700,000 (*FRUS*, 1696, December 29, 1948). Note that Winston Churchill, in an effort to dilute the force of the "right of return" claim for Arab refugees, and as part of his effort to move the British toward rapprochement with Israel (especially following the military clashes of the previous weeks), stated in the House of Commons on January 26, 1949, that "the one-half million Arab refugees" actually "came in" during the 25-year British administration of Palestine and obtained "employment under conditions we created."

2. On October 5, 1948, Clifford informed Lovett that the president declined "Griffis' idea of trying to get oil and other companies to help regarding the Arab refugee problem," including "personal messages" to them (Lovett, *Diary*).

3. *FRUS*, 1949, 600–610, telegrams of January 3, 1949. The American government basically dropped for the next several decades any pretense that its priority interest in Palestine was to promote the political interests of the Arab Palestinians themselves; this changed when the Palestine Liberation Organization obtained from the Arab League, in summit policy declarations of late 1973 and 1974, the ruling that it, and it alone, was the new sovereign authority for the West Bank and Gaza. This reshaped the diplomacy of the Arab-Israeli conflict into one whose focus was increasingly on the Israel-Palestinian conflict, as exemplified by Yasser Arafat's appearance shortly thereafter at the General Assembly of the United Nations. (But American policy at that time was tied to a written understanding with Israel that the United States would not negotiate with the PLO so long as it failed to recognize Israel's right to exist and to accept Security Council resolution #242 of 1967 and #338 of 1973.) See Sheehan's "How Kissinger Did It."

4. This message was Truman's third such personal admonition to Ben-Gurion; the first two took place in 1948 on 1 September and 30 December. As for this last one, McGhee, who was assistant secretary of state for the region at the time, would later describe it in his memoirs as "one of the strongest notes I'd ever seen" (*On the Frontline in the Cold War*, 45–46). McGhee added that "the Israelis, even under [that] extreme pressure ... refused to make any definitive statement on refugees or to separate the question from a general peace settlement" and (regarding which the present writer would strongly disagree) the Lausanne negotiations "floundered on this issue." In commenting on one of his trips at the time to Saudi Arabia, he writes that he said to Prince Faisal, "We deeply regretted Israel's action [of 'not permitting the refugees to re-

turn'] ... and our notes to Israel urging compliance *were known to his government* [emphasis added]. Fortunately, they [the Saudis] did not allow it to hinder U.S.–Saudi relations."

It is worth noting that McGhee, who would surely fail Lovett's personal test of what a truly objective American ambassador should bring to his post, was by background a geologist associated with a Middle East oil company, and, on his official swings through the region as a State Department official during the life of the PCC, he would skip visits to Israel in stated deference to the peace talk efforts being conducted at that time — although, as he explains in his memoirs (41–42), he "had long talks" by phone with Ambassador McDonald, who told him that the Arabs had proven that they could "not constitute a barrier to a Soviet threat in the Middle East." In the meantime, McGhee obviously did not hesitate to visit the other parties in those peace talks, especially Saudi Arabia, where he had past family and personal connections with Aramco and the Saudi government and felt at home when visiting company headquarters at Dhahran: "It was good to be back among oil men, many of whom were old friends" (64–65). He writes that, while at Riad, he complied with Ibn Saud's request (supported by U.S. ambassador James R. Childs) that he wear "Arab dress" in that "holy city," because it would then be easier to have him there as a "non-believer" (presumably, Childs was also in the habit of putting on Arab dress if necessary for his diplomatic duties).

5. See Jessup's 1974 oral history.

6. By April 1949, Ethridge had earned Israel's enmity for what it perceived as his one-sided views on, for example, the responsibility for the Arab exodus from Palestine and for the current stalemate on resolving that aspect of the problem. From Washington, Eban on 26 April warned his government that Ethridge was now "the primary factor in Israel's relations U.S.A. and UN," and that, therefore, it should take a "positive" line at the Lausanne negotiations (*PDC*, 592–93). Note that (a) Bevin, in that same month, while conversing with the ever-agreeable Ambassador Douglas, charged that the United States was the truly responsible party for the exodus due to its policies since 1945; (b) with Ethridge's resignation on 10 June, the State Department, and especially Truman, adopted a firm but less harshly critical line with the Israelis; and (c) Lie's senior assistant, the American Andrew Cordier, who was much respected in the State Department for his judicious views on Palestine and other matters, observed, as noted above, that the PCC was more a three-power body than a UN one, given its independent approach to peace negotiations (Cordier also faulted the PCC for discouraging direct talks between the parties).

7. That Truman's White House was receptive to this advice is suggested in a report by McClintock to Lovett that the president, soon after the election, was quoted as saying, "If the Jews hold me to my contract, they will have to keep theirs," which the State Department interpreted as meaning that Truman was holding to his stand that if Israel wished to keep all of the Galilee, it must give up the Negev — otherwise, as the phrase went at the time, Israel would be trying to have it both ways (*FRUS*, 1600). Even into 1949 (a) Lovett was telling British Ambassador Frank on 5 January that Israel "could not have it both ways" and that American policy as a PCC member was to adhere to Jessup's 20 November statement at the United Nations regarding the exchange of territory (Lovett, *Diary*); and (b) Truman, on 4 April, was writing to King Abdullah that his policy was as stated by Jessup — if Israel wanted territory beyond the original partition lines, then "it should offer territorial compensation" (*British Documents on Foreign Affairs*, 103ff). Interestingly, in March 1950, a meeting took place between McGhee and Jordanian officials, who, in connection with their inability to obtain from the Israelis a "corridor" from the Dead Sea to the Mediterranean, reminded him of that 1949 Truman message to Abdullah; McGhee's response was that this American policy was only a "general" one and "evidently had no influence on" the policy of the

Israeli government (Records the U.S. Mission to the United Nations, op. cit., file # 221). Also note Offner's conclusion that "Truman could not uphold his position that Israel should not expand its UN borders except through a negotiated exchange" (*Another Such Victory*, 305).

8. On January 24, 1949, Bevin told a visiting prime minister from Amman that the "Jews" would try and settle with one Arab state after another to their (the Jews') advantage, and that "Egypt was antagonistic both to Great Britain and to Transjordan" and was therefore refusing to work out a territorial arrangement with them over southern and eastern Palestine (*British Documents on Foreign Affairs*, 103ff).

9. On March 3, 1949, the Soviets urged the Security Council to take "prompt action" and approve the Israeli application.

10. As early as 1 February, the GOI thanked Bevin for having told its London representative, Joseph Linton, on 29 January, that he "never had any prejudices against Israel" (*PDC*, 410–12). Bevin had also mentioned that he hadn't been forewarned of America's 14 May recognition of Israel.

11. *British Documents on Foreign Affairs*, 1949 volume, 21–23 and 138; and 1950 volume, 65–67.

12. On December 14, 1948, following the passage of the Security Council resolution of 16 November and the Assembly resolution of 11 December, Bevin told Douglas that his policy of a "proper balance" required that he soon release (as he did by the end of January, just before according recognition to Israel) the 11,000 DPs on Cyprus. Ironically, however, the U.S.–run camps in Europe were still under a policy of restraining the Jewish DPs from officially leaving them without authorization as to destination, a policy that Sharett labeled as "fantastic" and contrary even to that of the United Kingdom. The State Department was holding to this policy for fear that allowing the DPs free entrance into Palestine would upset the armistice negotiations on Rhodes. However, in practice, the American military in Europe was administering the policy loosely, closing their eyes to those who simply picked up and left on their own, as individuals. By mid–February, with Bunche's concurrence, the policy was lifted and the camps began to empty out. The year 1949 would see the arrival in Israel of its one millionth Jewish citizen —10% of whom were living in kibbutzes and other collectives.

13. On January 19, 1949, that bank announced approval of the $100 million loan requested since June by Israel. The reason for that timing was, as recommended by McDonald, to help influence the upcoming 25 January elections for a constituent assembly away from pro–Soviet parties.

14. What actually was said at the press conference remains murky; for example, Lovett on December 28 told Clifford his problem arose from having only given a "no comment" in response to a question as to whether Marshall was told in advance of Truman's 24 October statement (Lovett, *Diary*). Since Lovett and the entire State Department had been put under wraps by Truman concerning Palestine until after the elections, one might second-guess Lovett for not finding an excuse to skip this 27 October event and its predictable question on that hot subject.

15. That the reference to "New York" represented in the minds of both Lovett and Marshall a reference to the alleged ability of the Jewish lobby in that city to obtain (and leak to the press) secret State Department information from sympathetic members of the U.S. and Israeli missions there is further exemplified by Marshall's 13 November explanation to Sharett as to why he had throughout October ducked meeting him: such a meeting would not have been a "normal" one between foreign ministers, given that "New York" immediately learned and used all such resultant confidential information (*FRUS*, 1579).

16. Roosevelt, who was in Paris completing her soon-to-be-successful effort to have the General Assembly adopt her committee's draft Human Rights Convention, was upset by what she saw as an anti–Israel resolution (passed on 4 November with only the Ukraine voting no and the Soviet Union abstaining), because, she believed, it required Israel, *inter*

alia, to withdraw its forces back to its pre-offensive 14 October lines without conditions and, barring such a withdrawal, implicitly threatened Israel, and only Israel, with sanctions under Chapter VII. However, Eban eventually succeeded in his argument to the Council that the resolution also required, as a condition of withdrawal, the opening of talks looking to an armistice and eventual peaceful resolution of the conflict in the Negev — this line was supported by Bunche, who helped the Council produce the more negotiations-oriented resolution of 16 November, referred to in the text above. Roosevelt's letter, as discussed in the preceding chapter, was addressed to Marshall and Truman and had as its premise that the president was not being kept fully informed of the situation by the State Department.

17. Lovett, on the basis of information provided by the British government to the American embassy in London, labeled the Israeli action a "terrible blunder" in his 10 January conversation with Niles (Lovett, *Diary*). He further assured Niles that "aerial photos" showed that IDF forces were still in Egyptian territory. (As noted in the present study, the facts were that all such forces had left Egypt proper by 9 January; also recall Crossman's point to the Israelis at this time that, if anything, the blunder was Bevin's for having overreached himself in ordering the British planes to enter the fighting zone, a move that neither the prime minister nor the British parliament, as Crossman correctly forecast, would support.)

18. Truman's message to Ben-Gurion was critical of the IDF having entered Egypt in disregard of Security Council resolutions and possibly triggering the application of the British treaty with Egypt; therefore, the president said he might have to reconsider his policy with Israel. In their formal and oral responses to the president via McDonald shortly thereafter, the Israeli leaders assured Truman that the IDF would be leaving Egypt very soon; regretted that Truman had transmitted the British view on the fighting "without comment"; noted that, although Egypt was still in Israeli territory, the United States was backing its bid to become a member of the Security Council for the next two years; and denied the American charge, based solely only on the reporting of the temporary U.S. representative in Amman, Wells Stabler, that Israel had laid down an ultimatum to Abdullah either to negotiate immediately, not an armistice agreement, but a "peace treaty," or to confront an IDF attack. The United States would later respond to these points, notably by explaining that it was only trying to protect Israel's own interests and avoid a clash with the United Kingdom at the Security Council; underlining that it was also pressing Egypt to cease its naval attacks on Tel Aviv, such as the ones of 31 December–1 January (and the bombing by plane of West Jerusalem on 2 January); and, finally, urging Israel to act on the 16 November Council resolution and negotiate a "peace in Palestine."

19. This declaration was accompanied by a strengthened program of increased military aid to Greece, Turkey and Iran (i.e., the northern tier of the confrontation with the Soviets in the Middle and Near East).

20. Brecher, *Foreign Policy System*, 265 (words in brackets are Brecher's own). Compare Ben-Gurion's view with McGhee's that the declaration had "provided the most specific U.S. assurances to protect Israel" (*On the Frontline*, 93–98, where McGhee also reports that Abdullah, who was assassinated on July 20, 1951, had once told him that "he had no fear of Israel" but he did of Ibn Saud and other Arab leaders). Dean Acheson, in his typical sardonic manner, dismissed the importance of the declaration as follows: with the U.S. intervention in Lebanon in 1958, the May 1950 declaration "was dead, if it had ever lived" (*Present at the Creation* [New York: W.W. Norton, 1969], 396; also see 258–59: "this book will not detail the time and effort spent on the Arab-Israel conflict ... a long record of failure" of our efforts).

21. Wilson, *Decision on Palestine*, 79–87; Frye, *The Near East and the Great Powers*, passim; and Sheehan, "How Kissinger Did It."

22. See Acheson, *Present at the Creation*, 171 and 177, where he describes the United

Nations as "a slightly mystical entity." Also, with further reference to previous citations in the present study regarding the 1946 Anglo-American Committee, note that Acheson, who was under-secretary of state at the time, writes on pages 169–82 that he regretted its ultimate failure and observes that, as a consequence, "Atlee had deftly exchanged the U.S. for Britain as the most disliked power in the Middle East"—surely a continuing truth today, whether merited or not. Finally, note that Lovett, in his oral history at Columbia University, said of Acheson that he was "one of my closest friends" with one flaw: "contempt for ignorance."

23. *British Documents on Foreign Affairs*, 1949 volume, 16–20.

24. But not only at the United Nations: Elie Kedourie once wrote that the intractability of the Palestine problem had its roots in the decision of the United Kingdom in 1939 to invite to a conference in London on that subject, in addition to the parties directly concerned within Palestine itself, the Arab states, thereby authorizing them to become involved in the dispute, with the result that the Arab Palestinians became the victims and dupes of "their neighbors' interested solicitude" (See "Britain, France, and the Last Phase of the Eastern Question," *Proceedings of the Academy of Political Science* 29, no. 3 (March 1969): 189–97, where Kedourie also faults the United Kingdom for having suggested and encouraged the establishment of the Arab League with the consequence of further shaping the Palestine question into more of an ideological issue than a traditional diplomatic one). Incidentally, the reader might recall that the British, at the 1947 Pentagon Talks described in this book, flatly denied to the Americans that they had been behind the creation of the Arab League.

25. Two particular examples come to mind for both the frivolity with which they were dreamed up and their lack of basis in reality. The first was Lovett's lighthearted conversation with Forrestal—at a time of unwarranted optimism regarding the prospects for General Assembly approval in May 1948 of the U.S.-proposed UN trusteeship over all of Palestine—in which he celebrated his own creative idea of placing Haifa and its oil facilities under U.S. control as one of the administering powers under that trusteeship. The second example is McGhee's similar revelation to his colleagues in the State Department in May 1950 of his having come up, sitting in his office, with the idea of declaring with the British (and eventually, when the declaration was finally issued, also with the French, despite initial British qualms) that the three would henceforth guarantee to the Arab states and Israel their existing borders and would additionally implement a strict policy of arms control—a trilateral policy that never had much impact in the field and would become irrelevant within a few short years with the end of the Western monopoly over arms supply to the region, the essential prerequisite for the success of such a policy, due to Soviet arms deals with Egypt.

26. *PDC*, volume for October 1948–April 1949, 3, meeting of 1 October.

27. For example, when Pablo de Azcaraté, a senior UN official based in Jerusalem, returned briefly to New York in early spring 1948, he was struck by the atmosphere of unreality prevailing in his organization at the time regarding plans for dealing with the Palestine situation (*PDC*, 583–86). A later example: Just prior to the vote on the November 4, 1948, Security Council resolution, the U.S. delegation reported that the French, in a working group, were now leaning toward a negative view of the draft due to Zionist pressure both in France itself and at the United Nations (*FRUS*, 1536–38). Similarly, in June 1949, the Canadian foreign ministry confessed that it was unable to follow the erratic American policy on Palestine, calling it a "revolving door."

28. A standard precept of secretaries of state is that, in practice, they are responsible for solving the problems of their own presidents and not those of presidents to follow.

Bibliography

Acheson, Dean. *Present at the Creation.* New York: W.W. Norton, 1969.

Baram, Phillip. *The Department of State in the Middle East.* Philadelphia: University of Pennsylvania Press, 1978.

Barger, Thomas C. "Middle East Oil Since the Second World War." *Annals of the American Academy of Political and Social Science* 401 (1961): 31–44.

Brands, H.W. *Inside the Cold War.* New York: Oxford University Press, 1991.

Brecher, Frank W. *Reluctant Ally: United States Foreign Policy Toward the Jews from Wilson to Roosevelt.* Westport, CT: Greenwood Press, 1991.

———. "Scholarship and the Diplomatic Roots of Israel." *Jewish Social Studies* 47, no. 2 (Spring 1985).

Brecher, Michael. *The Foreign Policy System of Israel.* New Haven: Yale University Press, 1972.

Brook, David. *Preface to Peace.* Washington: Public Affairs Press, 1964.

Bulletin. US Department of State. Washington, DC, 1946–.

Clifford, Clark. *Counselor to the President.* New York: Random House, 1991.

Cohen, Michael J. *Palestine to Israel.* London: Frank Cass, 1988.

———. *Truman and Israel.* Berkley: University of California Press, 1990.

———. "Truman and the State Department." *Jewish Social Studies* 43, no. 2 (Spring 1981): 165–78.

Crossman, Richard. *A Nation Reborn.* New York: Atheneum, 1960.

———. *Palestine Mission.* New York: Harper, 1947.

Crum, Bartley. *Behind the Silken Curtain.* New London: Milah Press, 1996 (c. 1947).

Dodge, Bayard. "Must There Be War in the Middle East?" *Reader's Digest*, April 1948, 34–45.

Donovan, Robert. *Conflict and Crisis.* Columbia: University of Missouri Press, 1977.

Eddy, William. *FDR Meets Ibn Saud.* New York: American Friends of the Middle East, 1954.

Feis, Herbert. *The Birth of Israel.* New York: W.W. Norton, 1964.

Forrestal, James. *Forrestal Diaries.* Edited by Walter Millis. New York: Viking, 1951.

Frye, N. *The Near East and the Great Powers.* Cambridge, MA: Harvard University Press, 1951.

Grose, Peter. *Israel in the Mind of America.* New York: Knopf, 1983.

———. "The President versus the Diplomats." In Louis and Stookey, *The End of the Palestine Mandate.*

Hahn, Peter. *Caught in the Middle East.* Chapel Hill: University of North Carolina Press, 2004.

Heller, Joseph. "Failure of a Mission: Bernadotte and Palestine, 1948." *Journal of Contemporary History* 14, no. 3 (July 1979): 515–34.

Hurewitz, Jacob, ed. *Diplomacy in the Near and Middle East: A Documentary Record: 1914–1956.* Princeton, NJ: Van Nostrand, 1956.

———, ed. *The Middle East and North Africa in World Politics: A Documentary Record.* New Haven: Yale University Press, 1975.

———. *The Struggle for Palestine*. New York: Schocken, 1976 (c. 1950).

———. "The United Nations and Palestine." In Frye, *The Near East and the Great Powers*, 91–105.

Ilan, Amitzar. *Bernadotte in Palestine, 1948*. London: Macmillan, 1989.

Israel, Government of. *Documents on the Foreign Policy of Israel*. Vols. 1–4, May 1948–December 1949. Jerusalem: ISA, 1981–1984.

———. *Documents on Israeli-Soviet Relations, 1941–1953*. 2 vols. ISA/WZO/Russian Federal Archives; London: Frank Cass, 2000.

———. *Political and Diplomatic Documents: Preliminary Volume, December 1947–May 1948*. Jerusalem: Israel State Archives (ISA) and World Zionist Organization (WZO).

Jessup, Philip. *The Birth of Nations*. New York: Columbia University Press, 1974.

———. *Oral History*. Columbia University, 1974.

Kaplan, Robert. *The Arabists*. New York: The Free Press, 1993.

Kedourie, Elie. "Britain, France, and the Last Phase of the Eastern Question." *Proceedings of the Academy of Political Science* 29, no. 3 (March 1969): 189–97.

Kennan, George F. *Memoirs, 1925–1950*. Boston: Little, Brown, 1967.

Knox, Charles F., Jr. *Papers*. Harry S Truman Library.

Koestler, Arthur. *Promise and Fulfillment*. New York: Macmillan, 1949.

Kohn, Hans. *Age of Nationalism*. New York: Harper & Row, 1962.

Krammer, Arnold. *The Forgotten Friendship: Israel and the Soviet Bloc, 1947–1953*. Chicago: University of Illinois Press, 1974.

Leahy, William. *Diary*. Library of Congress.

Lie, Trygve. *In the Cause of Peace*. New York: Harper & Row, 1954.

Lippman, Thomas. "The View from 1947: The CIA and the Partition of Palestine." *Middle East Journal* 61, no. 1 (Winter 2007): 17.

Louis, William. *The British Empire in the Middle East, 1945–1951*. New York: Oxford University Press, 1984.

Louis, William, and Robert Stookey, eds. *The End of the Palestine Mandate*. Austin: University of Texas Press, 1986.

Lovett, Robert. *Diary*. New York Historical Society Library.

———. *Oral History*. Harry S Truman Library, 1971.

———. *Oral History*. Columbia University, 1971.

Marton, Kati. *A Death in Jerusalem*. New York: Pantheon, 1994.

McDonald, James G. *Advocate for the Doomed*. Edited by Richard Breitman et al. Bloomington: Indiana University Press, 2007.

———. *My Mission in Israel*. New York: Simon and Schuster, 1951.

———. *Papers*. Columbia University.

———. *Refugees and Rescue*. Edited by Richard Breitman et al. Bloomington: Indiana University Press, 2009.

McGhee, George. *On the Frontline in the Cold War*. Westport, CT: Praeger, 1997.

Milstein, Uri. *History of the War of Independence*. Vol. 1: *A Nation Girds for War*. Lanham, MD: University Press of America, 1996.

Morgenthau, Hans. *Politics Among Nations*. New York: Knopf, 1955 (c. 1948).

Morris, Benny. *The Birth of the Palestinian Refugee Problem Revisited*. Cambridge: Cambridge University Press, 2004.

Naor, Moshe. "Israel's War of Independence as a Total War." *Journal of Contemporary History* 43, no. 2 (April 2008): 241–57.

Offner, Arnold. *Another Such Victory*. Stanford, CA: Stanford University Press, 2002.

Phillips, William. *Ventures in Diplomacy*. Boston: Beacon Press, 1953.

Quandt, William. "Uses and Abuses of History." *Middle East Journal* 62, no. 4 (Autumn 2008): 700–707.

Radosh, Allis, and Ronald Radosh. *Safe Haven*. New York: HarperCollins, 2009.

Randal, Jonathan. *Going All the Way*. New York: Viking, 1983.

Roosevelt, Kermit. "The Partition of Palestine: A Lesson in Pressure Politics." *Middle East Journal* 2, no. 1 (January 1948): 1–16.

Schoenbaum, David. *The United States and the State of Israel*. New York: Oxford University Press, 1993.

Sheehan, Edward. "How Kissinger Did It." *Foreign Policy* 12, no. 2 (Spring 1976): 3–70.

Silverberg, Robert. *If I Forget Thee, O Jerusalem*. New York: Morrow, 1970.

Slonim, Shlomo. "The 1948 American Embargo on Arms to Palestine." *Political Science Quarterly* 94, no. 3 (Autumn 1979): 495–514.

Snetsinger, John. *Truman, the Jewish Vote, and the Creation of Israel*. Stanford, CA: Hoover Institution Press, 1974.

Tal, David. *War in Palestine 1948*. London: Routledge, 2004.

Truman, Harry S. *Memoirs*. Vol. 2: *Years of Trial and Hope*. Garden City, NY: Doubleday, 1956.

Truman, Margaret. *Harry S Truman*. New York: Morrow, 1973.

United Kingdom, Government of. *British Documents on Foreign Affairs*, Part IV, Series B. Volumes for Near and Middle East, 1949–1950.

United Nations. Yearbook of the United Nations. Lake Success, NY: Dept. of Public Information, United Nations, 1947.

United States, Government of. *Foreign Relations of the United States*. Washington, DC: Department of State. "Near East" volumes for 1947–1949.

Urquhart, Brian. *Ralph Bunche: An American Life*. New York: W.W. Norton, 1998.

Weizmann, Chaim. *Trial and Error*. Philadelphia: Jewish Publication Society of America, 1949.

Weizmann, Vera. *The Impossible Takes Longer*. London: Hamish Hamilton, 1967.

Wilson, Evan. *Decision on Palestine: How the U.S. Came to Recognize Israel*. Stanford, CA: Hoover Institution Press, 1979.

Index

Abdullah, King of Transjordan (later, Jordan) 67, 71, 74–75, 103, 146, 189, 195, 197
Acheson, Dean 166, 172, 197–98
Altalena 89
American Jewish Committee 49, 51
American Zionist Emergency Committee (AZEC) 101
Anglo-American Committee of Inquiry on Palestine 36, 39, 57, 84, 90, 152, 163, 181, 187, 195, 198
Arab-Israeli Conflict 1, 84–90, 148, 164–65, 169, 197
Arab League 9, 63, 70–73, 87, 102, 108, 189, 198
Arab Legion 28, 67, 74–76, 108
Arab Liberation Army 25, 58, 127
Atlee, Clement 146, 198
Austin, Warren 48, 121; and reversal of Truman policy 5, 13–20, 46, 72, 97, 128; and U.S. recognition of Israel 28, 52, 175, 178–79
Australia 143
Azcaraté, Pablo de 198

Balfour Declaration 9, 38
Barkley, Albin 63
Barnes, Curtis 105
Begin, Menahem 160
Belgium 5, 16, 50, 60, 103
Ben-Gurion, David 32, 62, 93–94, 96, 99, 109, 115, 138, 146–47, 151–52, 162, 192, 194
Berlin Blockade 94, 157, 161, 187–88
Bernadotte, Estelle 135
Bernadotte, Folke 14, 51, 53, 55, 60–61, 63–65, 78, 80, 98, 154, 168
Bethlehem 105–106

Bevin, Ernest 8, 68–69, 80, 108, 115, 130, 145–46, 172, 181, 185, 187, 195, 196
Biffle, Leslie 81–82
Bohlen, Charles 19, 52
Brooklyn Institute of Arts and Sciences 35
Brownell, Herbert, Jr. 50
Bullitt, William 172
Bunche, Ralph 14, 53, 56, 98, 138, 140, 166–68, 187, 190, 194; and armistice negotiations, conduct of 70, 102, 142, 144, 146, 151, 154, 160, 162, 164, 192, 196; and Bernadotte assassination, attitude toward 135, 187; and Bernadotte Peace Plans, role in 55–56, 73, 78–80, 84–90, 100–102, 121, 128–30, 143, 146, 154, 157–60
Burdett, William 105, 132, 186
Byrnes, James 36

Cadogan, Alexander 69, 166–67, 186
Cairo 61, 71
Canada 16, 143, 159, 173, 193, 198
Celler, Emmanuel 132
Central Intelligence Agency (CIA) 49, 59, 63, 183–84
Childs, James 195
China 17, 137, 172
Churchill, Winston 194
Clark, Tom 184
Clay, Lucius 173
Clifford, Clark 2, 6, 19, 23, 36, 129, 131
Cohen, Benjamin 52, 121, 132
Cold War 1, 23, 139–40, 145–46, 164–65, 171, 187–88, 191, 107
Connelly, Matthew 46, 53
Cordier, Andrew 192, 195

203

Crossman, Richard 146, 176, 181
Crum, Bartley 39
Cunningham, Alan 57
Cyprus 154, 196
Cyrenaica 9, 173
Czechoslovakia 22, 25, 64, 116, 146, 171–72

Damascus 61
D'Arcy, J.C. 176
Dayan, Moshe 184
Democratic Party Plank 190
Dewey, John 129, 133, 137, 158, 190
Dodge, Bayard 180
Douglas, Lewis 28, 52, 108, 139–40, 145, 187, 189, 191, 193–94, 195
Dulles, John F. 96–97, 137, 144, 174, 190, 193

Eban, Abba 63, 93, 135–36, 138, 156, 167, 175, 190, 193
Eddy, William 182
Egypt 9, 44, 63, 70–71, 73, 108, 115, 145, 192, 196; and *passim*
Einstein, Albert 177
Epstein (later, Elath), Eliahu 11, 27, 28, 30, 52, 55, 63, 138, 180, 188, 189
Ethridge, Mark 152, 195
Evans, Harold 26
Evian Conference 35
Ewing, Jack 80
Exodus 42–43
Export-Import Bank 66, 100, 144, 154, 157, 196

Fahy, Charles 28
Faisal, Prince and Foreign Minister of Saudi-Arabia 31, 72, 194–95
Farouk, King of Egypt 71
Foreign Policy Association (FPA) 34, 91
Forrestal, James 7, 19, 26, 46–47, 50, 54, 63, 81–82, 92, 118, 134, 137, 154
France 14, 16, 50, 60, 64, 72–73, 103, 143, 145, 162, 163, 169, 180, 192, 193, 198

Glubb, "Pasha" John 71, 74
Goldmann, Nahum 49, 51, 63, 161
"Grady Group" 36–37, 90, 181
Greece 8, 172, 197
Griffis, Stanton 92, 96–97, 114, 186, 194

Gromyko, Andrei 20
Gross, Ernest 26, 28, 48, 52, 54, 185

Haganah 25, 57, 80
Haifa 48, 55, 61, 86–89, 130, 140, 173, 178, 184
Harrison, Earl 36, 116, 180
Hashemite Kings of Transjordan and Iraq 72–73, 108
Hebrew University 188
Helm, Knox 153
Henderson, Loy 11, 30–31, 44, 47, 51–52, 80–81, 121, 142, 163, 172–73, 192; role in Magnes visit 49, 180; role in McDonald appointment 54, 91; role in partition resolution 122–24, 174, 177; transfer overseas 55, 118–19
Hightower, John 51
Hilldring, John 43, 45, 49–50, 80–81, 117–19, 124
Hillenkoeter, Roscoe 49, 158
Holocaust 26, 144
Holy City of Jerusalem 105, 185, 190
Hurwitz, Jacob C. 163, 167, 173, 185

Ibn Saud, King of Saudi Arabia 72, 172, 182
India 63, 119, 173, 180
Indonesia 48
Iran 1, 8, 172, 197
Iraq 9, 72–73, 76, 119, 151
Irgun 25, 64, 75, 89, 99, 160
Israel: Galilee vs. Negev issue 64, 76, 78, 85, 87, 94, 101–102, 132, 145–46, 149, 188, 195–196; Jerusalem policy 59, 64, 75, 103–105, 108–109, 147–48, 150–51, 184, 185, 189; military conflicts 57ff, 74, 94–96, 109, 113, 129, 138, 141, 145–47, 154, 160, 183, 185, 191; Old City of Jerusalem 62, 74, 107–108, 147; policy toward Arab refugees 69, 74, 110ff, 149–50, 153, 195; policy toward U.S. and UN 60, 65, 96, 99, 109, 117, 146, 151–52, 193–95; policy toward USSR 161–62, 184, 191

Jacobson, Eddie 22, 179
Jessup, Philip 14, 29, 50, 89, 91, 97, 112, 118, 174, 179, 183, 185, 186, 191, 193
Jewish Agency 11, 17, 19, 36, 45, 50–51, 75, 125–26, 173–74

Johnson, Herschel 45, 50, 118, 122–23, 124, 175

Kashmir 48
Kedourie, Elie 198
Keeley, James 186
Keenan, Joseph 144, 152
Kennan, George 11, 172–73, 174, 180, 190
Kilgore, Harley 81–82
Kissinger, Henry 36, 164
Knox, Charles 31, 54, 60ff, 105, 180, 188
Kohn, Hans 168, 192
Korean War 48, 161
Krock, Arthur 133–34, 161

League of Nations: and Jewish refugees from Germany 35, 118, 126; and Palestine 5
Leahy, William 119–20, 182, 190, 191
Lebanon 72, 76
Lie, Trygve 10, 11, 13, 17, 18, 20, 88, 146, 162, 185, 192–93
Louis, William 188
Lovett, Robert: attitude toward Palestine policy 15, 19, 30, 47, 157, 191–92, 195; conversations with Clifford 28ff, 47, 51, 53–54, 60ff, 91–92, 96, 129, 133, 141, 155–61; relations with Truman 2, 56, 93ff, 101, 132–134, 146, 154–61, 181, 196

MacDonald, John 64, 98, 132
Magnes, Judah 49, 180
Marshall, George 21ff, 28, 55, 81, 92, 97, 101, 118, 131, 136, 154, 161, 172, 174, 176, 184, 191
Marshall Plan 9, 11
Masaryk, Jan 172
McCarthy Committee 91
McClintock, Robert 19, 28, 51–52, 54, 89, 96, 176; secret mission to Rhodes 55–56, 93, 100–102, 130–31, 187–89
McDonald, Barbara 95, 98, 188
McDonald, James: appointment to Israel 31–32, 37, 47, 54, 90, 92, 188; life and career 33ff, 59–60, 78, 92–93, 99–100, 153, 156, 162; at Paris General Assembly 95–97, 102
McDonald, Ruth 98, 153

McGhee, George 114, 186, 189, 194–96, 198
McGrath, Howard 81
McLean, Donald 184
Meir, Golda 25, 75, 177
Morgenthau, Hans 192
Morgenthau, Henry, Jr. 141, 158, 180

National Security Council (NSC) 7, 23, 43
Negev 9, 44, 59, 64, 67, 71, 76, 85, 95, 109, 124–25, 129, 145, 147, 154, 189, 192
Niebuhr, Reinhold 152
Niles, David 45, 49–50

Ottoman Empire 15

Palestine: Arab refugees from 66, 68–69, 85, 96, 110–14, 149–50, 189, 192, 194; and Arab Higher Committee (AHC) 72–74, 85
Palestine Liberation Organization (PLO) 194
Phillips, William 33, 39–40
Porter, William 174
Proskauer, Joseph 49, 51
Proust, Marcel 164

Republican Party Plank 54, 82, 121, 129, 181
Riley, William 114, 128, 162–63
Robeson, Paul 173
Rockefeller, John D., III 34
Roosevelt, Eleanor 3, 43, 79–82, 118, 120–21, 123, 131, 136, 141, 160, 191
Roosevelt, Franklin 182
Roosevelt, Kermit 180
Ross, Charlie 52
Ross, John 120, 189, 191
Rovere, Richard 32
Rusk, Dean 12ff, 26, 28, 31, 45, 52, 68, 96, 120, 155, 158, 168, 178, 190

Sadat, Anouar el 36, 164
Satterthwaite, Joseph 55, 119, 184
Saudi Arabia 11, 31–32, 71, 194–95
Schuman, Robert 144
Shertok (later, Sharett), Moshe 51, 95, 99, 109, 146–47, 193
Silver, Abba Hillel 50–51, 101, 156

"Six-Day War" 105, 186
Snetsinger, John 176
Soviet Union (USSR) 1, 8–9, 11, 14, 19, 26, 71, 82, 91, 94, 100, 116, 123, 127, 134, 139–40, 146, 161, 163; role in Israel 30, 39, 139–40, 173, 179, 196, 198; role in World War II 186; veto policy 5, 17, 103, 109, 128, 140, 143, 174, 183, 189, 190–91, 193, 196
Stabler, Wells 85, 197
"Stern Gang" 25, 64, 75, 98–99, 135
Suez Canal 9, 71, 145, 186
Sullivan, John 60
Syria 71–73

Taylor, Myron 35, 163
Thorp, Willard 19, 171, 175
Transjordan (later, Jordan) 9, 67, 70–71, 145–47, 150, 193
Troutbeck, John 101, 132, 188
Truman, Harry: personal attitudes toward Palestine issue 20–21, 46–47, 50–51, 79ff, 82–83, 89, 95, 97–99, 115, 121, 124–25, 129, 135, 137–38, 141, 144–46, 149, 160, 175, 178, 190, 194
Truman, Margaret 21
Truman Administration: internal tensions 2, 11–13, 18, 21, 79ff
Truman Presidential Library 21, 24, 79
Tuck, S. Pinckney 186
Turkey 1, 8, 63, 95, 143–44, 163, 172, 193, 197

United Kingdom: Arab policy 9, 44, 58, 67, 95, 110, 141, 145–46, 182, 184, 186; arms embargo on Middle East 11, 67; Palestine Mandate 5, 7, 11, 13, 17, 71, 117; "Pentagon Talks" 7ff, 94, 139–140, 191, 198; policy at UN 17, 25, 65, 77, 88, 98, 100–102, 122–23, 137, 139–40, 142–43, 155, 166–67, 184; policy toward Israel 52, 112, 141, 153, 160, 189, 193, 194, 196
United Nations (UN): Economic and Social Council (ECOSOC) 86; General Assembly resolutions 2, 9, 25, 58, 62, 84, 96–97, 129, 147; Jerusalem policy 59ff, 74, 106–109; Palestine Committee (UNPC) 10–11, 16ff, 173; Palestine Conciliation Commission (PCC) 70, 143–48, 150, 152–53, 163–64, 192, 193, 195; Security Council activities 5, 11ff, 23, 48, 53, 70, 79, 115, 134, 137–38, 142, 146, 175, 185, 192; Truce Commission (UNTC) 54, 60, 89, 98, 103, 132, 152, 185, 186; Truce Observation Team 60–61, 113, 128; Trusteeship Council 14, 25–26, 104, 107–108, 116, 189; UN Special Committee on Palestine (UNSCOP) 9, 44, 86, 106, 121, 166
United States: arms embargo 11, 52, 63, 77, 113, 155–56, 173–74; domestic pressure groups 11–12, 126, 168–69, 172, 173, 177, 180ff; Jerusalem policy 108–109, 113; military policy 60ff, 98, 119, 123, 138, 152, 155, 167–68, 172, 186; overall Palestine policy 1, 11, 19, 48, 60–68, 76–77, 79ff, 88–89, 92, 94, 97, 111; policy toward Jewish refugees in Europe 44, 66–67, 115–16, 117, 180, 184, 196; recognition of Israel 24ff, 46, 53–55, 80, 92, 111, 142, 145, 150ff, 180–182, 192; role in UN partition resolution 120–27; and "Tripartite Declaration of May 1950" 192

Vandenberg, Arthur 43, 133, 178, 190
Vatican 162–63, 185, 192
Vinson, Frederick 134
Voltaire 41

Wadsworth, George 44, 121, 186
Weizmann, Chaim 22, 27, 46, 53–54, 81, 144–45, 176, 179, 188–89, 192
Welles, Sumner 80
Wilkins, Fraser 51
Wilson, Evan 163, 176–77, 178, 190
World War I 14, 28
World War II 191; and Jewish refugees 34, 44, 57, 62, 66, 69, 105, 112, 115, 154, 172, 181, 196

"Yom Kippur War" 164

www.ingramcontent.com/pod-product-compliance
Lightning Source LLC
Chambersburg PA
CBHW032057300426
44116CB00007B/786